This is a study of how women figured in public reaction to the church from New Testament times to Christianity's encounter with the pagan critics of the second century CE. The reference to a hysterical woman was made by the most prolific critic of Christianity, Celsus, and he meant a follower of Jesus, probably Mary Magdalene, who was at the centre of efforts to create and promote belief in the resurrection. MacDonald draws attention to the conviction, emerging from the works of several pagan authors, that female initiative was central to Christianity's development; she sets out to explore the relationship between this and the common Greco-Roman belief that women were inclined towards excesses in matters of religion. The findings of cultural anthropologists of Mediterranean societies are examined in an effort to probe the societal values that shaped public opinion and early church teaching. Concerns expressed in New Testament and early Christian texts about the respectability of women, and even generally about their behaviour, are seen in a new light when one appreciates that outsiders focused on early church women and understood their activities as a reflection of the nature of the group as a whole.

*Early Christian women
and pagan opinion*

Early Christian women and pagan opinion

The power of the hysterical woman

MARGARET Y. MACDONALD

Department of Religious Studies
University of Ottawa

CAMBRIDGE
UNIVERSITY PRESS

Published by the Press Syndicate of the University of Cambridge
The Pitt Building, Trumpington Street, Cambridge CB2 1RP
40 West 20th Street, New York, NY 10011-4211, USA
10 Stamford Road, Oakleigh, Melbourne 3166, Australia

© Cambridge University Press 1996

First published in 1996

Printed in Great Britain at the University Press, Cambridge

A catalogue record for this book is available from the British Library

Library of Congress cataloguing in publication data applied for

ISBN 0 521 56174 4 hardback
ISBN 0 521 56728 9 paperback

For Duncan, Delia, and Jake

Contents

Contents

Preface

Although I have been working intensively on this book for about
five years, many of its themes have occupied my thoughts for much
longer. In preparing *The Pauline Churches* (Cambridge University
Press, 1988) I became fascinated with the question of how the reaction of non-believers to early Christian groups may have affected
life in the early church. *Early Christian women and pagan opinion* considers this question with a specific focus on early Christian women.

In conducting this study I was frequently required to venture
outside my own field of Early Christian Studies to consider the
work of anthropologists of Mediterranean societies and the work
of scholars in the area of women and religion. Given the interdisciplinary nature of my study, I set out deliberately to write a book
which I hope will interest specialists, but will also engage more
general readers. I have made extensive use of footnotes throughout which will offer scholars of early Christianity further information about textual backgrounds and related studies.

My investigation has been enriched by many conversations with
graduate students. In addition, I have received assistance from students working in conjunction with the Canadian Centre for
Research on Women and Religion at the University of Ottawa.
Steven Muir, a doctoral candidate in the Department of Religious
Studies at the University of Ottawa, deserves special mention for
editing, bibliographical work, and proof-reading.

For his judicious advice on the general shape of the book and
for organizing the initial reaction to my work in the form of very
valuable readers' reports, I would like to thank my editor at

Preface

Cambridge University Press, Alex Wright. I would also like to express my appreciation to two colleagues, Professor Naomi Goldenberg of the Department of Religious Studies at the University of Ottawa and Professor Eileen Schuller of the Department of Religious Studies at McMaster University, who have offered support in various forms.

During the course of conducting the research for this book I received funding from the University of Ottawa and the Social Sciences and Humanities Research Council of Canada. In particular, the support I received from the Faculty of Arts at the University of Ottawa as a complement to my SSHRC grant, which took the form of release from some teaching responsibilities, was instrumental in allowing me to complete my study in a timely manner.

The past five years of my life have involved not only the creation of this book, but also the birth of my two children, Delia and Jake. This book is dedicated to my husband Duncan and my two children who have all shared in the difficulties and the joys of the enterprise.

Abbreviations

ANF	A. Roberts and J. Donaldson (eds.), *The Ante-Nicene Fathers*
BAGD	W. Bauer, W. F. Arndt, F. W. Gingrich, and F. W. Danker, *Greek-English Lexicon of the NT*
Barn.	*Barnabas*
BTB	*Biblical Theology Bulletin*
CBQ	*Catholic Biblical Quarterly*
CH	*Church History*
1 Clem.	*1 Clement*
Clem. Alex. *Strom.*	Clement of Alexandria, *Stromateis*
Did.	*Didache*
GRBS	*Greek, Roman, and Byzantine Studies*
HDR	Harvard Dissertations in Religion
Herm. Man.	*Hermas, Mandate*
Herm. Sim.	*Hermas, Similitude*
Herm. Vis.	*Hermas, Vision*
HR	*History of Religions*
HTR	*Harvard Theological Review*
Ign. *Magn.*	Ignatius, *Letter to the Magnesians*
Ign. *Pol.*	Ignatius, *Letter to Polycarp*
Ign. *Smyrn.*	Ignatius, *Letter to the Smyrnaeans*
Ign. *Trall.*	Ignatius, *Letter to the Trallians*
JAAR	*Journal of the American Academy of Religion*
JAC	*Jahrbuch für Antike und Christentum*
JBL	*Journal of Biblical Literature*
JFSR	*Journal of Feminist Studies in Religion*

Abbreviations

JR	*Journal of Religion*
JRH	*Journal of Religious History*
JSNT	*Journal for the Study of the New Testament*
JSOT	*Journal for the Study of the Old Testament*
LCL	Loeb Classical Library
Mart. Pol.	*Martyrdom of Polycarp*
NHL	J. Robinson (ed.), *Nag Hammadi Library in English*
NovT	*Novum Testamentum*
NRSV	*New Revised Standard Version*
NT Apoc.	E. Hennecke and W. Schneemelcher (eds.), *New Testament Apocrypha*
NTS	*New Testament Studies*
Orig. *C. Cels.*	Origen, *Contra Celsum*
Pol. *Phil.*	Polycarp, *Letter to the Philippians*
RSV	*Revised Standard Version*
SBLDS	Society of Biblical Literature Dissertation Series
SBLMS	Society of Biblical Literature Monograph Series
SBLSP	Society of Biblical Literature Seminar Papers
SNTSMS	Society for New Testament Studies Monograph Series
SR	*Studies in Religion / Sciences Religieuses*
VC	*Vigiliae christianae*

Introduction

Defining the task

Among the second-century critics of early Christianity, Celsus was the most prolific. Unfortunately, we possess very little information about his life. His book *The True Doctrine*, written about 170 CE, no longer exists, and it is known to us only from a rebuttal composed by Origen some seventy years later, *Contra Celsum*. Luckily Origen quotes Celsus at length, and we are thus in a good position to recover much of what Celsus originally said. Of particular importance for this study is Celsus' remarkable interest in the presence of women among Jesus' followers, and in their role in the development of Christianity. In fact, Celsus describes the Christian resurrection belief as having been created by a 'hysterical woman' who was deluded by sorcery:

> But we must examine this question whether anyone who really died ever rose again with the same body ... But who saw this? A hysterical female, as you say, and perhaps some other one of those who were deluded by the same sorcery, who either dreamt in a certain state of mind and through wishful thinking had a hallucination due to some mistaken notion (an experience which has happened to thousands), or, which is more likely, wanted to impress others by telling this fantastic tale, and so by this cock-and-bull story to provide a chance for other beggars.[1]

The mention of a hysterical woman may be simply a general attempt to ridicule the beliefs of a cult which sprang from the

---

[1] See Orig. *C. Cels.* 2.55; 3.55; trans. Henry Chadwick (Cambridge University Press, 1953). The identification of the hysterical female as Mary Magdalene and the text as a whole are discussed fully in Part 1 pp. 104–9.

1

foolish imaginings of women; as we will see, other foreign religions had been critiqued similarly. But Celsus' knowledge of the Christian tradition is substantial enough that it is possible that he was familiar with the important role women play in resurrection accounts, and with the role of Mary of Magdala in particular. The lingering memory in early Christian circles about Mary as a follower of Jesus, a witness to the resurrection, and a herald of the news of the appearance of the risen Christ, is made clear by her prominence in New Testament traditions (Mark 16.1–11; Matt. 28.1–8; Luke 24.1–11; John 20.1–18) and in several gnostic writings from the second and third centuries CE.[2] Celsus noted that women continued to play a prominent role, acting as leaders in church groups after the death of Jesus, and he described the participation of women in Christianity's seditious evangelizing tactics. If Celsus' remarks were substantive rather than simply being a stereotypical attempt to chide early Christians, he was asserting that from its inception to his own day, Christianity had been very much a women's religion.[3]

Celsus' labelling of a woman with a talent for the invention of religious belief as 'hysterical' reflects a well-attested sentiment in the Roman Empire that women were inclined towards excesses in matters of religion. Commenting on Celsus' description of early Christianity as a lurer of women, the historian Ramsay MacMullen stated, 'Ardent credulity was presented as a weakness characteristic of the sex, pagan or Christian.'[4] At times this weakness took the form of addiction to religious matters, a trait said to be found only rarely in men.[5] At times it took the form of outright allegiance to a strange new religious group. According to the

---

[2] See for example: *Gospel of Philip*, 59.5–11; 63.32–6; trans. Wesley W. Isenberg, *NHL*; *Gospel of Mary*, 17; trans. Karen L. King, George W. MacRae, R. McL. Wilson, Douglas M. Parrott, *NHL*. For many other references see Kathleen E. Corley, *Private Women, Public Meals: Social Conflict in the Synoptic Tradition* (Peabody, Mass.: Hendrickson, 1993) 114 n.28.

[3] See Orig. *C. Cels*. 3.55. The notion of 'women's religions' is an important concept in the recent excellent study by Ross S. Kraemer, *Her Share of the Blessings: Women's Religions Among Pagans, Jews, and Christians in the Greco-Roman World* (Oxford and NY: Oxford University, 1992) 3.

[4] R. MacMullen, *Christianizing the Roman Empire (AD 100–400)* (New Haven and London: Yale, 1984) 39.

[5] See Strabo, *Geography*, 7.3.4 (C 297); trans. H. L. Jones (LCL 1924); cited in Kraemer, *Her Share*, 3.

Defining the task

ancient author Plutarch, fidelity to one's husband meant fidelity to his gods and the ability to 'shut the front door tight upon all queer rituals and outlandish superstitions. For with no god do stealthy and secret rites performed by a woman find any favour.'[6] The Greek term 'πάροιστρος', rendered here as 'hysterical', deserves special attention at the outset.[7] I have opted for this translation and not for the alternate, and no doubt less 'loaded', translation of πάροιστρος as 'frenzied'.[8] I have done so because 'hysterical' in the modern world is so strongly associated with women's behaviour which is out of control, with female nature that has gone morally and intellectually awry, with weakness and vulnerability inherent in the female sex. When Celsus' description of the woman witness to the resurrection is read in relation to his descriptions of other women these stereotypical perceptions about

---

6   Plutarch, *Moralia (Advice to Bride and Groom)* 140D; trans. F. C. Babbitt (LCL 1928). For more evidence that women were considered especially susceptible to strange religious impulses see Margaret Y. MacDonald, 'Early Christian Women Married to Unbelievers', *SR* 19:2 (1990) 229–31; Kraemer, *Her Share*, 211 n.1; MacMullen, *Christianizing*, 137 n.33.
7   Orig. *C. Cels.* 2.55; 2.59. See *Patristic Greek Lexicon*, G. Lampe (ed.) (Oxford: Clarendon, 1968) s.v. πάροιστρος. In adopting the translation of this term as 'hysterical', I am following Chadwick (see n.1 above). I am grateful to my research assistant Dilys Patterson for pointing out the fluid meaning of this word. I am also grateful to Steven Muir for the study he undertook of this term and its cognates. Some of the results of his investigation can be seen in 'Rebellion, Debauchery, and Frenzy in the Septuagint', *Nuntius* 16 .2 (1993) 19–21. Although this is not a common word, it is derived from the more common term οἰστράω which refers to the sting of the gadfly, and metaphorically to frenzy or madness. It often has a sexual connotation: Euripedes, *Bacchae*, trans. A. S. Way (LCL 1916) 32; 119; 1229 offers an especially appropriate illustration of this sense. See Henry George Liddel and Robert Scott, *A Greek English Lexicon* (Oxford: Clarendon Press, 1940), s.v. οἰστράω. The term πάροιστρος is to be distinguished from ὑστερικός, the Greek term from which the English 'hysterical' is derived. The literal meaning of ὑστερικός is 'suffering in the womb', a disease of women which produces such broad symptoms as apnea and convulsions. Although there are some convergences in meaning, in ancient literature ὑστερικός does not seem to be as directly associated with deranged behaviour as πάροιστρος. On the Greek term ὑστερικός see Liddell and Scott, *Greek English Lexicon*. In the medical writings of Soranus and Galen this condition is said to produce such symptoms as apnea, fainting, and convulsions. According to Soranus, deranged behaviour appears as a type of after-effect of ὑστερικός. See Galen, *On the Affected Parts*, 6.5; trans. Rudolph E. Siegel (Basel: S. Karger, 1976); Soranus, *Gynecology*, 3.4.26; trans. Owsei Temkin (Baltimore: John Hopkins, 1956). It is interesting to consider the implications of the association of involuntary celibacy with ὑστερικός in ancient medical writings. This point will be discussed further in Part 2.
8   Chadwick translates the term as 'hysterical' (see n.1 above). Note, however, that Harold Remus adopts the translation of Celsus' phrase as 'frenzied woman' in *Pagan-Christian Conflict over Miracle in the Second Century* (Cambridge, MA: Philadelphia Patristics Foundation, 1983) 107.

women emerge clearly. It is precisely these perceptions that I would like to recall for my readers in order that they might reflect upon how strongly stereotypes impinge upon characterizations of female behaviour both in ancient and modern societies – in order that they may sense the seemingly timeless imprint of stereotypes on the collective imagination.

I have, however, decided to set the stage for my discussion with Celsus' description of the hysterical woman for a further reason. The account moves quickly from testimony that a woman behaved in predictably deranged ways to an unwitting admission of the importance of her involvement in the telling of the tale. Moreover, while he clearly sought to downplay success, Celsus' efforts belie the fact that by the second century CE a significant population found the 'cock-and-bull' story to be convincing. The description of the 'hysterical woman' calls to mind the ambivalent attitude in antiquity towards religious talents displayed by women: these talents were both admired and held in great suspicion. For an illustration of this perception of religious talent we might consider the Sybil, a prophetess of obscure origin known to us from Jewish and pagan sources. Her proximity to early Christian circles is revealed by her appearance in an early second-century Christian text, *The Shepherd of Hermas*. During the course of his adventures Hermas mistakenly assumes that an elderly lady seen in a vision bearing a book of 'revelations' is the Sybil (she turns out to be the church).[9] Hermas' assumption and the disclosure of the woman's true identity are perhaps inspired by a need to respond to a common opinion of non-Christians about the prominence of female prophets and teachers in the early church. Celsus recounts that some early Christians are in fact 'Sybillists'.[10] Within early Christian groups the influence of women teachers was a subject of concern and could sometimes even elicit wrath, as is suggested by the haunting depictions of the suffering that will befall the prophetess Jezebel of the church at Thyatira (Rev. 2.19–23).[11]

The word 'hysterical' ($\pi\acute{\alpha}\rho o\iota\sigma\tau\rho o\varsigma$) employed by Celsus in

---

[9] *Herm. Vis.* 2.4.1. See *The Shepherd of Hermas* in K. Lake trans., *Apostolic Fathers II* (LCL 1913). On the origins of the Sybil see Robin Lane Fox, *Pagans and Christians* (New York, Alfred A. Knopf, 1986) 202–3.   [10] Orig. *C. Cels.* 6.34.

[11] See also Kraemer's interesting discussion of Jewish 'witches' in *Her Share*, 90, 108–9.

conjunction with the term 'sorcery' certainly calls to mind the notion of a deluded, deranged female, but we should be cautious about reading Celsus' clearly derogatory description as implying that the prototypic Christian (hysterical) woman was powerless or without influence. Important male figures in the development of Christianity receive similar categorization. In other places in Celsus' account (as recorded by Origen) πάροιστρος refers to the utterings of false prophets and messianic pretenders, which Origen takes to mean the prophets of Hebrew Scripture.[12] Furthermore, far from being simply deluded and immobilized by hysteria, the woman described by Celsus was an active witness, a teller of a fantastic tale. As will be discussed later in this volume, Christians could likewise describe women as both victims (e.g. 2 Tim. 3.6–7) and dangerous perpetrators (e.g. 1 Tim. 5.13) of fantastic tales. Thus, Christians and non-Christians shared the sentiment that women were inclined toward excesses in religious matters. The result, I will argue, was that early Christian women who risked public censure for their religious activities also were often the object of careful monitoring by those inside the church.

In order to gain a greater sense of the dual image of the hysterical woman as both deluded female and influential evangelist, it is valuable to assemble the references to women made by the first non-Christian observers of early Christianity. In Part 1 of this book I examine the comments of second-century pagan[13] authors who refer specifically to early Christian women. The early church works from the first and second centuries CE (including the New Testament) discussed in Parts 2 and 3 offer further indications of how women figured in public opinion about Christianity. My goal in Parts 2 and 3, however, also is to shed light on how public opinion about women in the church shaped early Christian teaching concerning women and, therefore, affected the lives of women. Generally, I aim to illustrate in this book the importance of the issue of female visibility in the relationship between the early church and Greco-Roman society. I seek to show what aspects of

[12] C.Cels.7.9–10.
[13] The word 'pagan' has no derogatory meaning in this book. It is employed in the usual sense adopted by scholars of the ancient world to distinguish Jews and early Christians from others in the Greco-Roman world.

the lives of early Christian women caught the attention of outside observers, and I consider how that attention may have been related to the increasing tension between church and society as the church moved into the second century.

To assess how church women figured in general *public opinion* is admittedly somewhat problematic. We have a few statements of intellectuals and government officials (representatives of elite social circles), which are the earliest descriptions of church members by non-Christians. These statements are of debatable value for determining *popular* reaction to Christianity. However, the second-century critiques of the early church which I analyse in Part 1 of this book reveal the strong influence of the rumours, impressions, and stereotypes which reverberate throughout society at all levels, elite and popular. In turn, the early Christian sources I discuss in Parts 2 and 3 disclose concern not only about highly visible behaviour of women which might cause reprisals from government officials, but also about the negative assessments which generally might result from chance encounters between outsiders and worshipping early church women. My contention in this book is that it is important to study the literary records of non-Christian observers of the church in conjunction with church texts which reveal sensitivity to the impressions of outsiders. In this way, we get a comprehensive picture: we see the importance of women in opinions about the church formed both in elite circles as well as the sectors of society that made up the remaining ninety-nine per cent of the population, the sectors of society from which virtually all early Christians came.[14]

A focus on the place of women in public opinion about the church can increase our knowledge of the history of early Christian women in two important ways. First, the remarks of non-Christian observers sometimes can offer details about the lives of early Christian women which either augment what is known on the basis of Christian sources or, more often, cause one to assess Christian evidence somewhat differently. For example, Lucian of

---

[14] Mary Ann Tolbert, 'Social, Sociological, and Anthropological Methods', in Elisabeth Schüssler Fiorenza (ed.), *Searching the Scriptures: Vol. 1, A Feminist Introduction* (New York: Crossroad, 1993) 269.

Samosata's description of Christian widows accompanied by children calls into question the tendency among scholars to polarize the lives of married early church women and unmarried early church women.[15] Secondly, a focus on how women figured in public opinion about the early church leads one to probe how the lives of early Christian women were shaped by stereotypical perceptions about women's roles in religion and society. I argue in this book that, for a variety of reasons, the early church threatened images of the ideal woman that existed in the ancient Mediterranean world. There was, in fact, such extensive convergence between notions of the ideal wife and mother in antiquity, despite a great range of time and geography, as to lead the ancient historian Mary Lefkowitz to offer the following assessment of the marital advice given by Plutarch in the second century CE: 'He was an antiquarian and historian and he studied and read enough to know that the concept of a married woman's role had not changed very much over seven hundred years.'[16] Early Christianity sometimes came to be seen as threatening the portrait of the ideal wife that typically included the virtues of chastity, proper care for husband and children, and exemplary management of the household. Instead of the ideal mother described by Tacitus whose greatest pleasure came from managing her own house and giving herself to her children, the early Christian woman was the wicked woman of Apuleius' *Metamorphoses* who combined secret religious rites with unchastity.[17] Instead of being discreet and modest, she was excessive and hysterical.

The writings of church authors from New Testament times onwards contain indications of the need to explain and direct the behaviour of women that arose in response to the critical remarks of outsiders and their unjust treatment of Christians. A key text for understanding early church response to public opinion about Christian women, 1 Timothy 5.3–16, suggests that the author of the Pastoral Epistles restricts the activities of young widows in

[15] See Part 3, pp. 227-30.
[16] Mary Lefkowitz, 'Wives and Husbands', *Greece and Rome*, 30 (1983) 46.
[17] See Tacitus, *Dialogus*, 28.4–5; Apuleius, *Metamorphoses*, 9.14. While the description in the *Metamorphoses* might refer to a woman who was a Jewish proselyte, it may also express a typical pagan observer's opinion of the Christian wife of a mixed marriage.

direct response to the community being reviled by outsiders. More accepting of Christian women's initiative and more vocal about the cruel treatment of Christians, Justin Martyr's *Apology* 2.2 explains how an exemplary Roman matron's efforts to divorce an immoral pagan husband culminate in the execution of her Christian teacher. 1 Timothy 5.3–16 and Justin's *Apology* 2.2 are examples of early Christian texts that I have selected for analysis in this book because they combine a discussion of women's behaviour with concern about the reaction of the outside world. Displaying a sensitivity to public perceptions about the activities of early Christian women, they lead us to reflect about the central issues involved in the church's interaction with Greco-Roman society. I have chosen to study particular texts produced in various church settings on the basis of their relevance for the topic, but there are no doubt other texts which are pertinent to the discussion. It is my hope that this investigation will serve as a point of departure for further exploration.

As a convenient way of managing the discussion, I have organized the early Christian material in relation to two themes. In Part 2 of the book, I deal with celibate early Christian women, including virgins, divorced women, and widows. In Part 3, I consider the lives of married early Christian women, both those who were married to Christian husbands and those who were married to non-believers. Although I have chosen this organizational framework, I do not mean to imply that there were diametrically opposite public reactions to early Christian married and unmarried women. In fact, I will argue that there is considerable overlap both in how married and unmarried women figured in public opinion about the church, and in early Christian responses to that public opinion. Not only by admitting celibate women, but also by accepting into membership married women unaccompanied by their spouses, church groups inevitably came into conflict with conventional ideals of female identity and behaviour. Yet, church authors also took great care to prescribe rules governing the lives of women (both married and unmarried) that matched the household ethics of Greco-Roman society. This 'balancing act' between challenge and acceptance of mainstream ethical values can be seen, for example, in the remarks of the author of 1 Peter. The effect of

1 Peter 3.1–6 is to legitimate the continuing relationship between Christian wives and pagan husbands. Such an effort flies in the face of Greco-Roman notions of marriage propriety which call for a woman to share the religion of her husband. In essence, 1 Peter sanctions a type of insubordination. But the author of 1 Peter also ensures that wives behave in the submissive, chaste, and reverent way that would appease a pagan husband and most likely also quiet any slander. Much of my study is devoted to understanding how women participated in the often ambivalent early church overtures to the Greco-Roman world.

The era which is relevant for the topic of early Christian women and public opinion about the Church begins in New Testament times and reaches to the Age of Constantine. However, with respect to the early Christian sources treated in this book, I have confined my study to the New Testament and Patristic material from the middle of the first century to the middle of the second century CE. There is inevitably a need to set realistic limits for a given research project. In addition, my choice to set my point of investigative departure at about 50 CE, when Paul was in the midst of his missionary campaign, and my end-point at about the time of the writing of Justin's Apology to Antoninus Pius around 156 CE, has been made because of a desire to understand the specific historical developments in this formative period of church history. In this study I am especially interested in the transition from a group (or groups) which would have appeared to observers as one Jewish faction among many, to a group (or groups) which by the early second century was clearly recognizable as a distinct entity, was increasingly subject to hostility, and was beginning to engage in sustained efforts at apology. This book aims to shed light on the part played by women in the increasing visibility of early Christianity and the growing dialogue between early Christianity and Greco-Roman society.

There is substantial overlap in terms of dates, social setting, and subject matter between New Testament works and the earliest church documents studied by Patristic scholars. Yet, the theological importance attributed to the New Testament in Christian circles has traditionally meant that the New Testament Canon continues to determine the division of labour between New

Testament scholars and scholars of the earliest Patristic literature. Probably because the parameters of fields of scholarship are generally slow to evolve, even scholars who are primarily interested in the historical study of early church texts have been reluctant to cross these self-imposed subject boundaries. In my opinion, this tendency has led to an incomplete understanding of the important developments in church history during the first half of the second century CE. Our understanding of the lives of early Christian women is strengthened, for example, when we analyse the developments evident in the Pastoral Epistles in light of similar developments apparent in the writings of Ignatius of Antioch, both works probably dating from the early second century CE and sharing similar interests in the development of church offices and the encouragement of Christian marriages. Moreover, scholars generally accept the thesis that the end of the first century CE onward was characterized by an increased 'patriarchalization' of the church that manifested itself in an appeal for Christian wives to be model wives according to Greco-Roman ideals of fidelity and subjugation; such patriarchalization is said to have occurred as a direct result of early Christian concern for their public image in the face of growing societal hostility.[18] But in order to evaluate the validity of this thesis it is vital to undertake a thorough overview of the part women played in the interaction between church groups and Greco-Roman society from Paul's day to the period when the last New Testament writings and earliest extra-canonical early Christian documents were produced.

Paul's letters are central to my study because they offer fascinating evidence from the earliest period of church history of patterns of life which could pose challenges to Greco-Roman society. Although Paul demonstrates some concern for social respectability which becomes even more developed in writings of his successors, 1 Corinthians 7 still provides fruitful material for exploring how the early church encouraged women to behave in highly controversial, if not counter-cultural, ways. For example, when Paul in 1 Corinthians 7.40 advised widows (without limiting his instruc-

---

[18] See discussion in Part 3, pp. 236–7 where I consider in detail the work of scholars who support this thesis.

tions to older women) to remain unmarried, the Apostle was confronting a society whose legislation called for the remarriage of widows. In contrast, material from the end of the first century CE to the middle of the second century CE has often been judged to be more concerned with appeasing tension between the church and world than with bold confrontation of societal ideals and laws concerning women.[19] It is in these texts that we can trace Christianity's earliest responses to increasingly hostile public opinion. From the correspondence of Ignatius of Antioch, for example, we gain insight into the reactions of a church subject to hostility during the reign of Trajan (98–117 CE). Encouragement to marry other Christians with the permission of the bishop clearly acts to protect the group – it is an injunction towards endogamy. When one compares Ignatius' cautious attitude towards celibacy with his endorsement of traditional marriage arrangements (Ign. *Pol.* 5.1–2), one is struck by this emergence of ethical sobriety at the beginning of the second century, a development which stands in contrast to Paul's rather bold encouragement of asceticism in the middle of the first century.

The reformulation of conventional social values into the paradigm of the ideal Christian couple had tremendous importance for early Christian women, and it certainly led to restrictions of women's activities and heightened encouragement of Christian wives to obey their husbands. Yet, I will demonstrate that it is misleading to view this development as being simply the result of quick (even mean-spirited) expediency in the face of growing concern about the church's public image. To understand the part played by ethical exhortations governing women's lives in early church response to increasingly hostile public opinion, we must be aware of Greco-Roman ideals concerning women and religion. In particular, we must recognize the symbolic significance of women's

---

[19] Commenting on the abandonment of Paul's preference for celibacy and virginity by the beginning of the second century, Elizabeth A. Clark has argued that 'the ordering of the household deemed normal by late ancient pagan society tended to prevail in Christianity as well'. See 'Early Christian Women: Sources and Interpretation', in *The Gentle Strength: Historical Perspectives on Women in Christianity*, L. Coon (ed.) (Charlottesville and London: University of Virginia, 1990) 21. For similar comments see Margaret Y. MacDonald, 'The Ideal of the Christian Couple: Ign. *Pol.* 5.1–2 Looking back to Paul', *NTS* 40 (1994) 105–6.

behaviour as an expression of group identity and group concern for reputation in ancient Mediterranean society.

The examination in Part 1 of the first non-Christian descriptions of the early church where reference is made to women will illustrate the symbolic significance of women's behaviour in ancient society, and it will shed light upon why women played such an important role in public opinion about the church. All of the sources in Part 1 are from the second century CE. Often impossible to date precisely, some of the material may have originated as late as about 170 CE, a few decades after the period mainly under discussion in this book. This is probably the case, for example, with Celsus.[20] But because of the enormous importance of this author's comments concerning early Christian women and because of obvious correspondence between his remarks and earlier treatments of the church by non-Christians, I have chosen to give Celsus an important place in this book. At first glance it may seem like questionable historical practice to place the critiques of second-century pagan authors in relation to early Christian sources that include much first-century material. But I argue here that it is precisely through studying the earliest literary references to church women by non-Christians, that one becomes alerted to indications in New Testament texts of the first encounter of church groups with expressions of public opinion which, at the outset, likely took the form of rumour and impression.

It is fitting that we consider the remarks of the first pagan critics of early Christianity from the time of Pliny the Younger's correspondence at the beginning of the second century to Celsus' era, for in so doing we will move progressively from scanty and impressionistic descriptions of early church groups to much more detailed and systematic treatments of early Christianity. From Celsus we will hear of women being at the centre of Christianity's inception, of women being involved in the development of core beliefs and of women who were evangelists. As we turn to early Christian sources in Parts 2 and 3 the mounting tension between Christians and the larger society that can be sensed with respect to female

---

[20] On the difficulty of dating Celsus see Robert M. Grant, *Greek Apologists of the Second Century* (Philadelphia: Westminster, 1988) 132–9.

visibility will gain new significance. Much will be revealed about the complexity of the involvement of women in the interaction between early Christianity and Greco-Roman society. We will discover women at the centre of early Christianity's offensiveness, but also at the heart of its appeal.

Women's studies in early Christianity and cultural anthropology

This study is a contribution to the current interest in the recovery of information about the lives of early Christian women in the Greco-Roman world. I am sensitive to Bernadette Brooten's warning that the history of early Christian women must be more than the study of male attitudes towards women; the primary focus should be on women.[21] Yet since in this book I am dealing with how the activities of church women cut across the ideals about women in Greco-Roman society and how public opinion helped to shape the ideals about women upheld in early Christianity, a major part of this study necessarily explores the attitudes of male authors. With that said, women remain at the centre of this investigation in the sense that my primary concern will be to ask how women were affected by, and in turn how they affected, the ideals that touched their lives.[22]

There is no doubt that the current interest in the history of early Christian women is related to the capacity of the sources somehow to reflect, and even to address, the experiences of modern women both inside and outside the Christian tradition. For example, the story of the *Acts of Paul and Thecla*, discussed in Part 2 of this book, illustrates the hostility which continues to be bestowed on women by family and society when they circumvent cultural norms. Yet, while modern women have sometimes seen their own situations reflected in the accounts of the lives of women in the ancient world, scholars are becoming wary of supposing that the motives, expectations, and desires of women in antiquity easily can be

---

[21] See B. Brooten, 'Early Christian Women and Their Cultural Context: Issues of Method in Historical Reconstruction' in *Feminist Perspectives on Biblical Scholarship*, A. Y. Collins (ed.) (Chico, Calif., Scholars, 1985) 80.   [22] Ibid., 82.

understood in modern terms.[23] Whether we consider the cultural codes governing the face-to-face contact of life in the city, laws concerning marriage and family, or even the attitudes about procreation and the physical demands of bearing children, we continue to encounter the 'otherness' of Greco-Roman society. We enter a world where physiognomical handbooks present scrutiny of others as an essential survival skill,[24] a world where divorced women often had no rights to their children,[25] a world where the physical demands of multiple pregnancies were so great as to lead one scholar to conclude: 'Un mari amoureux était une catastrophe.'[26] It is in this world that we must place the concern in early church circles about the public perception of worshipping women, the quiet determination of Christian women to be submissive to their non-believing husbands, and the bold enterprise of church virgins and widows to remain holy in body and spirit.

To ensure an appreciation of the 'otherness' of the society where Christianity had its origins, one obviously must strive to explore the intersection between early Christian texts and Greco-Roman society. Thus, this work is fundamentally a historical study. Yet, I have learned a great deal from scholars who, influenced by the methodologies of the social sciences, claim that the deliberate use of models (simplified representations of real-world objects, events, or interactions) can lend greater precision and control in dealing with historical evidence, can increase awareness of previously unconscious frames of reference, and thus can act as a corrective to the tendency for modern anachronistic presuppositions to dominate one's reading.[27] Allowing the 'foreign' New Testament world to emerge, ready to challenge current interpretations of

---

[23] See for example Carol Meyers, *Discovering Eve: Ancient Israelite Women in Context* (New York and Oxford University Press, 1988) 34; M. Lefkowitz, 'Wives and Husbands', 31–2; Gillian Clark, *Women in the Ancient World* (Oxford: University, 1989) 1–2.

[24] See M. W. Gleason, 'The Semiotics of Gender: Physiognomy and Self-Fashioning in the Second Century C. E.', in *Before Sexuality: The Construction of Erotic Experience in the Ancient World*, D. M. Halperin, J. J. Winkler, F. I. Zeitlin (eds.) (Princeton: University Press, 1990) 389.   [25] See G. Clark, 'Roman Women', *Greece and Rome* 28 (1981) 205.

[26] See Aline Rousselle, 'La Politique des Corps: Entre Procréation et Continence à Rome', in *Histoire des Femmes en Occident, L'Antiquité* vol. 1 (Georges Duby and Michelle Perrot (eds.), Paris: Plon, 1991) 346.

[27] For an extensive discussion of models and their usefulness in the historical enterprise see T. F. Carney, *The Shape of the Past: Models and Antiquity* (Lawrence, Kansas: Coronado,

texts, has been especially important for scholars making use of the insights from cultural anthropology. They have noted anthropology's sensitivity to anachronism and ethnocentricity in the study of cultures, and they have sought to avoid these tendencies in the reading of biblical texts. In addition, they have called for the use of models which facilitate the cross-cultural comparison of the social context of the interpreter with the object being interpreted.[28] I have found anthropology of Mediterranean societies to be especially suggestive for the present study. Of the models emerging from the work of anthropologists which are of importance in this investigation, the honour/shame syndrome and the 'men: public domain/ women: private domain' dichotomy are especially significant and will be examined in detail below.

Social-scientific interpretation

Doing interdisciplinary work requires considerable methodological sophistication and it is not without risk. Much has been written about the use of social-scientific models in biblical interpretation and it is impractical to repeat all the theoretical

1975). Carney has had an enormous influence on how biblical scholars define and employ models; see Bruce Malina, 'The Social Sciences and Biblical Interpretation', in *The Bible and Liberation: Political and Social Hermeneutics*, N. Gottwald (ed.) (New York: Maryknoll, 1983) 14, 24 n.14. On models and the study of early Christianity see Philip Francis Esler, *Community and Gospel in Luke-Acts: The Social and Political Motivations of Lucan Theology* (Cambridge University Press, 1987) 24–6; M. Y. MacDonald, *The Pauline Churches: A Socio-Historical Study of Institutionalization in the Pauline and Deutero-Pauline Writings* (Cambridge: University, 1988) 26–7; Bruce Malina, *Christian Origins and Cultural Anthropology: Practical Models for Biblical Interpretation* (Atlanta: John Knox, 1986); B. Holmberg, *Sociology and the New Testament: An Appraisal* (Minneapolis: Fortress, 1990) 12–15; John H. Elliott, *What is Social-Scientific Criticism?* (Minneapolis: Fortress, 1993) 40–8; see also pp.124–6 where Elliott collects the major social-scientific models being employed in New Testament criticism.

28 The seminal work on the New Testament and Cultural Anthropology has been undertaken by Bruce Malina. Malina speaks of New Testament 'foreigners' in *The New Testament World: Insights from Cultural Anthropology* (London: SCM, 1981). See also Jerome H. Neyrey, *Paul, in Other Words: A Cultural Reading of His Letters* (Louisville, Kentucky: John Knox Press, 1990) 12–14; B. Malina and J. Neyrey, *Calling Jesus Names: The Social Value of Labels in Matthew* (Sonoma, California: Polebridge, 1988) 145–51; Elliott, *What is Social-Scientific Criticism?* 45. The anthropological approaches to the study of the New Testament may be distinguished from the sociological approaches, but it is impossible to arrive at absolute divisions between the methodological realms; see Tolbert, 'Social, Sociological, and Anthropological Methods', 256–7.

discussions here.[29] Yet, it is useful to explore methodological issues which seem particularly relevant for this study. Consideration of general questions that have arisen about the use of social-scientific methods for the interpretation of ancient texts will lead us to discuss how anthropological studies might help us define an approach to the study of early Christian women.

By comparing early Christian texts with the findings of anthropologists of modern Mediterranean societies I will be comparing early Christianity to phenomena from different historical situations.[30] The benefit of engaging in comparison between early Christianity and movements, groups, and societies of another time is that often much more is known about them than about the early church. But, as has been frequently noted, the danger lies in the temptation for scholars to use modern data to fill in gaps in the evidence from the past. Moreover, the desire to discover analogy must be balanced with the realization that no phenomenon ever corresponds perfectly to another.[31] If one notes, for example, that a woman's domestic behaviour both in modern rural Greece and in Greco-Roman society is understood as indicative of the stability of both household and of society as a whole, we must not assume that 'home', 'family', and 'marriage' mean exactly the same thing in both contexts. However, when anthropologists note that it is common in Mediterranean societies to link a wife's suspicious absence from the house, disregard for housework, or excessive gossiping, with perceptions about her basic moral nature,[32] we may raise interesting new questions about how to read ancient references to feminine vices: Hermas' wife who 'does not refrain her tongue with which she sins' (*Herm. Vis.* 2.2.3), or the young widows censured by the author of the Pastorals for 'gadding about from

---

[29] Two recent works offer thorough discussions: Holmberg, *Sociology and the New Testament*; Elliott, *What is Social-Scientific Criticism?* In contrast to Holmberg, Elliott evaluates both anthropological and sociological approaches.

[30] On the comparative method in the social-scientific interpretation of religious traditions see Gerd Theissen, 'The Sociological Interpretation of Religious Traditions: Its Methodological Problems as Exemplified in Early Christianity', *The Social Setting of Pauline Christianity* (Edinburgh: T & T Clark, 1982) 192–5. On the comparative method see also Holmberg, *Sociology and the New Testament*, 114–17; Esler, *Community and Gospel*, 9–12.   [31] Theissen, 'Sociological Interpretation', 194.

[32] See for example, Juliet du Boulay, *Portrait of a Greek Mountain Village* (Oxford: Clarendon, 1974) 131–3.

house to house' (1 Tim. 5.13). This type of 'distant' comparison, as opposed to the more widely used method of comparison of phenomena from the same historical context, does not involve the verification of hypotheses in the first instance, but it may assist in the formulation of new hypotheses worthy of further exploration.[33] These hypotheses must then be verified with data from the ancient sources.

A second benefit of engaging in cross-cultural, and indeed transhistorical, comparison is that it may help us bridge the gap between the society in which we live and the ancient world which is so remote. It may seem that the way to avoid anachronism and ethnocentrism in the study of ancient societies is to devote one's attention exclusively to them. However, the large gaps in evidence and the puzzling findings that the historian must face means that it is all too easy to read between the lines, assuming we understand the situation based on our own experiences. When dealing with the New Testament we encounter the additional difficulty of working with a text whose very familiarity and continued connection with our own culture rid it somewhat of its power to surprise us.[34] I am not claiming that it is possible to be free of all the presuppositions and priorities that are tied to our cultural context when we deal with ancient texts.[35] In fact, a major contribution of feminist biblical scholarship has been its ability to demonstrate that value-neutrality is not only an impossible dream, but it is also a goal that prevents scholars from becoming aware of the political context of their own work and its public responsibility.[36] My historical research in this book has been inspired by the questions of our own time; from introduction to choice of models to conclusions. Yet I

---

[33] On 'close' and 'distant' comparison and their differing roles in the verification and formulation of hypotheses see Esler, *Community and Gospel*, 10.

[34] See James L. Resseguie, 'Defamiliarization and the Gospels', *BTB* 20 (1990) 147–53.

[35] Note that Malina seems to imply that it is possible to do this when he argues that the approach he develops in *Christian Origins and Cultural Anthropology*, is 'consistently comparative, heading off ethnocentrism from the very outset', p. iv. See the interesting review of Malina's book by Susan R. Garrett in *JBL* 107 (1988) 532–4. Garrett argues that 'Malina's omission of any discussion of the theoretical underpinnings of [Mary] Douglas' model fosters an impression of the model as absolute – as somehow untainted by the ethnocentrism that it aims to circumvent' (p. 533).

[36] See Elisabeth Schüssler Fiorenza, 'The Ethics of Biblical Interpretation: Decentring Biblical Scholarship', *JBL* 107 (1988) 10–11.

also believe that there is a need both to approach ancient people with the kind of respect we give other contemporary cultures and to savour the richness of a world which, in many ways, is very foreign to us. If we introduce a third cultural group into our dialogue between Greco-Roman society and our own, we may be more successful in this task. To experience a society as 'other' and then to compare that group with ancient society, may allow the distinctive nature of various elements of ancient society to stand out more sharply. The distance between our world[37] and modern Mediterranean society may alert us to the distance between our world and ancient Mediterranean society.

The findings of anthropologists of the Mediterranean have been employed with increasing frequency over the past few years by historians of antiquity and of the early church, researchers of formative Judaism, and biblical scholars in the hope of shedding light upon cultural systems which may seem quite alien in our contexts. The attraction of scholarship to the societies of the modern Mediterranean is probably due to the fact that these societies are distinct enough, both from our world and from the ancient people who are the primary focus of the investigation, to allow for truly cross-cultural investigation. Yet the choice of working with the investigations of anthropologists of the modern Mediterranean, is also related to the perception that modern Mediterranean societies are sufficiently similar to ancient Mediterranean societies to make comparison meaningful.[38] While anthropologists argue in favour of the existence of a distinct Mediterranean cultural region primarily (though not exclusively) on modern evidence, early Christianity scholars have extended this notion of unity to encompass ideas about historical continuity. For example, Jerome H. Neyrey makes the following statement in his investigation of how

[37] I am aware that my world in a Canadian context is somewhat different from the world of a reader in an American or British context, and quite possibly dramatically different from readers in other social locations. I have nevertheless chosen to speak of 'our world' as a means of referring to the many values and presuppositions that I share in common with readers who have been influenced by what has sometimes been called 'North-Atlantic' culture.

[38] This is in keeping with Theissen's outline of comparative procedures. He speaks of the comparison of *substantively related* religious movements in differing historical situations. See Theissen, 'Sociological Interpretation', 193. The emphasis is mine.

Mediterranean perceptions of women shaped the way Mary was presented and perceived: 'The Mediterranean cultural area was, and still is, a world divided according to gender: every person, place, object, action is known either as male or female.'[39] Without debating the validity of this particular statement, it is important to be aware of the problem of circular reasoning which may be involved in using modern groups to explain and analyse early Christianity.[40] While the cultural resemblances may be a testimony of a cultural content indigenous to the area and which may predate Christianity itself, the strong presence of Christianity in the Mediterranean region (particularly in the Greek rural life discussed in this book) means we also must admit that some of the analogy may be due to the mirroring or development of early Christian tendencies.

As we compare the societies of early Christianity to modern Mediterranean societies we distance ourselves significantly from our own context far more than we would in a comparison between early Christianity and a modern North American religious group. Furthermore, by considering points of contact between modern Mediterranean societies and early church groups we are taking into consideration analogies between symbol systems which encompass far more than narrowly defined religious meanings. These factors add considerable cross-cultural validity to the enterprise. However, we need to be careful about building models of Mediterranean society based on a kind of indiscriminate amassing of ancient and modern evidence. Scholars have done a good deal to alert us to the foreign nature of the ancient world in relation to our world by means of comparison with alternate social contexts, but the question of cultural continuity requires further examination. While the assumption that ancient Mediterranean people were 'just like us' may stand disproven, the assumption that modern Mediterranean people were 'just like' the ancients could prove to be misleading in new ways. More thought needs to be given to how we deal with the apparent continuity between the

---

[39] See Jerome H. Neyrey, 'Maid and Mother in Art and Literature', *BTB* 20 (1990) 65.

[40] On the problem of circular reasoning in social-scientific interpretation of the New Testament see Holmberg, *Sociology and the New Testament*, 110. See also my response to Holmberg in 'The Ideal of the Christian Couple', n.16, p.108.

modern Mediterranean region and ancient societies in a manner that does not gloss over historical variation. Moreover, assumptions about 'otherness' must not blind us to the possibility of certain elements of continuity existing between ancient society and our own.

Closely related to the methodological reservations that I have raised about the comparison of the early church to groups in different historical contexts is the fear that social-scientific methods may prevent the detection of historical particularities. Rather than beginning with an assumption about the repetitiveness of human behaviour (which is implicit in social-scientific methodologies), one scholar warns that we should be intent on discovering what is distinctive about early Christianity.[41] However, the study of ancient texts gains a new dimension when it is concerned not only with the shape of particular situations, but also with the structure of social situations which characterize many repeated situations.[42] In this book, for example, the incorporation of ethnographic findings concerning the symbolic significance of female behaviour in Mediterranean villages is central to the analysis of the role of stereotypes in the descriptions of Christian women by non-believers. Yet, despite the convincing arguments one might raise in favour of incorporating insights from the social-sciences in the interpretation of ancient texts, dangers remain. Interpreters must remain watchful for the historical arrow that can shatter one's careful reconstructions. Bengt Holmberg expresses a central consideration very well when he states: 'All application of a model or theory in historical or interpretive research underlies the risk of regularizing the bewildering diversity of the source material past the point where one is still looking for inherent generalities and patterns to where one arrives at harmonization and standardization of the evidence.'[43]

Is it possible to avoid completely the harmonization and standardization of evidence when using models? Probably not, for

---

[41] See E. A. Judge, 'The Social Identity of the First Christians: A Question of Method in Religious History', *JRH* 11: 2 (1980) 213. For an example of a second scholar who is sceptical of the use of social-scientific methodologies see C. S. Rodd, 'On Applying a Sociological Theory to Biblical Studies', *JSOT* 19 (1981) 95–106.

[42] See J. H. Elliott, *A Home for the Homeless* (London: SCM, 1982) 9.

[43] Holmberg, *Sociology and the New Testament*, 155.

models are themselves 'constructed by shedding the concrete and rich differences that clothe the similarities'.[44] In dealing with the subject of the present study I am convinced that the best prevention against reductionism is to allow social-scientific and historical modes of interpretation to act as a means of control and correction for one another.[45] Studies of early Christianity which rely on the social sciences usually include 'abstract, generalizing frameworks' which have seemed to some readers to be 'quite unrelated to the texts they purport to illuminate'.[46] In an effort to curtail vagueness and to touch the rich and concrete detail of the lives of early Christian women, I have focused quite intently on the workings of particular texts and I have relied deeply on the findings of ancient historians. In the study of early Christian women and public opinion about the church it is very important not to stare past the complexities of Augustan marriage legislation and the particularities of a world that was fearful of the attraction of Roman women to eastern cults.

Feminist interpretation

Despite the fact that recent investigations of ancient women in the fields of classics, biblical studies, formative Judaism, and early church history display various methodological perspectives, there have been comparatively few which make explicit use of social-scientific models.[47] Feminist biblical scholars have drawn attention to the frequent 'omission of any consideration of gender' in social-

---

[44] See Malina, *Christian Origins and Cultural Anthropology*, 29–30. Malina discusses the nature of models as 'simplified approximations of more complex real world realities; their value consists in the understanding that they can generate and the interpretations that they can corroborate. They are not intended to be statements of absolute truth, and they need to be validated. Moreover, they are abstractions based on similarities only and are constructed by shedding the concrete and rich differences that clothe the similarities.' On the judicious use of models see Holmberg, *Sociology and the New Testament*, 154–5.

[45] See Elliott, *A Home*, 4.

[46] Garrett, Review of Malina, *Christian Origins and Cultural Anthropology*, 534.

[47] On feminist scholarship and interdisciplinary biblical scholarship see Meyers, *Discovering Eve*, 6–23. Meyers notes a certain reluctance in feminist inquiry to take an interdisciplinary approach in biblical scholarship (p. 20). Meyers' own social-scientific perspective for the study of ancient Israelite women aims to correct this deficiency. See especially her use of the work of feminist anthropologists to critique the notion of patriarchy in biblical scholarship (pp. 24–46). With respect to early Christian women, two major works which draw on the findings of anthropologists should be considered. In *Her Share of the Blessings*,

scientific research on Christian origins[48] and to the neglect of feminist scholarship by practitioners of social-scientific criticism.[49] Given the desire of scholars who appeal to social-scientific insights to guard against ethnocentrism and anachronism, it is ironic to hear them being charged with adopting models uncritically, without acknowledging the possibility of bias inherent in the models themselves. Feminist scholars have pointed out that instead of exploring the theoretical frameworks and political implications of models fully, some practitioners of social-scientific criticism accept models uncritically. It is assumed that models have been 'scientifically tested' within the disciplines of sociology and anthropology; they act to disengage one from modern concerns, and they offer complete protection from value-judgment. Mary Ann Tolbert, for example, recently has argued that 'insistence on the differences between North American culture and ancient Mediterranean culture revealed by the use of anthropological models cannot be taken, as it sometimes seems to be, as evidence that the use of such models protects the interpreter from his or her own modern values, concerns, and presuppositions'.[50] In response

Kraemer makes use of Mary Douglas' grid/group model to understand the religious experiences of women in antiquity. In *Private Women, Public Meals*, Corley makes use of anthropological insights on food and meal innovation to evaluate the significance of the presence of women at meals in the Gospels. Other studies of early Christianity which use anthropological insights to understand the lives of early Christian women include: Stuart L. Love, 'Women's Roles in Certain Second Testament Passages: A Macrosociological View', *BTB* 17 (1987) 50–9; Stuart L. Love, 'The Household: A Major Social Component for Gender Analysis in the Gospel of Matthew: A Macrosociological View', *BTB* 23 (1993) 21–31; Stuart L. Love, 'The Place of Women in Public Settings in Matthew's Gospel: A Sociological Inquiry', *BTB* 24 (1994) 52–65; Maryanne Stevens, 'Paternity and Maternity in the Mediterranean: Foundations for Patriarchy', *BTB* 20 (1990), 47–53. (There are several essays in this issue of *BTB* which study Mary employing anthropological insights); Elizabeth A. Clark, 'Sex, Shame, and Rhetoric: En-gendering Early Christian Ethics', *JAAR* 59 (1991) 221–45; Alicia Batten, 'More Queries for Q: Women and Christian Origins', *BTB* 24 (1994) 44–51; Carol Schersten LaHurd, 'Rediscovering the Lost Women in Luke 15', *BTB* 24 (1994) 66–76; Jerome H. Neyrey, 'What's Wrong With This Picture? John 4, Cultural Stereotypes of Women, and Public and Private Space', *BTB* 24 (1994) 77–91.

[48] Tolbert, 'Social, Sociological, and Anthropological Methods', 268.

[49] Elisabeth Schüssler Fiorenza, *But She Said: Feminist Practices of Biblical Interpretation* (Boston: Beacon, 1992) 86, n.11, p. 236; see also pp. 83–6.

[50] Tolbert, 'Social, Sociological, and Anthropological Methods', 268. Here Tolbert refers to the work of Bruce Malina, one of the most important proponents of the use of anthropological models in New Testament interpretation. For similar comments see Schüssler Fiorenza, *But She Said*, 84.

to Tolbert, it should be noted that social-scientific interpreters of the biblical world often make use of models precisely in an effort to bring their modern values into the open and to introduce interpretative categories which are as close to the biblical world as possible. Yet, the suspicion of claims of value-neutrality has been so central to the development of feminist readings of early church texts that it must be considered carefully in any attempt to draw upon insights from the social sciences to study early Christian women.

Since the appearance of her ground-breaking work, *In Memory of Her: A Feminist Theological Reconstruction of Christian Origins* (1983), Elisabeth Schüssler Fiorenza has continued to challenge interpreters of biblical texts with respect to the theoretical underpinnings and the contemporary relevance of their work. In her presidential address at the 1987 meeting of the Society of Biblical Literature, Schüssler Fiorenza called for an 'ethics of accountability' which must shape scholarship. Noting the Bible's role in the inspiration of noble causes, but also in the legitimation of dehumanizing ones, Fiorenza awakens the scholar to the contemporary ramifications of the interpretative task:

If the Bible has become a classic of Western culture because of its normativity, then the responsibility of the biblical scholar cannot be restricted to giving 'the readers of our time clear access to the original intentions' of the biblical writers. It must also include the elucidation of the ethical consequences and political functions of biblical texts in their historical as well as in their contemporary sociopolitical contexts.[51]

While the present study extends beyond the New Testament text to include far less well-known and less revered texts, as a whole it treats a body of literature that has undeniably shaped the images of women which form part of our western culture.[52] At various points I entertain the important question of the original intention

---

[51] Elisabeth Schüssler Fiorenza, 'The Ethics of Biblical Interpretation', 15. In this citation Fiorenza refers to K. Stendahl, 'The Bible as a Classic and the Bible as Holy Scripture', *JBL*, 103 (1984) 10.

[52] The formative significance of the Patristic era for contemporary experience is an important theme in E. Pagels' work. For example, see the introduction to *Adam, Eve, & the Serpent* (London: Weidenfeld and Nicolson, 1988) xvii. On the place of Christian teaching on women in the development of the Western tradition see Clark, *Women in the Ancient World*, 2–3.

of ancient authors; but in seeking to understand how women figured in public opinion about the church in the first two centuries of its existence and how this affected church teaching itself, I also consider the ethical consequences and political functions of the texts in their historical contexts. Influenced by the theoretical discussions of social-scientific interpretation of early church texts, I endeavour to be explicit about the distance (and proximity) between ancient Greco-Roman culture and our own. My desire is that the present work will both offer insight into early Christianity in its Greco-Roman context, and also lead to some critical reflection about the patterns of behaviour encoded in our culture. For example, I hope that this study will cause the reader to reflect on the trans-historical survival of expectations concerning female behaviour which continue to shape the lives of women in various ways. I hope that my study will raise questions about why the violation of stereotypes can elicit a violent reaction within societies. I also hope that this window into the lives of women, who risked relations with their families to enter a new religious group, will lead to a further appreciation of the challenges faced by all women who strive to lead 'multi-dimensional' lives.

Consideration of the methodological limits and possibilities of social-scientific interpretation of early church texts in light of feminist critique leads to an obvious, but difficult, question: How does one move from issues of contemporary relevance to ancient texts without simply blurring the lines between social settings and participating in overt reductionism? I remain convinced that a cautious, heuristic use of social-scientific models can help one articulate one's theoretical framework, can facilitate control of historical evidence, and ultimately contribute to a better understanding of the lives of early Christian women.

In the following investigation I have made use of anthropological models and studies of Mediterranean culture in order to facilitate the task of mapping out the distance between the ancient world and our own. This conceptual distance grants both worlds the kind of 'relative' status that will enable us to evaluate them critically. In many respects, I consider much of the present study to be a dialogue between cultures. I have found comparison of texts to the findings of anthropologists of Mediterranean societies extremely useful in guarding against the danger of assimilating the lives of early Christian women to our own experience.[53] Investigators of the lives of early Christian women are accustomed to identifying meanings in early church texts by male authors which are incongruent with contemporary attitudes about the way society should be organized and with views about human dignity. Yet, we must also be open to discovering evidence of activities and ideals of women which are not in keeping with contemporary aspirations. Thus, as will be discussed in this book, the choice for a woman to remain unmarried and, hence, free from the 'bonds' of traditional marriage may have less to do with the contemporary search for male/female equality than might first appear. Or, to offer a second example, the husband/ wife: Christ/ church comparison which is attached to a hierarchical vision of marriage in Pauline literature may lead one initially to conclude that one has discovered a straightforward example of the oppression of woman; but 'contextualization' of the text may reveal a surprising picture of the importance of the woman in the preservation of the identity of both family and church.

Feminist scholars have added their voices to the general call for interpreters of early Christian texts who employ social-scientific insights in their research to immerse themselves in the critical evaluations of the analytical tools they adopt and to become familiar with theoretical and methodological discussions between social scientists themselves.[54] While this endeavour inevitably raises the exigencies of the task, it is worthwhile. Through attending to dialogues between anthropologists I have arrived at what I believe to be some of the most interesting questions to raise in relation to ancient texts. For example, the tendency to associate the value of honour exclusively with men and the value of shame exclusively

---

[53] See Fiorenza's comments about keeping alive the 'irritation' of the original text in 'Ethics of Biblical Interpretation', 14.

[54] Holmberg, *Sociology and the New Testament*, 108–14; Fiorenza, *But She Said*, 84. In her feminist evaluation of social-scientific methods of biblical interpretation, Tolbert includes an interesting discussion of the current state of feminist critique of both sociology and anthropology; see 'Social, Sociological, and Anthropological Methods', 259–64. LaHurd, a practitioner of social-scientific interpretation, has recently discussed the methodological challenges involved in the use of anthropological models to study early Christian women; see 'Rediscovering the Lost Women in Luke 15', 72–4.

with women in Mediterranean societies has recently been critiqued; this leads me to consider how celibate women in Pauline Christianity may sometimes have been responsible for defending their own honour and the honour of church communities.[55] By being attentive to discussion among anthropologists of Mediterranean societies that question the assumption that there is a simple correspondence between the opposition of symbols such as nature/culture, pollution/purity, public/private, or sacred/profane and gender roles, I can raise questions about how we should read the depictions by non-Christians of Christian women as neglectful of household responsibility and early Christianity as a home-based religion. Moreover, the above discussions have shaped my reflections concerning how we should evaluate female involvement in the early church in terms of the categories 'public' and 'private'.[56] My study has also been influenced by the consensus emerging in feminist anthropological studies that patterns of male dominance and sexual asymmetry are subject to considerable cultural variation, and that quick assumptions should not be made about correlations between ideology and the actual shape of female power.[57] Such considerations have informed my analysis of the negative characterizations of early Christian women by non-believers and have led me to re-evaluate commonly held interpretations of such texts as 1 Peter 3.1–6 which have been understood as representing a return to patriarchy in light of a concern for public image. In fact, the closely related 'honour and shame' and 'public: male/ private: female' models, which have been the subject of critical assessment in Mediterranean anthropology, and the concept of power in anthropological discussions of women and culture, are so important for

[55] For a recent assessment of the categories 'honour' and 'shame' in Mediterranean anthropology see David Gilmore, 'Introduction: The Shame of Dishonour', in Gilmore (ed.), *Honour and Shame and the Unity of the Mediterranean* (Washington DC: American Anthropological Association, 1987) 5–8.

[56] See Jill Dubisch, 'Culture Enters through the Kitchen: Woman, Food, and Social Boundaries in Rural Greece' in Dubisch (ed.), *Gender and Power in Rural Greece* (Princeton, NJ: University, 1986) 207–8.

[57] See Michelle Zimbalist Rosaldo and Louise Lamphere (eds.), *Woman, Culture, and Society* (Stanford, California: Stanford University, 1974) 13; Michelle Zimbalist Rosaldo, 'The Use and Abuse of Anthropology: Reflections on Feminism and Cross-Cultural Understandings', *Signs* 5 (1980) 417; Dubisch (ed.), *Gender and Power in Rural Greece*, 17–18.

the present study that I have chosen to give them detailed attention at the outset.

Honour and shame

The values of honour and shame have played such a prominent role in anthropological studies of Mediterranean regions that they are seen as fundamental to the assumption that 'the Mediterranean Basin represents a cultural unity' and, hence, are related to the very inception of 'a Mediterranean focus in cultural anthropology'.[58] In recent years, biblical scholars have turned to anthropological studies of honour and shame and have found these concepts so enlightening as to lead one commentator to declare confidently that honour and shame are 'the core values of the Mediterranean world and of the Bible as well'.[59] Anthropologist David D. Gilmore offers a succinct description of the classic understanding of the honour and shame model:

Honour and shame are reciprocal moral values representing primordial integration of individual to 'group.' They reflect, respectively, the conferral of public esteem upon the person and the sensitivity to public opinion upon which the former depends. . . Since all face-to-face societies are moral communities where public opinion arbitrates reputation, all such societies may be said to have some form of honour and shame. . . However, what seems descriptively outstanding about the Mediterranean variant is the relationship to sexuality and gender distinctions. . .[60]

---

[58] See David Gilmore, 'Introduction: The Shame of Dishonour', 2–3. Gilmore here evaluates the development of the honour and shame model since the appearance of the classic work, Jean G. Peristany (ed.), *Honour and Shame: The Values of Mediterranean Society* (London: Weidenfeld and Nicolson, 1966). See Gilmore, pp. 2–21 which includes a comprehensive bibliography.

[59] See Joseph Plevnik, 'Honour/Shame', in John Pilch and Bruce J. Malina (eds.), *Biblical Social Values and Their Meaning: A Handbook* (Peabody, MA.: Hendrickson, 1993) 95. The seminal work on honour and shame in the New Testament was by Bruce J. Malina; see *New Testament World*, 25–50. See also Halvor Moxnes, 'Honour, Shame, and the Outside World in Paul's Letter to the Romans', in Jacob Neusner (ed.), *The Social World of Formative Christianity and Judaism* (Philadelphia: Fortress, 1988) 207–18; Bruce J. Malina and Jerome H. Neyrey, 'Honour and Shame in Luke-Acts: Pivotal Values of the Mediterranean World', in Neyrey (ed.), *The Social World of Luke-Acts: Models for Interpretation* (Peabody, Mass.: Hendrickson, 1991) 25–65. For an extensive bibliography on honour and shame see Elliott, *Social-Scientific Criticism*, 126.

[60] Gilmore, 'Introduction: The Shame of Dishonour', 3.

Introduction

The relevance of this model for an understanding of early Christian responses to public scrutiny is obvious. In Part 2 I will argue that in 1 Corinthians 7 there are indications that Paul (and the community) has been the recipient of public appraisal and that he is sensitive to public opinion. In trying to understand how Paul's focus on the chastity of women may be related to this sensitivity, it will be especially important to consider how the Mediterranean concept of honour and shame may relate to sexuality and gender distinctions.

In general, anthropological studies have identified *honour* as a value embodied by males and *shame* (here, in a positive sense, as concern for reputation) as embodied by females. Male honour is related to the struggle to preserve the shame of kinswomen. Female shame is demonstrated through sexual chastity. Therefore, male reputation is linked to female sexual conduct. When males are not successful in maintaining the chastity of females, their honour is diminished in relation to other males.[61]

Anthropologists have been interested in exploring how the honour/shame syndrome may be related to economic power and the control of resources. What has been identified as distinctive about Mediterranean regions (in contrast to other societies where affluence is rooted in the control of women and their labour) is that Mediterranean women are valued especially for their chastity, an immaterial resource. The struggle for control of this resource – fundamental to the acquisition of male honour – is characterized by competition and precarious social relations. The struggle does not simply involve two parties, male and female, as one might first expect, but three: 'the masculine experience of sexuality becomes broadened conceptually to encompass a triad involving two men – or groups of men – and a woman, who is reduced to an intermediating object'.[62] Thus when seeking to understand 1 Corinthians 7, we might ask how the virgin holy in body and spirit might act as

---

[61] Ibid., 4. The way honour and shame are portrayed as gender-specific in Mediterranean culture has been of great interest to biblical scholars. See, for example, Malina and Neyrey, 'Honour and Shame in Luke-Acts', 41–4; Plevnik, 'Honour/Shame', in Pilch and Malina (eds.), *Biblical Social Values*, 96.

[62] Gilmore, 'Introduction: The Shame of Dishonour', 4. On female chastity as a resource see the important work by Jane Schneider, 'Of Vigilance & Virgins: Honour, Shame and Access to Resources in Mediterranean Society', *Ethnology* 10 (1971) 1–24.

a mediator between Paul (and the male members of his community) and the male-dominated outside world.

Societies that exhibit the values of honour and shame tend to depict women as being vulnerable to a predatory male sexuality. Anthropologists have explored the relationship between these values and the tendency to 'protect' women through the sexualized division of community space into private and public spheres and through the introduction of physical barriers such as veiling: 'There are indeed few societies outside the Latin and Muslim worlds where women must not be "seen", as though this amounted to the provocative flaunting of a scarce resource.'[63] The discussion of pagan critique of early Christianity in Part 1 will demonstrate that church women could be accused of being too frequently absent from the home, remiss in domestic affairs, and ultimately, of being sexually immoral. Such aspersions cast on female characters in the early church were combined with a general dismissal of early Christianity (especially pronounced in Celsus' criticism) as a religion located in women's quarters. An understanding of the relationship between the honour and shame syndrome and the distinction between female: private space and male: public space can lead us to a greater awareness of the ramifications of this kind of accusation for the male church authors. In precarious attempts to establish public esteem, these writers felt compelled to respond to challenges to their honour from outsiders, and they sought to direct and control the behaviour of female church members.

The inability to ensure that women demonstrate an appropriate sense of shame entails a threat to masculine identity. Likewise, too close an association with domestic affairs on the part of men can lead to a negation of masculine identity. Anthropologists have gathered examples from various Mediterranean communities of the shaming that occurs when men are viewed as being 'too much of the house'.[64] Early church authors of the first and second centuries CE do not tell us explicitly that they have been accused of being 'too much of the house', but as I will argue in subsequent

---

[63] Gilmore, 'Introduction: The Shame of Dishonour', 5. On the relationship between honour and shame and the gender division of space in the ancient world and early Christianity see Neyrey, 'What's Wrong With This Picture?', 80–1.

[64] Ibid., 14; see discussion pp. 8–16.

sections, they frame their ethical exhortations in such a way as to suggest that they experienced such a sentiment. At the very least, it is clear that early Christians were building a household-based movement that would be depicted as suspiciously female-oriented by the pagan critics of the second century.

Public, male / private, female

Both at a symbolic level and in terms of concrete daily activities, women in Greco-Roman society were associated with the private domain of the home. Very early in church history, Christians articulated serious concerns about arrangements within the home and about the model behaviour of women in the home (e.g. Col. 3.18–4.1; Eph. 5.21–6.9). When one examines early Christian exhortations concerning marriages between believing women and non-believing men, the topic of household norms emerges repeatedly. How a believing woman should behave within a household which had a non-believer at its head becomes the subject of serious deliberation (e.g. 1 Pet. 3.1–6). Within the church community, such marriages were clearly of 'public' interest: once a household of a non-believer had been infiltrated by one Christian, there was hope for the further expansion of the group as a whole. The way the household functions as a kind of crossroads between public and private life in early Christianity is a fascinating subject that deserves further study. At this point it is important to recall some generally held conclusions about the household and the involvement of women in early Christianity.

Paul's letters offer several indications that the *ekklesia* (church) gathered in houses (e.g. Rom. 16.5; 1 Cor. 16.19; Phlm. 2). Moreover, as noted above, the household seems to have provided an important arena for conversion. Scholars now recognize that because so much important activity took place in a sphere traditionally associated with women, possibilities for women's involvement in leadership roles must have been greatly increased. Evidence from the Pauline corpus and from Acts which speaks of women as leaders of house-churches has been judged to be especially significant (Phlm. 2; 1 Cor. 16.19; Rom. 16.5; Col. 4.15; Acts

16.14–15, 40).[65] Although we can detect a reduction of options for women's involvement within the more developed hierarchical structure evident at the end of the first century CE, the study of Ignatius of Antioch contained in Part 3 of this book makes it clear that we must be wary about concluding too quickly that the situation changed dramatically during the period we are discussing.

In her recent work, *Her Share of the Blessings: Women's Religions Among Pagans, Jews, and Christians in the Greco-Roman World*, Ross S. Kraemer has turned her attention to the significance of the symbolic use of familial language to express the nature of relationships within the Christian communities, a phenomenon obviously related to the gathering of communities in private homes. According to Kraemer, women's ability to reject traditional roles was facilitated by the use of the familial metaphor: 'By rendering the public realm an extension of the domestic, women were able to exercise power and public functions without explicitly challenging the division of society into public and domestic realms, and the association of women with the domestic.'[66] I believe that Kraemer is correct in identifying a connection between the combination of the public and domestic spheres and the support of women's activities in church circles. Yet, I am struck by the resemblance between what Kraemer identifies as facilitating women's abilities to reject traditional roles – the bringing of the public into the domestic sphere – and the reasons given by non-Christian commentators for why Christianity is such a destructive force in society. As I will demonstrate in Part 1, second-century critics recognized that the early church rendered the public an extension of the domestic, and they attacked Christianity for blurring the conventional distinction between public: male space and private: female space. My desire to understand how the public reaction to early Christian women may have influenced their lives has led me to see the fluid relationship in church communities between the private and the public as being more problematic for women than Kraemer's

---

[65] E. Schüssler Fiorenza, *In Memory of Her: A Feminist Theological Reconstruction of Christian Origins* (London: SCM, 1983) 177–8.

[66] Kraemer, *Her Share*, 142; see 141–2. Here Kraemer compares the adoption of the familial metaphor in early Christianity with the use of titles 'such as "mother of the city" as a means of legitimizing the roles of women benefactors in Greco-Roman cities' (p.142).

Introduction

interpretation admits. If early Christian women did not explicitly challenge either the division of society into public and domestic realms or the association of women with the domestic sphere, why were they accused of doing so by the pagan critics of the second century and what was the effect of this accusation on their lives? Much of Part 1 of this book is devoted to answering this question. But as a means of setting the stage for the discussion, we must evaluate the use of the slippery terms 'public' and 'private' as a means of categorizing the ideals of Greco-Roman society and their influence on male and female behaviour.

In the literature of Greco-Roman society, it is not difficult to find evidence of the public/private dichotomy being used to describe the roles of men and women. In the first century CE Philo expressed an ideal of rigid separation between the male sphere of public life and the female sphere of household management, in relation to the Jewish women of Alexandria:

> Market-places and council-halls and law-courts and gatherings and meetings where a large number of people are assembled, and open-air life with full scope for discussion and action – all these are suitable to men both in war and peace. The women are best suited to the indoor life which never strays from the house, within which the middle door is taken by the maidens as their boundary, and the outer door by those who have reached full womanhood.[67]

Throughout the Empire, among Pagans, Jews, and Christians we hear expressions of the ideal 'spatial' distinction related to sex.[68]

To understand the significance of this distinction, scholars increasingly are drawing upon insights from anthropological

---

[67] See Philo, *The Special Laws*, 3.169–75; excerpt from Ross Kraemer, ed., *Maenads, Martyrs, Matrons, Monastics: A Sourcebook on Women's Religions in the Greco-Roman World* (Philadelphia: Fortress, 1988) 29–30.

[68] For other examples consider Tacitus, *Dialogus*, 28.4–5; Plutarch, *Moralia*, 138A–146A; 1 Corinthians 14.33–6; 1 Timothy 5.13–15; Tertullian, *On the Apparel of Women*, 13; John Chrysostom, *Against Judaizing Christians*, 2.3–6; 4.3. For more evidence of this dichotomy see J. P. Hallett, *Fathers and Daughters in Roman Society* (Princeton: University, 1984) 7–8, 29–30 n. 46. The association of women with the private sphere and men with the public sphere has been the subject of recent studies of early Christianity which may be consulted for further examples. See Corley, *Private Women, Public Meals*, 15–17, 24–79; Karen Jo Torjesen, *When Women were Priests: Women's Leadership in the Early Church and the Scandal of their Subordination in the Rise of Christianity* (San Francisco: Harper, 1993) 111–32; Neyrey, 'What's Wrong with this Picture'; Love, 'The Place of Women in Public Settings'.

studies of traditional Mediterranean societies. It is generally recognized by anthropologists that in such societies, men are associated with the public sphere (commerce, politics, the marketplace, cafés, fields, the place of assembly, etc.) and women are associated with the private sphere (the home). In addition, this spatial division is an important means of maintaining the values of honour and shame discussed previously. In his study of classical Athens, D. Cohen has expressed succinctly the model of gendered public and private space that is operative in the work of several anthropologists:

The house is the domain of secrecy, of intimate life, and honour requires that its sanctity be protected. Any violation of the house is an attack on the honour of its men and the chastity of its women, even if the intruder be only a thief. The separation of women from men and the man's public sphere within this protected domain is the chief means by which sexual purity is both guarded and demonstrated to the community.[69]

An ancient historian might reply that this picture of the division between the spheres of men and women seems far more applicable to the wife of classical Athens than to the Roman woman. The Roman wife was more publicly visible, had greater freedom of movement and exerted more influence (indirectly, but often very effectively) in that most public of domains, the world of politics.[70] Yet, we must not assume that emergence from behind the walls of a house necessarily implies an abandonment of the separation between the men's public, outside sphere and the women's private, inside sphere. In discussing the issue of the emancipation of Roman women, Jane F. Gardner has warned that women's highly visible activities were frequently more formal than real, their offices were largely honorific, and a woman's political influence still was 'exercised on a personal basis, on private occasions in

---

[69] D. Cohen, 'Seclusion, Separation and the Status of Women in Classical Athens', *Greece and Rome* 36 (1989) 6. See the following studies by anthropologists: J. Campbell, *Honour, Family, and Patronage* (Oxford: Clarendon, 1967) 95–103, 268–91, 301–20; du Boulay, *Portrait of a Greek Mountain Village* 100–200; P. Bourdieu, 'The Sentiment of Honour in Kabyle Society' in J. G. Peristany (ed.), *Honour and Shame: The Values of Mediterranean Society* (London: Weidenfeld and Nicolson, 1965) 191–241; J. Pitt-Rivers, 'Women and Sanctuary in the Mediterranean', in *The Fate of Shechem; or, the Politics of Sex* (Cambridge University Press, 1977) 113–25.   [70] See Clark, *Women in the Ancient World*, 17–20.

private houses'.[71] In her important study of representations of women at meals in the Synoptic Gospels, Kathleen E. Corley has argued that women in the Greco-Roman period were beginning to attend public meals (especially in the Latin West) and this was related to their greater visibility in the public sphere generally. But Corley also notes frequent summons for women to return to the home, for 'social ideology concerning women's behavior in the public sphere was not advancing at the same rate as the actual behaviour of women'.[72] Karen Jo Torjesen has noted similar societal tension in her study of women's leadership in the early church. When such factors as social status and skills enabled a woman in Greco-Roman society to adopt leadership roles, she was always vulnerable to being 'attacked for abandoning women's social space, the household, and for forsaking the womanly virtue of chastity, which meant keeping her sexual presence far from the public eye'.[73] All of these studies make it clear that however successful women were in penetrating the public sphere in Greco-Roman society, they remained subject to symbol systems that associated them with the home and acted to circumvent their activities.

Recent studies of women's religious activities in pagan contexts have also illustrated the involvement of the public/private distinction in cultural systems of the ancient world. An abundance of evidence exists for women's cultic offices 'not only for traditional Greek and Roman worship, but for new, imported, and transformed cults, including numerous so-called mysteries, and Roman Emperor worship'.[74] In a world where religion was tied to the

---

[71] Jane F. Gardner, *Women in Roman Law and Society* (London and Sydney: Croom Helm, 1986) 264–5. On this topic see also Ramsay MacMullen, 'Women in Public in the Roman Empire', *Historia* 29 (1980) 208–18, especially, p. 214; Hallett, *Fathers and Daughters*, 31.

[72] Corley, *Private Women, Public Meals*, 25. Corley's work is valuable for the present study because it draws attention to the importance of meal practices in the visibility of early Christian women and it highlights concerns in the Synoptic Gospels about propriety. Her work has shown me that the kind of questions that I have applied to texts that fall mainly into the Pauline tradition, might fruitfully be asked of the gospel material as well. In her work, however, the terms public and private appear to be fairly 'static' concepts. In this book I hope to illustrate the somewhat ambiguous nature of the categories public and private when applied to early Christianity and the consequences of this ambiguity for the lives of women. Corley's findings will be discussed further in Part 1.

[73] Torjesen, *When Women Were Priests*, 113.   [74] Kraemer, *Her Share*, 84.

public institutions of cities and state, women (and men) could be called upon to bear the enormous costs of financing the performance of public religious festivals and entertainments and to underwrite the cost of public buildings.[75] Ross Kraemer has noted that, particularly in Greek cities during the Hellenistic and Roman periods, women's priesthoods and cultic offices must be evaluated in relation to the whole system of benefactions.[76] In their role as benefactors women could act independently and Kraemer (somewhat in contrast to the remarks of Gardner cited above) warns that we should take seriously evidence suggesting that women held titles and served in offices in their own right (i.e. not only because their husbands held titles).[77]

However, our understanding of women's patronage must be tempered by other factors. Kraemer draws attention to the work of Riet van Bremen on women and wealth, who argues that the encouragement of women to participate in public life must be understood in light of 'an ideology which minimized the public nature of this behavior, by depicting and conceptualizing the city as an extended family, thus rendering public benefactions familial solicitousness writ large'.[78] The language of benefaction includes references to fathers and mothers of the city and to sons and daughters. In other words, wealthy women who were visible in the public domain were praised 'in terms that posed no threat to the traditional ideology of gender differences and appropriate roles for women'.[79] Thus, we have an example of the private domain (the home) becoming the symbol for the public, but the lines of division still functioning to preserve gender differentiation.

In the early church as well, the private can be used to express the nature of the public. While the Epistle to the Ephesians clearly is

[75] Ibid., 84–5, 86–7.   [76] Ibid., 87.

[77] Ibid., 86–7. She draws attention to the important study by Bernadette J. Brooten, *Women Leaders in the Ancient Synagogue* (Chico, Calif.: Scholars, 1982). See also R. A. Kearsley, 'Asiarchs, *Achiereis* and the *Archiereiai* of Asia', *GRBS* 27 (1986) 183–92.

[78] Ibid., 87–8, citing Riet van Bremen, 'Women and Wealth', in A. Cameron and A. Kuhrt (eds.), *Images of Women in Antiquity* (Detroit: Wayne State University, 1985) 236–7. For a similar argument see Natalie Boymel Kampen, 'Between Public and Private: Women as Historical Subjects in Roman Art', in Sarah B. Pomeroy (ed.), *Women's History and Ancient History* (Chapel Hill and London: University of North Carolina, 1991) 218–48.

[79] Kraemer, *Her Share*, 88.

concerned with the inner arrangement of the individual household of believers (Eph. 5.21–6.9), this text also calls the *ekklesia* the household of God. The addressees are told that they are no longer strangers and sojourners, but fellow citizens with the saints and members of the household of God (Eph. 2.19; cf. Gal. 6.10; 1 Tim. 3.14–15). Despite the fact that the *ekklesia* meets in individual houses and uses the household both as an arena for evangelization and a model for its own organization, the church clearly also has a public dimension. The household of God extends far beyond any individual dwelling or even city, to embrace the whole world (cf. Eph. 2.10).[80] It is an entity dedicated to winning over both Jew and Gentile: in essence, it seeks to transform society.

The interrelationship between the public and private which is so obvious in early Christian texts has intriguing implications for church women. As noted earlier, the merging of the public with the private sphere in early Christianity heightens the possibility of women assuming leadership roles. When one encounters Paul's female co-workers there is no evidence of a reduced participation in the Apostle's public ministry in comparison to male workers. This is illustrated well by the example of Euodia and Syntyche who are said to be struggling in the gospel with Paul, together with Clement and the rest of Paul's fellow workers (Phil. 4.2–3). These women likely travel and engage in other activities which are crucial to the task of evangelization. Nevertheless, to call the ministry of these women 'public' is somewhat misleading, for much of it must have taken place 'in-house'. As Jerome H. Neyrey has noted in his study of John 4 (the story of the Samaritan woman) even where cultural expectations of females in the public sphere appear to be blatantly violated, this early church text calls hearers to become insiders – to enter a fictive-kinship circle, a private, household world – where there may be new standards for what is appropriate.[81]

The specific focus of this book on how women figured in public opinion about the church will make the categories of public and

---

80 On the nature of the 'church' (translation of the Greek term ἐκκλησία), see Ernest Best, 'Church', *Harper's Bible Dictionary*, Paul J. Achtemeier (ed.) (San Francisco: Harper & Row, 1985) 168–9. On the life of house-churches combining elements of the private and public spheres see Torjesen, *When Women Were Priests*,126.

81 Neyrey, 'What's Wrong with This Picture?', 88–9.

private, when applied to early church women, appear even more slippery. The attempt to evaluate the significance of women's behaviour is complicated by the fact that even if activities took place within the context of a network of house-churches and activities were generally of the kind that would not draw public attention, women could not count upon shelter from public view. Our study of pagan critique of early Christianity will alert us to the fact that these women were visible and vulnerable. In a world where privacy was rare, even church meetings which took place in private dwellings were subject to scrutiny and speculation (1 Cor. 14.23–5). Enthusiastic re-enactment of the proclamation that in Christ 'there is neither male nor female (Gal. 3.28)', which involved ritual removals of head-coverings during prophecy (1 Cor. 11.2–16) might be judged to be 'Bacchic': frenzied, debauched, foreign, and altogether suspicious behaviour.[82] Women who travelled for mission purposes might be seen as away from home far too frequently. Too much gadding-about might offer opponents an occasion to revile them (1 Tim. 5.13–14).

There is no doubt that the relationship between private and public in early church life is complex. Before we turn to the analysis of specific texts, we should consider that many scholars have warned that by relying too heavily on this dichotomy we run the risk of simplistically categorizing women's behaviour. The methodological reservations may be divided usefully into three major points:

(1) Researchers estimate that use of the concepts of public and private in discussions of women's lives often gives a false impression of uniformity: not enough attention is paid to chronological, geographical, and even architectural variation.[83] While the

---

[82] Note that Antoinette Clark Wire sees the public/private dichotomy at work in Paul's response to the problem of head covering. She suggests that the women are aiming to introduce what they practise in their own homes within the more public arena of the house-church. See *The Corinthian Women Prophets: A Reconstruction through Paul's Rhetoric* (Minneapolis: Fortress, 1990) 183. On Bacchic (Dionysian) rituals see Part 1.

[83] On architectural and geographical variation see Wendy Cotter, 'Women's Authority Roles in Paul's Churches: Countercultural or Conventional?' *NovT* 36 (1994) 350–72. On the question of cultural variation in general see Rosaldo and Lamphere (eds.), *Women, Culture, and Society*, 13; Pauline Schmitt Pantel, 'The Difference Between the Sexes: History, Anthropology and the Greek City', in Michelle Perrot (ed.), *Writing Women's History* (Cambridge MA: Blackwell, 1992) 72–5; Meyers, *Discovering Eve*, 32–3.

private/public dichotomy reflects a pattern of gender asymmetry which can be observed across cultures, it is nevertheless important to be alert to cultural variations.

(2) In speaking of the distinction between public and private, it is necessary to avoid assumptions based on modern western experience. One scholar asks the penetrating question: 'Our present-day values give primacy to the public sphere, but can we legitimately translate those values to societies in which matters of kinship and family (the domestic realm) cannot be so easily separated from economic and political matters (the public realm)?'[84]

(3) Finally, we must recognize that the dichotomy of private and public is a static concept: it may conceal the dynamic movement and interaction between realms which occurs in real societies. A primary association with one domain does not preclude involvement or influence in the other. We should think about how women act at the crossroads between private and public. An anthropologist working on rural Greece, Jill Dubisch, has concluded that rather than women being simply situated on one side of the equation, 'women are concerned with maintaining boundaries, mediating between realms, and transforming substances suitable for one realm into those proper for another'.[85]

These ideas have alerted me to aspects of the lives of early Christian women that would otherwise have escaped me. For example, to think of women as mediators between realms is enormously suggestive for understanding the shape of the lives of early church women married to non-believers, women who lived on the divide between church and world. That one should not think of women's association with the home as a kind of rigid seclusion is made clear by the nature of these women's activities and the scope of their influence both inside and outside of the church. Even wives who seem as restricted in the household as early Christian women married to non-believers, are capable of extending their influence far beyond the walls of the house, as I will discuss in Part 3.

---

[84] Meyers, *Discovering Eve*, 32. See also Meyers' interesting comments concerning problems in using the term 'patriarchy' to characterize the experience of ancient women, 24–46.
[85] Dubisch, 'Culture Enters through the Kitchen', 208.

Cross-cultural comparison helps us to become aware of meanings associated with the household life which may diverge considerably from our contemporary experience. For example, by observing what happens when a woman in a Greek village is seen as being too often away from home, we are in a better position to understand the consequences of mixed marriages in early Christianity. Frequent absences may carry implications for her family's respectability that we may not otherwise recognize. Practices which to us may seem completely unrelated to sexuality, are understood as a reflection of a woman's lack of chastity and as a violation of the honour of her husband.

In order to appreciate how variations in the public/private dichotomy may have affected the activities of women in early Christianity, it is necessary to investigate fully the specific activities of women in particular churches located in particular cities. More work needs to be done which incorporates the findings of disciplines related to ancient history, including archaeology, in order to avoid giving a false impression of uniformity when describing the experiences of early Christian women.[86] One of the most important insights that has emerged from scholarship on early Christian women is that we must not take the cultural ideal of the 'woman at home' at face value: what goes on in actual practice may differ substantially from what society prescribes. However, because of my specific focus in this book on public opinion (which often stares past the particulars of history), I am actually also very interested in the impression of uniformity one gains when considering the abundance of evidence that links gender with the public/private dichotomy. Although I have been concerned throughout this study with the divergence between 'image' and 'reality', I am also very interested in how 'image' influences and shapes reality. Thus I am concerned with the impact on the lives of women of such statements of conventional wisdom as that made by the historian Tacitus in the late first century CE. He looked back to the 'good old days', when household responsibilities were taken seriously in

---

[86] An example of a study that sets out to understand the activities of early Christian women in relation to the life of a specific city, Philippi, is Lilian Portefaix, *Sisters Rejoice: Paul's Letter to the Philippians and Luke-Acts as Received by First-Century Philippian Women* (Stockholm: Almqvist and Wiksell International, 1988).

the Roman family and wives were neither idle nor indifferent: 'In the good old days, every man's son, born in wedlock, was brought up not in the chamber of some hireling nurse, but in his mother's lap, and at her knee. And that mother could have no higher praise than that she managed the house and gave herself to her children.'[87] Against a background of growing unease about the stability of the family and of concern for the production of Roman heirs, the cultural ideal of the division between the female: domestic sphere and male: public realms was proclaimed.[88] During times of crisis, including confrontations with new religious groups such as Christianity which were thought to be a threat to society, we would expect especially strong expressions of traditional values and accepted beliefs.[89] Influenced by a desire to support traditional political and social institutions and to encourage the stability of society, Celsus criticized Christianity for contributing to household disruption. This disruption was directly opposite to the domestic harmony that was the object of Tacitus' longing.

The lives of early Christian women no doubt differed from one another in many ways due to personal factors such as family relations and wealth. In addition, there were factors related to particular geographic locations such as the level of animosity Christians experienced in each location. Notwithstanding these factors, early Christian women remained subject to overarching cultural ideals which reminded them of their primary responsibility to the household. The importance of these ideals will be evident in Part 1 as we analyse the collection of non-Christian references to early Christian women. We will discover that even if these women displayed quiet, reverent, and chaste behaviour – doing nothing overtly in opposition to even the most conservative interpretation of the public/private dichotomy – they could still be accused of violating the cultural ideal of the woman 'at home'. As we move on to analyse the early Christian texts in Parts 2 and 3, we will gain

---

[87] Tacitus, *Dialogus* 28.4–5; trans. E. S. Forster and E. H. Heffner (LCL 1931–70).

[88] On concern for heirs and the stability of the Roman family see J. P. V. D. Balsdon, *Roman Women: Their History and Habits* (London: Bodley Head, 1962) 14, 75, 197–8.

[89] Note that Robert Wilken describes Celsus as one who 'supports traditional values and defends accepted beliefs'. See *The Christians as the Romans Saw Them* (New Haven and London: Yale, 1984) 95.

a greater sense of the effect of this accusation on their lives, and we will discuss how this accusation may have been related to the advice they received in church circles.

A social-scientific concept of power

Understanding the significance of women's activities – their meaning and relative importance within the context of the Greco-Roman world – remains at the heart of the enterprise of all scholars who find themselves at the crossroads between early Christian studies and the field of women and religion. In order to address the issue of significance I have found it useful to reflect upon the concept of *power* and its place in anthropological discussions of women and culture. I believe that allowing my historical study to be informed by social-scientific insights has alerted me to the fact that women's activities are far more varied than is often assumed, has prevented me from taking hierarchical descriptions of female/male interaction at face value, and has helped me to become sensitive to possible disparity between ancient and modern world-views and aspirations.

Noting the substantial amount of informal influence and power exercised by women in a variety of social contexts, Michelle Zimbalist Rosaldo in her article 'Women, Culture, and Society: A Theoretical Overview' (1974) makes the distinction between power as 'the ability to gain compliance', and culturally legitimated authority as 'the recognition that it is right'.[90] Drawing attention to a tendency among social scientists to neglect the exercise of power by women, Rosaldo offers the following reminder:

---

[90] See Michelle Z. Rosaldo, 'A Theoretical Overview', in Rosaldo and Lamphere (eds.), *Women, Culture, and Society*, 21. Rosaldo refers to the distinction between authority and power in classic social-scientific thought inspired especially by Max Weber; see her discussion p. 21 n.2. In the same volume see also the theoretical remarks of L. Lamphere, 'Strategies, Cooperation, and Conflict Among Women in Domestic Groups', 97–112. The distinction between power and authority made by social scientists has been of particular importance for Bengt Holmberg in his examination of Pauline Christianity: *Paul and Power: The Structure of Authority in the Primitive Church as Reflected in the Pauline Epistles* (Philadelphia: Fortress, 1980). The concepts of power and authority in anthropological discussions have been featured in two recent investigations of women and Christian origins. See Batten, 'More Queries for Q', 45–6; LaHurd, 'Rediscovering the Lost Women in Luke 15', 70–2.

'while authority legitimates the use of power, it does not exhaust it, and actual methods of giving rewards, controlling information, exerting pressure, and shaping events may be available to women as well as men'.[91]

The distinction between power and authority has been more recently examined by Jill Dubisch in her introduction to a collection of essays edited by Dubisch, *Gender and Power in Rural Greece* (1986). While Dubisch concurs with Rosaldo on the importance of the distinction between power and authority, she calls for greater analytical precision and she considerably expands the body of questions we may raise in relation to this distinction. She argues that:

while it may be somewhat useful to distinguish between illegitimate and legitimate exercises of power, between power and authority, this distinction should not blind us to the fact that not only may both be effective (and illegitimate power may be even more effective than legitimate power, since the way it is used is less circumscribed by social rules), but also they may be both culturally recognized.[92]

As an example of this kind of cultural recognition, which may vary from the quite explicit to the more tacit, Dubisch mentions the tendency for Greek men to attribute the quality of *poniria* ('cunning' or 'deviousness') to Greek women. She believes that this conviction represents a cultural acknowledgment of the ability of women to get their own way, a cultural acknowledgment of female power even though it may be deemed illegitimate power. The whole question of the relationship between illegitimate and legitimate exercises of power is itself a complicated one according to Dubisch, for one must be aware that men and women may not agree about what is and is not 'legitimate'.[93]

In discussing the important question of the ways in which women exercise power, Dubisch notes that it is too limiting to think exclusively in terms of personal influence. In many societies power is exercised by women indirectly through the agency of others. This fact leads Dubisch to suggest that it is perhaps more useful to think of different spheres of power. To offer an example familiar

---

[91] Rosaldo, 'A Theoretical Overview', 21.
[92] Dubisch (ed.), *Gender and Power in Rural Greece*, 17–18.   [93] Ibid., 17–18.

to students of ancient society, the female patron may be best understood as exercising power through the sphere of patronage with its network of clients and obligations.[94] The domestic, household sphere is identified by Dubisch as a highly significant arena in modern Greek society as it was similarly in Greco-Roman society. Women's roles within this network of relationships are important for the society as a whole. However, modern Western thought has tended to devalue the household sphere, searching for the seat of power within the public domain, and this focus undoubtedly has contributed to a lack of appreciation of the variety of manifestations of power linked to the domestic, household sphere in different societies.

Dubisch also points out that anthropologists have argued that submission to authority structures which confine women to the domestic sphere actually have created avenues for women to exercise power: 'ironically women's power may stem from submission to the system that seeks to deny it to them . . . it is through their acquiescence to the cultural value system that women find not only satisfaction, but also the route to power'.[95] A woman increasingly may succeed in exercising power as she emulates more closely the maternal or wifely ideal encompassed by the cultural value system under whose conceptual canopy she stands. But, it is also important to note that the power that a woman may wield inside may well extend to the outside. A respectful or devious wife may make or break a husband's reputation in the public world.[96] In the end, we must remain aware of the possible interrelationships between the inside and the outside: 'By ridding ourselves of the preconception that women's activities are "only" domestic, we begin to realize the relationship of such activities to the "larger" system.'[97]

The distinction between authority and power nuanced by the methodological points raised above will serve as an important model in this book for assessing female involvement in the early church. In order to illustrate the usefulness of this distinction it

[94] See Caroline F. Whelan, 'Amica Pauli: The Role of Phoebe in the Early Church', *JSNT* 49 (1993) 67–85.   [95] Dubisch (ed.), *Gender and Power in Rural Greece*, 18.
[96] Ibid., 18–20.   [97] Ibid., 26.

is valuable to consider how it sheds light on one text which is paramount to the present study, 1 Peter 3.1–6:

Wives, in the same way, accept the authority of your husbands, so that, even if some of them do not obey the word, they may be won over without a word by their wives' conduct, when they see the purity and reverence of your lives. Do not adorn yourselves outwardly by braiding your hair, and by wearing gold ornaments or fine clothing; rather, let your adornment be the inner self with the lasting beauty of a gentle and quiet spirit, which is very precious in God's sight. It was in this way long ago that the holy women who hoped in God used to adorn themselves by accepting the authority of their husbands. Thus Sarah obeyed Abraham and called him lord. You have become her daughters as long as you do what is good and never let fears alarm you. [trans. *NRSV*]

Although we must leave thorough analysis of this text to later in this volume, some initial remarks about the exercise of female power are useful for understanding the interests of this study as a whole. This passage offers several instructions concerning the behaviour of Christian wives, but our main focus will be on the remarkable interest expressed in the Christian wives of unbelievers who, it is hoped, will win their husbands 'without a word by their conduct'.

In instructing the Christian wives of unbelievers to live modestly, quietly, and in submission to their husbands, the author of 1 Peter clearly is acknowledging the authority structures which define relationships in the household. Women are being called upon to demonstrate shame and render the honour of their households above suspicion. Such close proximity to the unbelieving world means that it is prudent for wives to go about their business quietly. The risk of danger is implied by the exhortation never to let fears alarm them. While it may seem that little more can be said about instructions which clearly reinforce hierarchy in male/female relations, when we recall the distinction discussed above between authority and power, we may detect new levels of meaning. Although the author reinforces the authority of the unbelieving husband, in stating the possibility that the husband may be won by the example of his wife, he/she nevertheless expresses what Dubisch has called a 'cultural acknowledgment of female power'.

This acknowledgment takes place despite the fact that it is clearly illegitimate power according to the norms of the non-believing world. Moreover, it might even be said that the author of 1 Peter's acknowledgment of female power is itself quite indirect, even cautious. One may reasonably ask: realistically, how can a husband be won 'without a word'? Even if it is the case that moral example was a more powerful evangelizing tool in the ancient world than in our modern context, at some point ideal behaviour would need to give way to teaching.

It is useful to recall what was said previously about understanding the exercise of female power in terms of spheres of influence. The domestic sphere of the believing woman enabled her to touch not only the life of her husband but many other lives with her own pious example and inspired speech. Slaves and children come immediately to mind, but the setting of the extended household of the Greco-Roman city may also have offered opportunity for interaction with clients and business associates of various kinds.[98] Christian texts offer examples of the faith spreading from women to their children, from the time of the composition of 2 Timothy, which describes Timothy's faith as a faith that dwelt first in his grandmother Lois and in his mother Eunice (2 Tim. 1.5); to the time of Augustine, so fervently evangelized by his mother Monica. By remaining married to an unbeliever and by emulating the life of an ideal mother and wife, a woman gains societal approval and therefore increasingly may succeed in exercising power. In other words, the denial of a woman's authority in relationship to her husband in the household and the reinforcement of the 'traditional' female life that occurs in 1 Peter 3.1–6 by no means completely thwarts female power. In addition, while this power clearly is exercised in the domestic sphere, it extends its influence deeply into the public sphere; it contributes to the spread of a new religious movement that will defy political authorities in its determination to worship the one God and will come to threaten the very order of the society as a whole.

---

[98] See discussion in W. Meeks, *The First Urban Christians: The Social World of the Apostle Paul* (New Haven and London: Yale University, 1983) 30.

Introduction

This brief discussion of 1 Peter 3.1–6 serves to illustrate how theoretical reflection about the distinction between power and authority can help us explore the place of women in encounters between church groups and non-believers. It also demonstrates how such theoretical reflection can help us guard against understanding women's association with the private sphere and men's association with the public sphere simply as static realities; we are impelled to explore how women's roles in the dynamic exchanges between the private and public spheres were related to the interaction between the church and the world. Although I have chosen to illustrate the theoretical perspective being adopted in this book with reference to an early church text, 1 Peter 3.1–6, the social-scientific insights on power, honour and shame, and the relationship between the female: private and male: public spheres highlighted in this introduction will be shown to be equally useful for elucidating the non-Christian descriptions of early Christian women discussed in Part 1. They will be especially useful in analysing the negative characterizations of church women as immoral and neglectful of home-based responsibilities and the depictions of Christianity as a religion which takes matters of public concern and endeavours to sequester them in clandestine private spaces.

This book is entitled *Early Christian women and pagan opinion: the power of the hysterical woman* because I have found that women who were labelled as deviant nevertheless had enormous power in the construction of a new religious movement. Obviously this power was deemed illegitimate by a critical outside world, but as I will show, this power, despite its substantial influence in the birth of the early church, only gained a legitimate status in the church itself to a certain degree. Powerful women do not necessarily become authorities. If the title smacks of irony, it is because I have encountered irony in my findings at every turn. Where I thought I had discovered the circumvention of female activities by hostile public reaction, I discovered surprising ingenuity and bravery on the part of early Christian women. Where I thought I had discovered silenced women, I found missionaries with quiet but powerful voices. Where I thought I had discovered a celibate utopia comprised of women who had been liberated from traditional family responsibilities, I discovered women caring for children. Where I thought I had discovered female symbolism which did nothing but enshrine the ideal of the male-dominated woman, I discovered female mediators between realms, mediators between the church and the world, even between the realms of the human and the divine.

PART ONE

Pagan reaction to early Christian women in the second century CE

The following constitutes an examination of the comments of second-century pagan authors who refer specifically to early Christian women. While many Christian works from the first and second centuries CE (including the New Testament) offer general indications of public opinion of the early church, the authors examined in this section explicitly characterize early Christians as outsiders to mainstream society. In concentrating on these earliest reactions, we are able to witness a new religious group gaining public attention for the first time. In studying these texts, we obtain a greater understanding of that fascinating period before Christianity became a recognizable force in the Roman Empire, when it was still a little-known movement, fiercely setting out to forge an identity.

Obviously, we cannot grasp fully how women figured in public opinion of early Christianity without taking into account how other religious groups in the Greco-Roman world were judged for the effect they had on women. Fortunately, David L. Balch provides a thorough investigation of how women featured in Greco-Roman criticism of various Eastern religions.[1] Balch's analysis has led him to conclude that, 'Roman ideals resulted in certain stereotyped criticisms of the Dionysus cult, the Egyptian Isis cult, and Judaism: they produced immorality (especially among Roman women) and

---

[1] See D. Balch, *Let Wives be Submissive: The Domestic Code in 1 Peter* (Chico, Calif.: Scholars, 1981), 65–80.

sedition.'[2] Some of the texts analysed by Balch will also be discussed here when comparison can be shown to be especially relevant, but the reader is encouraged to consult Balch's *Let Wives be Submissive: The Domestic Code in 1 Peter* as an important complement to this book.

There have been several excellent studies of pagan critique of early Christianity in the past number of years which not only have shed light upon the interplay between early Christianity and the Greco-Roman world, but also have illustrated how pagan sources can add to our knowledge of early Christianity itself. Stephen Benko collected the major components of pagan criticism of Christianity during the first two centuries CE (1980) and then he expanded his findings in his book *Pagan Rome and the Early Christians* (1984).[3] More extensive surveys and discussions extending to later periods can be found in the classic work by Pierre de Labriolle, *La réaction païenne; étude sur la polémique antichrétienne du 1er au VIe siècle* (1948)[4] and the more recent study by Robert L. Wilken, *The Christians as the Romans Saw Them* (1984).[5] As early as 1970 Jeanne-Marie Demarolle examined how Christian women were viewed by the third-century critic, Porphyry.[6] However, there as yet exists no comprehensive study of how early Christian women figured in public opinion about the church. It is my hope that this book will redress this imbalance and complement the results of existing investigations of the pagan reaction to the birth of Christianity.

It is important that I make clear at the outset that it is impossible for me to offer an exhaustive study of the comments of the second-

---

[2] Ibid., 74. Balch argues that, 'Judaism, and later Christianity, inherited criticisms which Greeks and Romans originally directed against the Dionysus and the Isis cults' (p. 67). However, he only briefly considers some of the relevant criticisms of Christianity which involve references to early Christian women as they relate to his argument about the apologetic function of the household code in 1 Peter (p. 86). The brevity of his discussion is no doubt related to the fact that most of the references come from a period later than that which Balch primarily is considering.

[3] See S. Benko, 'Pagan Criticism of Christianity during the First Two Centuries AD', in H. Temporini and W. Haase (eds.), *Aufstieg und Niedergang der römischen Welt* (Berlin and New York: Walter De Gruyter,1980) 1055–1118 and *Pagan Rome and the Early Christians* (Bloomington: Indiana University, 1984).

[4] Pierre de Labriolle, *La réaction païenne: étude sur la polémique antichrétienne de 1er au VIe siècle* 2 edn (Paris: L'artisan du livre, 1948). [5] Wilken, *Christians as the Romans Saw Them*.

[6] Jeanne-Marie Demarolle, 'Les femmes chrétiennes vues par Porphyre', *JAC* 13 (1970) 42–7.

century pagan critics of early Christianity in the context of this volume. Therefore, I have relied on other scholars to offer information about the social setting of these texts and to explain some of the general issues in question. Moreover, it would be impractical to include the complete record of their comments; thus, I have cited only those texts which mention women explicitly or contain material which is fundamental to my argument. My main contribution lies in the highlighting of the importance of female visibility in pagan critiques of early Christianity, an aspect of these texts which has previously been ignored, and to illustrate how paying attention to this visibility can help us understand early Christian texts. In Parts 2 and 3 I will illustrate how Greco-Roman critique was reflected in early Christian texts, and I will explore how both critique and reaction affected the lives of early Christian women.

Pliny

The first specific reference to early Christian women by a pagan author occurs in the correspondence between Pliny the Younger and the Emperor Trajan. As governor of Pontus-Bythinia between 111 and 113 CE, Pliny was charged with bringing the province's affairs in order. The letter in which he consults with the Emperor about the appropriateness of the actions he has taken concerning Christians mentions only two specific persons: two female slaves (*ancilla*) who were called deacons (*ministra*). In order to gain information about the early church Pliny had these women tortured: 'This convinced me that it was all the more necessary to find out what the truth was by the torture of two female slaves who were called deaconesses. I found nothing else but a depraved and excessive superstition (*superstitio*).'[7]

---

[7] See Benko's translation of Pliny's letter 10.96–7 in 'Pagan Criticism', 1068–9. Other translations include *Pliny*, trans. W. Melmoth (LCL 1915); and Betty Radice, *The Letters of the Younger Pliny* (New York: Penguin Books, 1963). See detailed discussion in W. H. C. Frend, *Martyrdom and Persecution in the Early Church* (New York: University, 1967) 162–6. The Latin text of Pliny's letter reads: '*Quo magis necessarium credidi, ex duabus ancillis, quae ministrae dicebantur, quid esset veri et per tormenta quaerere.*' Scholars believe that the Latin *ministra* corresponds to the Greek διάκονος, but this is not certain. See Bonnie Bowman Thurston, *The Widows: A Women's Ministry in the Early Church* (Minneapolis: Augsburg Fortress, 1989) 134 n. 53.

If we place this very brief passage within the context of the letter as a whole and draw upon some information from sources of the same period, we are able to extract a substantial amount of information about the lives of these women and the probable reasons why they came to Pliny's attention. Although trials and torturing have already occurred, Pliny nevertheless turns to Trajan for advice before proceeding any further. He poses a series of questions about such matters as whether one should treat youth and adult alike, and about whether allowance should be made for Christians who purportedly change their mind. Pliny wonders whether having the mere name (*nomen ipsum*) 'Christian' is enough to warrant punishment, or whether there must be evidence of specific crimes attached to the name. It is clear from what follows that Christians have been denounced to Pliny, sometimes in such a way that the accuser offered little, if any, supporting evidence or information. Pliny was willing to adopt harsh measures despite having minimal knowledge about early Christianity, and despite having heard accusations against Christians that often amounted to little more than a label of membership in a group. His attitude indicates the powerful role rumour and impression played in defining relationships between groups in the Greco-Roman world.

Pliny offers few details about the early Christians who were apprehended. He notes that the Christians include both citizens and non-citizens and represent all age groups, all classes, and both sexes. He describes the Christian movement as posing a risk not only to cities, but also to villages and agricultural areas. But in addition to Pliny's observations about the general makeup of the early Christian group, we must consider carefully his references to the two female deacons. If we focus on these two women, we immediately come up with an obvious question: how did these particular slave women come to Pliny's attention? The fact that these women had a prominent ministerial role in the Christian community – a ministry apparently not hampered by their status as slaves – was in all likelihood a significant factor in their visibility and subsequent arrest.[8] It is impossible to be certain about the specific activities of

---

[8] Although it cannot be ruled out completely, there is no evidence to suggest that being a slave-deacon was less of an honour than being a deacon who was freeborn. The mention

such second-century female deacons, but even if they were limited to those of the more traditional type of the deaconess of the third and fourth centuries CE (care of the sick and poor, the instruction of female proselytes, providing assistance during the baptism of women), there is still much that may have contributed to the visibility of these women. For example, among the special duties of the deaconess (which will be discussed in a subsequent chapter) was ministry to women in pagan households to which it would have been too dangerous to send a male minister.[9] Perhaps the pagan head of a household who found his household penetrated by unwanted Christian ministers was among the informers alluded to in Pliny's correspondence. We should also entertain the possibility that the arrest of the slaves was a means of deflecting the blame away from a master or mistress with suspicious Christian tendencies.

The visibility of the two women interrogated by Pliny may have been related to their status as slaves. There are indications in early Christian texts that the slaves of pagan households could damage the reputation of the church in the wider society. The author of 1 Timothy (a text roughly contemporary with Pliny's letter) calls for the Christian slaves of pagan households to respect their masters in order that the doctrine of God would not be blasphemed (1 Tim. 6.2; cf. *Const. Apost.* 8.32). The correspondence of Ignatius of Antioch, which like Pliny's letter dates from the reign of Trajan, includes a strong exhortation discouraging slaves from attempting to secure their freedom (Ign. *Pol.* 4.2–3). Such efforts might very well bring unwanted attention to the church and lead to misunderstanding about the nature of the group's social ethos and priorities. This text also warns against the church being responsible for the funds required to secure a slave's manumission. The purchase of the slaves of a pagan master would be an especially risky practice for a group which was aiming to foster the right impression in society at large.

of female deacons supports the existence of this church office for women at the beginning of the second century. The Pastoral Epistles, contemporary with Pliny's letter, offer further evidence of this office. The evidence from Pliny would support a translation of 1 Timothy 3.11 as female deacons, and not wives of deacons. See note 7 above.

[9] See *Constitutions of the Holy Apostles* 3.15 (*ANF* 7.431) cited in R. S. Kraemer (ed.), *Maenads*, 239–40.

When we consider Christian exhortations which clearly were intended to limit the activities of slaves (such as those from Ignatius to Polycarp), we cannot assume that these injunctions reflect the actual situation in the church. There may be divergence between teaching and reality, as the mention in Pliny's letter of deacon slaves being tortured illustrates. Further, there is the possibility that in some early church circles, slaves were encouraged to take on dangerous and unconventional roles, despite the dominant tone of caution one finds in Christian literature from the beginning of the second century. As is often the case with texts on women from this period, one is left wondering whether such circumspection reflects ambivalence about the powerful contribution that subordinate members of the household were in fact making to the expansion of the early church, despite the shadow of suspicion their activities might cast on the group. A slave who was also a deacon might have a prominent interest in the conversion of the unbelieving members of the household. She would have access not only to other slaves, but presumably also to the children of the household and perhaps to its mistress. A slave who shared devotion to Christ with her mistress might accompany her to Christian gatherings[10] and she might well be called upon to orchestrate the arrangements required for continued participation. As will become clear, both the pagan critiques of early Christianity and early Christian texts themselves suggest that the early church was seen as having a contaminating influence on the household, and it is likely that slaves played a major part in the spreading of this contagion.

Another relevant factor to the situation of the two female slave deacons that Pliny arranged to have tortured may be the loss of business opportunities, mentioned in the Acts of the Apostles (Acts 16.16–21 cf. Acts 19.23–5).[11] Acts includes an intriguing account of Paul and Silas being accused before the magistrates in Philippi for causing a disturbance through the advocacy of 'customs illegal for us Romans to adopt and follow' (16.21). This charge is the result of Paul's exorcizing a slave girl. She had been possessed by a spirit who told fortunes, and her owners had made her the centre of a

---

[10] See note 18 below.
[11] See Fiorenza, *In Memory of Her*, 265. Benko, 'Pagan Criticism', 1070.

lucrative business. Her new state meant the end of this business opportunity, and thus Paul and Silas were accused of failing to respect property rights and household structures (Acts 16.16–21). It is easy to imagine similar scenarios in which a slave owner was enraged because of the loss of revenues resulting from a slave's passion for following Christ. For example, a once talented and highly desired slave prostitute who had become a source of frustration for an owner might be disposed of by accusing her of being a Christian.[12]

Pliny's question to Trajan about whether or not specific crimes must be associated with the name Christian in order for offenders to merit punishment has intrigued commentators[13] and it is worth considering in relation to women. Pliny proceeded as though the name Christian were enough; Trajan supported this basic assumption, but he forbade the 'hunting out' of Christians, made allowances for them changing their minds, and cautioned against accepting anonymous accusations. When we read Pliny's letter we get the impression that he was convinced on principle that early Christianity was an enemy of the state and that adherence to the cult itself was punishable. But there are indications here that he nevertheless set out to find specific crimes of subversion. He may have been looking for confirmation of the rumours he had heard. Initial inquiry led him to discover 'stubbornness and inflexible obstinacy' which deserved punishment. Christians who were questioned subsequently revealed that their so-called crimes included:

[coming] together on a certain day before daylight to sing a song with responses to Christ as a god, to bind themselves mutually by a solemn oath, not to commit any crime, but to avoid theft, robbery, adultery, not to break a trust or deny a deposit when they are called for it. After these practices it was their custom to separate and then come together again to take food but of an ordinary and harmless kind, and they even gave up this practice after my edict, when in response to your order I forbade associations.[14]

---

[12] On slave prostitutes see Lilian Portefaix, *Sisters Rejoice*, 27–8; see also Gardner, *Women in Roman Law and Society*, 250–3.

[13] Benko devotes a whole chapter of his *Pagan Rome* to this; see pp. 1–29; see also his 'Pagan Criticism', 1070–2; Wilken, *The Christians*, 23–4.

[14] From Benko's translation of Pliny 10.96 in 'Pagan Criticism', 1069.

The description of early Christian rites here seems innocuous enough, but Pliny gives the impression that he had approached his inquiries with the expectation of discovering something far more sinister, especially with his assessment that the food was 'ordinary and harmless'. Pliny may have been influenced by the Roman historian Livy's description of the suppression of Bacchic (Dionysian) rituals in Italy, written during the reign of Augustus (27 BCE–14 CE). This well-known episode occurring in the early second century BCE involved the migration of a cult from Greece to Italy, a cult which was accused of holding night meetings involving feasting, promiscuity, and 'meetings of men and women in common'.[15] From later in the second century also comes evidence that Christians were accused of rites involving meals where human flesh was consumed.[16] Having considered early Christian frescos and textual evidence for meal settings and eucharist celebrations, Kathleen Corley has noted an interest in table etiquette and sensitivity about the impressions Christians might make at a public banquet. She is especially interested in concern about women's proper association with the private sphere and the perception that the presence of church women with men at public meals is immoral.[17] Women were closely associated with meal practices in public opinion about the church. What this means for our evaluation of Pliny's innocuous description of Christian rites is that language which might first appear as banal and lacking in specific accusations may still encode deep suspicions about the presence of women at early Christian celebrations.

Pliny's account suggests that whatever information he was able to gather initially, or perhaps more importantly, whatever impres-

[15] See Livy, *Annals*, 39.8–19, trans. E. Sage (LCL 1936). For a thorough summary of that text see Benko, 'Pagan Criticism', 1066–7. For a discussion of the relationship between Pliny and Livy's description of the Bacchanalia see Ibid., 1072; Wilken, *The Christians*, 6–17; R. M. Grant, 'Pliny and the Christians', *HTR* 41 (1948) 273.

[16] See description of early Christianity by Marcus Cornelius Fronto discussed below.

[17] Corley, *Private Women, Public Meals*, 75–9. She refers especially to the fresco from the catacomb of St Priscilla known as the '*Fractio Panis*', which depicts a eucharist shared by women only and to Clement of Alexandria's instructions concerning the attendance of women at banquets (*Paedagogus* 2.7). The primary focus of Corley's book is the Synoptic tradition; however while discussing women in the context of Greco-Roman meals, she refers to the comments of Marcus Cornelius Fronto recorded by the third-century Christian, Minucius Felix (p. 76) which are discussed in detail below.

sion he took away from the initial interrogations, was insufficient to convince him of the group's harmlessness. He set out to gather more information by the torture of two female slaves who were called deaconesses. His efforts resulted in the discovery of 'nothing else but a depraved and excessive superstition'.[18] It is impossible to tell if the torture of the slave women led him to uncover additional information about early Christian activities, but the fact that he does not furnish further details leads one to suspect that his efforts were unsuccessful. The presence of female slave leaders in the group may have been enough to conjure up suspicion of sexual immorality given the association in the Greco-Roman world between slavery, sexual availability, and prostitution.[19] Pliny does not hesitate to offer a categorical final judgment: Christianity was a depraved and excessive superstition (*superstitio prava, immodica*). Pliny's language is characteristic of assessments of oriental religions, including Judaism, in the first and second centuries CE.[20] If we focus on the issue of the involvement of women in these foreign superstitions, we find accusations of the indiscriminate defilement of women and immodest mingling of men and women.[21] Added to these perceived characteristics of 'foreign superstitions' was the well-attested sentiment, discussed in the Introduction, that women were especially susceptible to their proselytizing tactics. Roman readers might have had their suspicions confirmed that Christianity was a women's religion, in hearing that the two Christians Pliny had tortured were slave women who had the role of *ministra*, a title which is sometimes given to pagan cult officers.[22]

In the end, Pliny's comments are quite ambiguous, for although

[18] Pliny's torture of slaves for information also calls to mind Livy's description of the Bacchanalia in *Annals* 39.8–19. A freedwoman named Hispala Faecenia brought the rites to the government's attention in 186 BCE. When informing on the nature of rites she noted that she had attended the Bacchanalia with her mistress when she was a slave. See Benko, 'Pagan Criticism', 1066; Kraemer, *Her Share*, 43–5. On Livy see note 15 above.

[19] Corley, *Private Women, Public Meals*, 48–52.

[20] See Benko, 'Pagan Criticism', 1075. Similar language is used in Livy's description of the Bacchanalia described above. Two other pagan authors contemporary with Livy who make references to early Christianity (but with no explicit mention of women) use similar language: see Suetonius, *Nero* 16.2; Tacitus, *Annals* 15.44. On superstitions see also Plutarch, *De Superstitione*, esp. ch. 2.

[21] D. L. Balch has collected the evidence for the cult of Dionysus (Bacchanalia), Isis cult, and Judaism in *Let Wives*, 65–80.

[22] This has been noted by Kraemer, *Her Share*, 182 n.88.

he seems to be aware that he has discovered a group which lacks the characteristics of the strangest of foreign groups, he nonetheless uses language that would conjure up accusatory imagery in the minds of his readers. The effect of Pliny's ambivalence and somewhat unsystematic approach in dealing with the issue of early Christianity (supported by Trajan's reply) was to create a situation for members of the early church which was ambiguous. This is not to say that these Christians were conscious of this ambiguity the way a modern person would be, who has been schooled in the tradition of Jean-Paul Sartre to expect life's absurdities. Rather, a second-century Christian in Asia Minor might express an awareness of the treachery of Satan which could lead to slander of the community at the hands of outsiders (e.g. Ign. *Trall.* 8.1–2). However, early Christians from this period did voice injustice and irony. Pliny's operative policy of punishing Christians who were so in name, without finding evidence of specific criminal activities, is echoed in early Christian texts themselves. In the middle of the second century the Christian apologist Justin Martyr told of the trial of a Roman Christian, Ptolemaeus, who had come to the attention of authorities on account of his being denounced as the instructor of a pagan's wife. Ptolemaeus was sentenced to death, and a Christian who witnessed the events protested with this interesting comment: 'What is the ground of this judgment? Why have you punished this man, not as an adulterer, nor fornicator, nor murderer, nor thief, nor robber, nor convicted of any crime at all, but only that he is called by the name of Christian?'[23] In 177 CE Tertullian expressed a similar sentiment: 'all that is cared about is having what the public hatred demands – confession of the name, not examination of the charge'.[24] In the same work Tertullian told of the ironic, cruel treatment of Christian wives who had reformed their behaviour. Instead of rejoicing in the now chaste behaviour of his wife, the unbelieving husband cast her out of the house.[25]

Tertullian's remarks remind us that even Christian women who exhibited behaviour considered model and womanly by the

---

[23] See Justin, *Second Apology*, 2, trans. A. Robert and J. Donaldson (*ANF* 1.188).

[24] Tertullian, *Apology*, 2 (*ANF* 3.18–19) cited in Benko, *Pagan Rome*, 3.

[25] Tertullian, *Apology*, 3 (*ANF* 3.20). On this sentiment see also *Recognitions of Clement*, 2.29.

standards of the day might not escape serious or even life-threatening consequences. Confessing Christ, rejecting worship of the
gods, and being a member of a group labelled as subversive to
home and state would be enough to lead to accusation. If we consider the nature of the activities of the two female slave deacons
mentioned by Pliny we must be careful not to assume too quickly
that their arrest was related to some type of sensational or revolutionary emancipatory behaviour. We should be aware of the fact
that even quite conventional behaviour might be negatively interpreted by outsiders. Despite the brevity of the reference to women
in Pliny's letter to Trajan, when taken in the context of the letter
as a whole, there is much interesting material to consider as we
reflect on the issue of female visibility. Having been alerted to the
possibility that what Christian women experienced at the hands of
outsiders, and even within church communities themselves, had as
much to do with the appearance as with the reality of their actions,
we may now move on to consider subsequent references to early
Christian women in pagan critique.

Marcus Cornelius Fronto

In one second-century source, the involvement of women is used
to illustrate the clandestine nature of early Christianity. Unlike
Pliny's correspondence, there are no reports of incidents involving
specific women. Yet women are present at the level of impression
and appearance; their very visibility is used as evidence for crime.
Marcus Cornelius Fronto (100–166 CE), the Roman orator and
tutor of Marcus Aurelius, is believed to be the author of a critique
of Christianity. This critique was later used in a work titled
'Octavius' by the Christian apologist Minucius Felix (200–240
CE).[26] Minucius Felix's work cites pagan criticisms of Christianity
and it then offers a defence of Christianity against paganism. The

---

[26] Benko has stated that the arguments used by the pagan in *Octavius* are probably based on
'a now lost, anti-Christian oration by Marcus Cornelius Fronto'. See Benko, *Pagan Rome*,
54; 74, notes 1–2; Benko, 'Pagan Criticism', 1081–2. Although Minucius Felix claims to
have derived information from Fronto in *Octavius* 9.6, some scholars have been less optimistic about the extent to which Minucius Felix based his dialogue on Fronto's work.
W. H. C. Frend, for example, speaks of 'fragmentary paraphrase', but he is nevertheless
confident that the speech reflects general Roman opinion around 150–160 CE; see

following excerpts are highlights from the anti-Christian polemic probably based on Fronto's thought:

is it not scandalous that the gods should be mobbed by a gang of outlawed and reckless desperadoes? They have collected from the lowest possible dregs of society the more ignorant fools together with *gullible women (readily persuaded, as is their weak sex)*; they have thus formed a rabble of blasphemous conspirators, who with nocturnal assemblies, periodic fasts, and inhuman feasts seal their pact not with some religious ritual but with desecrating profanation; they are a crowd that furtively lurks in hiding places, shunning the light; they are speechless in public but gabble away in corners. . . They recognize each other by secret marks and signs; hardly have they met when they love each other, throughout the world uniting in the practice of a veritable religion of lusts. Indiscriminately they call each other brother and *sister*, thus turning even ordinary fornication into incest by the intervention of these hallowed names. . . On a special day they gather for a feast with *all their children, sisters, mothers—all sexes* and all ages. There, flushed with the banquet after such feasting, they begin to burn with incestuous passions . . . the light is overturned and extinguished, and with it common knowledge of their actions; in the shameless dark with unspeakable lust they copulate in random unions, all equally being guilty of incest, some by deed, but everyone by complicity.[27] (Emphasis mine)

In keeping with stereotyped critiques of illegitimate cults during this era, the speaker is concerned with how women figure in the immoral activities of the group.[28] The speaker describes the efforts of early Christians to seek out and corrupt women. Women are viewed as being inherently susceptible to such tactics. But if we probe the description further, we obtain interesting information about how the church is seen as violating the proper distinction between public and private domains. Described as a gang of des-

---

Martyrdom and Persecution, 252–3, 269. For further information about whether Minucius Felix based his dialogue on Fronto's work see also Albert Heinrichs, 'Pagan Ritual and the Alleged Crimes of the Early Christians', in P. Granfield and J. Jungman (eds.), *Festschrift Johannes Quasten* (Münster: Aschendorff, 1970) 26–7. See also note 27 below.

[27] *Octavius* 8–9, in *The Octavius of Marcus Minucius Felix*, trans. G. Clarke (New York: Newman, 1974). On the use of Fronto in *Octavius* see pp. 8–9, 221–4, n. 123. Cf. *ANF* 4.177.

[28] Cf. for example, Tacitus' description of the Jews in *Histories* 5.5: 'Toward every other people they feel only hate and enmity. They sit apart at meals, and they sleep apart, and although as a race they are prone to lust, they abstain from intercourse with foreign women; yet among themselves nothing is unlawful.' *Histories*, trans. C. Moore (LCL 1931).

peradoes which is in opposition to the gods, early Christianity is perceived as a public threat. Women are present at 'public' church meals; men and women gather together for feasts without any consideration of propriety. However, what is cited as especially reprehensible in this case is that this public disorder operates through secret tactics, seeking the seclusion of the private domain. Meetings are held at night; words are exchanged in corners; all members of the family, including children, are present. Presumably, the author has in mind the kind of clandestine activities that might take place in a private home. The home, which should protect women and children from such destructive forces, becomes the very site of their corruption.

The reference to familial language ('indiscriminately they call each other brother and sister') is especially intriguing, given that usage of such language has been judged by scholars of early Christianity to be a sign that early church groups brought the public: male domain into the domestic: female sphere, and hence, opened up avenues for women's activities that might not otherwise be available in society at large.[29] There is a recognition of the blurring of lines between inside and outside in the accusation that Christians turn 'even ordinary fornication into incest': the common immorality of the outside world becomes indecency in the home. In essence, this text reveals the perception, which becomes even more strongly pronounced in Celsus' critique, that the heart of Christianity's threat lies in rendering the public sphere an extension of the private. In aiming to understand what this meant for early Christians, it becomes immediately clear that the private: household world of early Christianity did not shelter one from the public gaze. However much the reality of church as 'new family' facilitated the involvement of women, it clearly also heightened Christianity's offensiveness and left women vulnerable to scrutiny.

While the critique of early Christianity recorded in the above speech is obviously polemical, and as always we must be aware of the distinction between appearance and reality, it nevertheless may offer substantial insight into how early Christians in the second

---

[29] See Introduction, 30–1.

century operated. Having studied the growth of Christianity from 100 to 400 CE Ramsay MacMullen notes a decline in references to missionary effort starting at the turn of the second century.[30] In responding to the puzzling issue of under what circumstances most conversions actually took place, MacMullen points to the importance of the somewhat sequestered settings of home and work where news could be exchanged and healings and exorcisms performed.[31] He concludes that early Christians were essentially cautious when it came to large-scale public appearances.[32]

If MacMullen's conclusions are correct, then early Christian texts encouraging visibility and public declarations of faith must be analysed carefully. It is worth considering one example which may have points of contact with Fronto's polemic. Writing in the early to mid-second century, the author of the Pastoral Epistles is intent on encouraging community gatherings involving preaching, teaching and the public reading of scripture (1 Tim. 4.12–15; cf. 5.19–21; 2 Tim. 2.2).[33] However, at times almost imperceptibly, the focus of these exhortations changes from the internal assembly to relations between the church and the world. Clearly the Pastoral Epistles voice an interest in conversion (e.g. 1 Tim. 2.3–4; 2 Tim. 4.2–5), despite any attendant risks of persecution entailed in proselytizing. Indeed opponents are to be countered with 'sound speech that cannot be censured' in order to avoid any possibility of the slander of the community (Tit. 2:7–8). The focus on the public sphere in the Pastoral Epistles seems to have two dimensions. On the one hand there is an encouragement of community members to gather together openly as well as an interest in the public dimension of ministry. On the other hand there is concern with the impression made on outsiders and with giving the mission a universal appeal.

The two-dimensional focus on the public domain in the Pastoral Epistles is probably related to two interrelated problems. The way these texts focus on the public sphere may be a response to pagan

---

[30] MacMullen, *Christianizing the Roman Empire*, 33–4. [31] Ibid., 36–42.
[32] Ibid., 40.
[33] On the public nature of teaching in the Pastoral Epistles see Abraham Malherbe, 'In Season and Out of Season: 2 Timothy 4:2, *JBL* 103 (1984) 240–1. See also my discussion in *Pauline Churches*, 175–6. The Pastoral Epistles are discussed further in Part 2, pp. 154–78.

accusations of secretive activity, a response which aims to quiet pagan attack. Yet, the public emphasis may also be a response to an internal problem. It has been suggested that there is a connection between appeals to the public nature of Timothy's ministry (1 Tim. 4.12–15; 2 Tim. 4.2–5) and the tactics of false teachers who were thought to pose an internal threat to the group by sneaking into the household, upsetting the faith, and capturing 'silly women' (2 Tim. 3.6; cf. Tit. 1.11).[34] If this is the case, we have here an example of an early Christian author aiming to admonish community members by warning them to avoid the kind of behaviour of which, in all likelihood, they themselves had been accused during the course of pagan critique.[35] In other words, an early Christian author is capable of attributing the same vice to members of the internal group that has been used to label the group by outsiders. Moreover, pagan opinion concerning the vulnerability of women to conversion to Christianity is reworked within a church context into the vulnerability of women to allegedly heretical teaching. This is an example of a phenomenon we will encounter frequently during the course of our study: external values and labels are appropriated by the group during the process of self-definition. Such appropriation illustrates the importance of the perception of outsiders in the development of a community's sense of boundaries setting it apart from both internal enemies and the external world.[36]

As is typical for early Christian authors of this period, the author of the Pastoral Epistles appears to be waging a battle on two fronts – internal enemies and outsiders – and it is often not easy to see clearly the author's line of vision. This dual perspective is evident in the teaching on widows in 1 Timothy 5 where young widows (probably under the influence of the 'false teaching' mentioned above) are said to be wasting time, wandering from house to house saying what should not be said, and contributing to the slander of

[34] Malherbe, 'In Season', 242.
[35] There are several indications in the Pastoral Epistles that community members are experiencing criticism at the hands of outsiders. I have collected the evidence in *Pauline Churches*, 167–70.
[36] See interesting discussion in A. P. Cohen, *The Symbolic Construction of Community* (London and New York: Tavistock, 1985) 74–5.

the community. The author's recommendation is unambiguous: the young widows should marry, have children and manage their households (1 Tim. 5.11–15). Not only does this exhortation curtail the expansion of an unacceptable ascetic teaching (1 Tim. 4.3), but it also quiets the behaviour of women which was drawing unwanted attention from outsiders.[37] Women become relegated to their proper place in the private domain of the household. But it is important to realize that such strong efforts to reinforce the traditional boundaries separating the male, public sphere from the female, private sphere were destined to have only limited effect. By virtue of its interest in transforming society and of its physical manifestation as an association of house groups, the household of God (1 Tim. 3.15) would remain visible as a movement where the private and public merged, and gender distinctions were threatened.

To return to Fronto's polemic, it is important to recognize that the secretive nature of the church's activities did not curtail speculation and detailed comment on those activities by outsiders. Christian rites were visible enough at least to generate rumours: all notions of table etiquette and propriety have been abandoned, promiscuity and incest are said to be rampant, brotherhood and sisterhood language reaches far beyond symbolic proportions. Fronto states that immorality involves all ages and sexes, but it is important to note his effort to be more precise about the nature of the scandal. He stresses the involvement of women, sisters, and mothers in the feasts: the corruption of women and children undoubtedly is a sign of the group's sinister nature. Church authors from the second century onward demonstrate an awareness that Christians are accused of such things.[38] But what is remarkable is that church authors can also apply such descriptions to distinguish their 'authentic' views from various 'heretical' groups. In the middle of the second century Justin, for example,

[37] I have discussed the teaching on women in the Pastoral Epistles in detail in *Pauline Churches*, 176–89. Here I draw on the interesting work of Dennis R. MacDonald, *The Legend and the Apostle: The Battle for Paul in Story and Canon* (Philadelphia: Westminster, 1983) where he explores a possible relationship between the false teaching condemned by the author of the Pastoral Epistles and the Apocryphal *Acts of Paul and Thecla*.

[38] Minucius Felix is a case in point here. See also Justin, *Dialogue with Trypho* 10 (*ANF* 1.199); *First Apology* 29 (*ANF* 1.172); Tertullian, *Apology* 7 (*ANF* 3.23).

claimed (in the style of Fronto) that some gnostic groups 'over-turned the lamp', had promiscuous intercourse and ate human flesh.[39] According to Clement of Alexandria, the Carpocratians (a libertine gnostic group) held their wives as common property.[40] Later in the same century, Irenaeus explained that as part of their previous religious lives some Christian women had taken part in promiscuous rites.[41] From the fourth-century Christian author Epiphanius of Cyprus comes an especially dramatic account of the Christian group known as Phibionites which has much in common with Fronto's description of the Christians from the second century. According to Epiphanius, the members of this group have 'their women in common'. During the course of a meeting a husband 'says to his own wife, stand up and perform the *agape* [make love] with the brother'.[42] At the end of his account Epiphanius claimed that his detailed knowledge of the group was based on personal experience; he had been lured into the group by attractive young women.[43]

When we see the similarity between what pagans said about Christians and what Christians said about internal enemies, we are left with many questions about the influence of stereotypical categories and about historical accuracy. It is not enough today to say that pagan critique was based exclusively on the activities of so-called extremist early Christian groups. Scholars now read church authors very much aware of the possibility of an exaggerated difference between what was heretical and what was orthodox. If we recall the need to wage a battle on two fronts, the attempt to communicate the message, 'it may be true of them, but not us' should come as no surprise. Neither should we be surprised that Christians adopted conventional polemical language and concepts

---

[39] Justin, *First Apology* 26 (*ANF* 1.172); cf. Tertullian, *Apology* 7 (*ANF* 3.23).

[40] Clem. Al. *Strom.* 3.5–10, trans. H. Chadwick, *Alexandrian Christianity*, Library of Christian Classics vol. 2, H. Chadwick and J. Oulton (eds.) (London: SCM, 1954).

[41] Irenaeus, *Advursus omnes Haereses*, 1.6.3 (*ANF* 1.324).

[42] *Panarion*, 26.4–5, trans. Benko. For citation of entire text see Benko, *Pagan Rome*, 65–6; for information about translation see 77 n.47. See also Stephen Benko, 'The Libertine Gnostic Sect of the Phibionites According to Epiphanius', *VC* 21 (1967)103–19.

[43] Benko, *Pagan Rome*, 88 n. 48, citing *Panarion*, 26.17.1ff. For discussion of these fascinating texts which condemn the practices of various groups see Benko, 'Pagan Criticism', 1083–8; *Pagan Rome*, 54–78; Wilken, *The Christians*, 19–21.

to make accusations against alleged heretics, including charges about the corruption and inappropriate visibility of heretical women. But rather than seeing the similarity between pagan impression of Christians and Christian impression of deviant groups as evidence of the historical unreliability of this material, it is important, given the great diversity in early Christianity, to take seriously the possibility that rumours among the pagans do reflect the actual practices of some groups.

Even those texts which have been transmitted in Christian tradition as representative of orthodoxy give indications that the negative comments of outsiders were based on the observations of actual rites, which were then subject to a variety of interpretations. Early in the second century, Ignatius of Antioch sought to ensure that the bishop would have authority over the *agape* (Ign. *Smyrn.* 8.2). Although the *agape* here is usually understood in conjunction with the Eucharist, we cannot be certain of the specifics of his reference. The fact that this kind of language was used in relation to a gathering would be enough to raise suspicion, even if the 'love feast' was not of the kind corrupted by the immorality of false teachers mentioned in Jude 12 or of the kind ascribed to the Phibionites by Epiphanius in the fourth century.[44] Even in the earliest New Testament period, there are indications that religious rites were subject to public scrutiny. Paul clearly is afraid that the gift of tongues will be misunderstood by outsiders (1 Cor. 14.22–5). This kind of concern for propriety may also underlie his awkward response to the practice of women uncovering their heads when the community gathers for prayer and prophecy (1 Cor. 11.2–16). This behaviour may have been inspired by Paul's own teaching of the principle that in Christ, 'there is no male and female' (Gal. 3.28), a teaching which Pauline Christianity shares in common with aspects of Syrian early Christianity and Valentinian Gnosticism, and which may draw its origins from a saying in a baptismal rite that predates Paul. Although Paul seems to have been convinced of the importance of avoiding such interpretations, in other circles this teaching was interpreted as referring to the transcendence of

---

[44] Benko, 'Pagan Criticism', 1089. See also Pliny's allusions to the Eucharist discussed above.

sexual differentiation and the return to androgynous perfection.[45] Unity was an ideological goal which could be enacted in many dramatic forms in early Christianity, and these practices could have varying effects on public opinion.

Although offering no mention of the activities of specific early Christian women, the remarks attributed to Marcus Cornelius Fronto have enabled us to reflect about the place of women in the charge of immorality which figures in pagan critique. Women, along with their children, are depicted as engaging in promiscuous rites and of violating the appropriate order of society, including the lines of division between private and public. As is the case with Pliny's remarks, we find in Fronto's polemic a strong curiosity about the rituals of early Christianity, including dining practices. This text is especially interesting because of the repeated focus on the visibility of women in the those rites. It does seem, however, that as we move from Pliny to Fronto we have left the firm grounds of history and have moved to the more speculative world of impression, rumour, and stereotype. But as we begin to think about the complicated question of the relationship between pagan critique and the content of early Christian literature, we will see that, with respect to women at least, this speculative world is no less important than the bedrock of historical fact. Through very real activities, and at times even by their silent presence or semblance of visibility, early Christian women became the indicators par excellence of perversion or of sanctity.

Lucius Apuleius

From about the middle of the second century comes an account which may reflect the charge that Christianity led to the immorality of women. Lucius Apuleius (123–?), the well-known poet, philosopher, and rhetorician from North Africa, was educated in

---

[45] See D. R. MacDonald, *There is No Male and Female: The Fate of a Dominical Saying in Paul and Gnosticism* (Philadelphia: Fortress, 1987). According to MacDonald, Galatians 3.27–8 originated in a saying of Jesus recorded in the *Gospel of the Egyptians* (Clem. Al. *Strom.* 3.13.92) and found in similar versions in *2 Clement*, 12.2 and the *Gospel of Thomas*, 37, 21a, 22b. See my discussion of MacDonald's work in Margaret Y. MacDonald, 'Women Holy in Body and Spirit: The Social Setting of 1 Corinthians 7', *NTS* 36 (1990) 165–8.

such important ancient centres as Carthage, Athens, and Rome. He wrote a work which reveals a hostile pagan reaction to the activities of a woman who may well be a Christian. In his *Metamorphoses* (or *The Golden Ass*) he tells the colourful tale of one Lucius, who was transformed by magic into an ass for a time. As part of his adventures when he is in animal form, Lucius finds himself sold to a baker. Here he finds himself in an opportune position to observe what might otherwise have remained strictly between husband and wife:

The baker who purchased me was otherwise a good and very modest man but his wife was the wickedest of all women and he suffered extreme miseries to his bed and his house so that I myself, by Hercules, often in secret felt pity for him. There was not one single vice which that woman lacked, but all crimes flowed together into her heart like into a filthy latrine; cruel, perverse, man-crazy, drunken, stubborn, obstinate, avaricious in petty theft, wasteful in sumptuous expenses, an enemy to faith, and chastity, she also despised the gods and instead of a certain religion she claimed to worship a god whom she called 'only'. In his honour she practiced empty rites and ceremonies and she deceived all men and her miserable husband, drinking unmixed wine early in the morning and giving her body to continual whoring.[46]

The reference to the worship of 'a god called only' means that Apuleius' description of the wicked woman could refer to either a Jewish proselyte or a Christian woman. It calls to mind for example, Juvenal's satirical description (offered in the midst of an attack on the religious corruption of Roman women) of an old Jewish beggar woman who is paid to interpret dreams and is called 'an interpreter of the laws of Jerusalem, high priestess with a tree as temple, a trusty go-between of high-heaven'.[47] However, the

---

[46] Apuleius, *Metamorphoses* 9.14, translation by Benko in 'Pagan Criticism', 1090. See also Benko's discussion of the date, provenance, and meaning of this text, 1090–1. I prefer Benko's translation here but see also trans. by W. Adlington, rev. S. Gaselee (LCL 1915). For support of the thesis that this passage refers to Jewish or Christian worship, see J. Gwyn Griffiths (ed. and trans.) *Apuleius of Madauros: The Isis-Book (Metamorphoses, Book XI)* (Leiden: E. J. Brill, 1975) 345, 359; and the discussion of Marcel Simon, "Apulée et le Christianisme", in Antoine Guillamont and E-M. Laperrousaz (eds.), *Mélanges d'Histoire des Religions* (Paris: Presses Universitaires de France, 1974), 299–305.

[47] Juvenal, *Satire* 6; cited in Kraemer, *Maenads*, pp. 41–2. See discussion in Kraemer, *Her Share*, 90, 109. In this work, Juvenal speaks of the wine feasts and sexual activities in various suspicious religious groups, including the cult of Isis. See Balch, *Let Wives*, 77 n.12; R. E. Witt, *Isis in the Greco-Roman World* (Ithaca, NY: Cornell, 1971); Sharon Kelly Heyob, *The Cult of Isis among Women in the Greco-Roman World* (Leiden: Brill, 1975).

possible reference to the Eucharist ('unmixed wine') suggests a Christian context.

The fact that the unfortunate baker suffered 'miseries to his bed' leads us to question whether what lies behind Apuleius' description is the refusal of sexual favours, inspired either by asceticism or by an unwillingness to be intimate with someone who is not a Christian. Although the picture painted is overwhelmingly one of sexual immorality, we will find that Apuleius likely is drawing upon a series of stereotypical vices which are associated with too frequent absence from the home. The depiction of a woman as a whore in fact might be due to the woman's behaviour that is ascetic, not promiscuous. As I will discuss in detail in Part 3, in his 'Second Apology', Justin tells of a Christian woman from Rome who was married to a pagan and was repulsed by the thought of intercourse with one who belonged to the unbelieving world.

However we understand her actions, the woman's problematic sexual behaviour in Apuleius' account is depicted as extending beyond the walls of the household. The accusation of sexual immorality of the woman (she is man-crazy, an enemy to chastity, and a whore) is in keeping with Fronto's comments about Christian women being involved in immoral acts. However, Apuleius' text is far more specific about the nature of female vice and about female culpability. While in Fronto's polemic the attraction of women to early Christian rites is the result of their inherent credulity, in Apuleius' description the woman is depicted as bold, uncontrollable, and capable of deception. She is completely lacking in shame, the very basis of her husband's honour.

Apuleius' description, which might represent a popular assessment of a husband who was unlucky enough to find himself sharing his house with a Christian wife, is similar to a later text which speaks in general about the consequences of the illegitimate religious activities of women. Here damage to husband, bed, and house are also in view. The early fourth-century CE author known as Pseudo-Lucian spoke of wives who 'leave the house immediately and visit every god that plagues married men, though the wretched husbands do not even know the very names of some of these . . .' Their return is not characterized by the resumption of normal wifely duties. Rather, the moment they arrive, wives choose to have 'long baths, and by heavens, sumptuous meals accompanied by much coyness towards the men'.[48] As in Apuleius' account we find here a description of the illegitimate religious activities of the woman, coupled with disdain towards the husband. One of the most interesting features of Pseudo-Lucian's text is that it makes explicit what is often implied in other writings: the suspicious comings and goings of women for dubious religious reasons are an assault on the social order which separated the female or private sphere from the male or public sphere and, ultimately, a threat to the core values of honour and shame.

When read in relation to the text from Pseudo-Lucian, Apuleius' description of the woman who worships 'the god called only' offers valuable insight into the nature of public opinion concerning marriages between pagan husbands and early Christian women. I will examine these marriages in detail in Part 3. It is important at this point to consider the kind of women's behaviour which would elicit criticism, including a barrage of accusations of having stereotypical vices. Given that early Christian women lived in a world which believed that women were inclined towards religious fanaticism and which accused unauthorized cults of leading women to behave immorally, we would expect that pagan members of a household and neighbours of a Christian woman would be sensitive to even the subtlest signs of illicit behaviour. In fact, the texts we have been considering do alert us to some of these signs. Scruples about food or curious feasting, suspected extravagance or laziness with respect to household duties, a lack of interest in relations with one's husband or in family matters generally might lead to questions. One early Christian text reminds us that something as simple as a sudden preference for plainer, more modest clothing could be noted by outsiders as significant. When Tertullian exhorted Christian women on the importance of avoiding luxurious clothes, he recorded the objection made by some women that the Christian name should not be blasphemed on account of a derogatory change in their former style of dress.[49]

---

[48] Lucian, *Amores*, 42; trans. M. D. MacLoed (LCL 1913), cited in Portefaix, *Sisters Rejoice*, 54–5. Portefaix also cites Strabo C297 (*Geography* 7.3.4), see her discussion on pp. 54–5.
[49] See Tertullian, *On the Apparel of Women*, 2.11 (*ANF* 4.24).

The most obvious and suspicious signs of Christian activities which are alluded to both in pagan critique and in early Christian literature are intrusion within the house by mysterious visitors, and/or frequent absences from the home. The departure of a woman to attend an early morning rite could lead quickly to an eruption of rumours about her adulterous behaviour, however innocent her intent. One fascinating early Christian text from the fourth century CE illustrates that early Christians were aware of the possibility of dangerous shifts in public opinion. The *Constitutions of the Holy Apostles* tells of the special ministry which the deaconess has to women who are part of unbelieving households: 'sometimes thou canst not send a Deacon, who is a man, to the women in certain houses, on account of the unbelievers. Thou shall therefore send a woman, a Deaconess, on account of the imaginations of the bad.'[50]

It appears that rumours of sexual promiscuity were hovering over relationships between believing men and the daughters and wives of non-believers. In light of the possibility of scandal, it would be prudent to send out a woman minister, whose entry into the non-believing household would be less likely to be noticed. One of the most fascinating aspects of this text is that it admits the need for discretion, even secrecy, in Christian groups. In fact, the Christian woman in view here seems bound to remain in the house and requires discreet visitations. Such precautions are hardly surprising when one considers that a woman's marital infidelity (implicit in her decision to join the church without her husband) could have life-threatening repercussions. As I will discuss further in Part 3, early Christian sources indicate that marriages between believing women and pagan men could lead to persecution.

Apuleius' description of the woman who worships 'the god called only', the text from Pseudo-Lucian on the suspicious

---

[50] *Constitutions of the Holy Apostles*, 3.15 (*ANF* 7.431); cited in Kraemer, ed., *Maenads*, 239. This work from fourth-century Syria incorporates material from earlier works including the *Didache* and the *Didascalia Apostolorum*. See *New Catholic Encyclopedia* (New York: McGraw-Hill, 1967) 689–90. In the text cited here, the *Constitutions* are essentially an adaptation of the *Didascalia*, a work from third-century Syria. The *Constitutions* are, however, more explicit than the *Didascalia* with respect to the specific dangers involved in sending a deacon to a pagan household. See R. H. Connolly (ed.), *Didascalia Apostolorum* (Oxford: Clarendon, 1969), ch. 16, pp. 146–8.

religious activities of women, and the instructions concerning the duties of the deaconess in the *Constitutions* all reflect a phenomenon that has been observed by anthropologists of Mediterranean societies: intrusions into the house and/or frequent absences from the house can be potent signs of a woman's infidelity and general unsuitability as a wife. The remarks of anthropologist Juliet du Boulay about modern Greek village life seem equally applicable to ancient society:

absence from the home or irregularities in customary activities which cannot be minutely and indisputably accounted for in society, will almost inevitably be taken as evidence of surreptitious liaisons . . . since, according to the conception of feminine nature, a woman's shame is the seat of her virtue, lack of virtue in aspects of life completely unrelated to sexuality may, if occasion arises, be referred back to a woman's basic moral nature.[51]

If we allow Du Boulay's remarks to inform our understanding of the consequences of public censure for the life of marriages between pagan men and early Christian women we arrive at the following picture: a woman's mysterious comings and goings for religious purposes, and/or her entertainment of secret visitors were a sign of her lack of restraint, probably promiscuity, and they ultimately meant that the woman was shameless and immoral. Such actions could have serious repercussions. Harsh laws would punish the Roman woman if rumours of her behaviour became actual charges of adultery, although if her husband was unfaithful he incurred no legal punishment unless the other woman was married. It was the *wife's* sexual purity which determined the household's reputation and legal standing in the community.[52]

With the help of cultural anthropology, we see how easy it was for women who joined new religious groups to be depicted in the

---

[51] Du Boulay, *Portrait of a Greek Mountain Village*, 130; see p.133.

[52] Roman law on adultery is complicated, but it is clear that it 'was intended primarily to preserve the chastity of women within marriage'. Penalties might involve partial loss of dowry and property, banishment, hard labour and, under certain circumstances, even death. See excellent discussion by Gardner in *Women in Roman Law and Society*, 128; see pp. 127–31. On adultery laws see also P. Brown, *The Body and Society : Men, Women and Sexual Renunciation in Early Christianity* (London and Boston: Faber and Faber, 1988) 23. In these last two paragraphs I have been following closely, but developing further, the argument articulated in my article, 'Early Christian Women', 230–1.

contemptuous fashion of Apuleius' description of the baker's wife. Moreover, we realize that the role of women in the speculative world of impression, rumour, and stereotype could have had serious consequences for their lives. Suspicions about vices of various shapes and sizes quickly become charges of sexual infidelity and immorality. In both Apuleius' account and the similar text from Pseudo-Lucian, husbands are portrayed as objects of pity and wives are accused of deceit. But there is another side to these negative portraits. If we recall the remarks in the Introduction to this book about the tendency to attribute the quality of cunning or deviousness to women in modern Greek society, we will be able to consider how such negative presentations actually may function as cultural acknowledgments of the ability of women to 'get their own way'. Thus, when ancient women are said to be sneaking out of their homes to attend mysterious early morning rites or to worship strange gods about whom their husbands have never even heard, we are, in a sense, reading an acknowledgment of their power, even if it is clearly illegitimate power according to those who are in positions of authority. As we consider the early Christian material in subsequent chapters we will probe the shape of that power. In fact, the next text may already provide us with some understanding of such power. The remarks of the following author return us once again to the particulars of history and prevent us from concluding too quickly that pagans only *thought* they saw a women's religion.

Lucian of Samosata

Robert Wilken describes Lucian (115–200 CE) as, 'a satirist who wrote humorous essays and dialogues about life in the Roman world' – a satirist who 'pokes fun at the gullibility of the Christians'.[53] Lucian tells the tale of the philosopher Peregrinus (d. 165), also known as Proteus, who converts to Christianity during the course of his travels to Palestine. His new-found faith leads to his arrest, and while in prison he receives some intriguing visitors:

[53] Wilken, *The Christians*, 45. On Lucian see also Remus, *Pagan-Christian Conflict*, 165–6.

Then at length Proteus was apprehended for this and thrown into prison, which itself gave him no little reputation as an asset for his future career and the charlatanism and notoriety-seeking that he was enamoured of. Well, when he had been imprisoned, the Christians, regarding the incident as a calamity, left nothing undone in the effort to rescue him. Then, as this was impossible, every other form of attention was shown him, not in any casual way but with assiduity; and from the very break of day aged widows and orphan children could be seen waiting near the prison, while their officials even slept inside with him after bribing the guards. Then elaborate meals were brought in, and sacred books of theirs were read aloud, and excellent Peregrinus – for he still went by that name – was called by them, 'the new Socrates' . . . Indeed, people came even from the cities of Asia, sent by the Christians at their common expense to succour and encourage the hero. They show incredible speed whenever any such public action is taken; for in no time they lavish their all. So it was then in the case of Peregrinus; much money came to him from them by reason of his imprisonment, and he procured not a little revenue from it.[54]

The text goes on to describe the major characteristics of Christianity in terms already familiar to us from the previously discussed pagan comments: the 'poor wretches' are convinced that they are going to be immortal. They deny the Greek gods. They have common property and consider one another to be 'brothers'. Yet, despite the fact that this text probably reflects conventional assessments about the Christians in many parts of the Empire,[55] if we place it in relation to what we know from early Christian sources, there is significant evidence to suggest that we have here a fairly accurate picture of historical events. In particular, the mention of widows visiting Peregrinus is striking. An alternate translation of γράδια χήρας as 'old hags called widows' better captures Lucian's satirical tone which is in keeping with well-documented derogatory characterizations of older women and their activities.[56] But the presence of conventional representations does

---

[54] Lucian, *The Passing of Peregrinus,* 12–13, trans. A. M. Harmon (LCL 1936). See commentary on this text in C. P. Jones, *Culture and Society in Lucian* (Cambridge Mass. and London: Harvard University, 1986) 121–4.   [55] See Benko, 'Pagan Criticism', 1095.

[56] This is the translation adopted by C. H. Turner in 'Ministries of Women in the Primitive Church', *Constructive Quarterly,* 7 (1919) 439; also cited in Bonnie Bowman Thurston, *The Widows,* 74. See Liddell-Scott, *Greek-English Lexicon,* s.v. γραῖδιον in support of the translation as 'old hag'. Dennis R. MacDonald has collected some interesting evidence on the characterization in Greco-Roman society of old women, and the stories told by old women, in *The Legend and the Apostle,* 13–15.

not mean that we should assume there is no reality reflected in this account. The visibility of the widows in the story of Peregrinus will come as no surprise to anyone who has even the most basic knowledge of the involvement of women in early Christianity. While it is impossible to be certain about the precise shape of the ministry of widows in the period we are discussing, New Testament evidence such as that in Acts and in the Pastoral Epistles, coupled with material from the Apostolic Fathers and the *Apocryphal New Testament*, leaves no doubt that from very early on widows played a prominent role in the life of the church, and by the beginning of the second century CE some even participated in some sort of order of widows.[57]

Being far more than objects of the church's benevolence, by the second century CE widows provided service for church groups.[58] The fact that widows were seen waiting near Peregrinus' place of imprisonment at the break of day suggests that they had congregated there to pray. As the text makes clear by its reference to meals and to sacred books, the imprisonment of early Christians meant that both prisoners and onlookers would be involved in various rites. But if we are to appreciate the full impact of reference to widows in *The Passing of Peregrinus* we must also examine the related reference to children. The mention of orphans, in conjunction with widows, also is in keeping with evidence from early Christian literature where the care of widows is paired with the care of orphans as a duty of the church (Jas. 1.27; *Herm. Man.* 8.10; *Barn.* 20.2; Ign. *Smyrn.* 6.2). Moreover, Lucian's text confirms the impression that widows were responsible for the care of orphan children in the church. Having brought up children and cared for the afflicted are listed as prerequisites for enrolment in the office of widows by the author of the Pastoral Epistles, and there is no reason to doubt that women would have continued in these roles after their acceptance into the order (1 Tim. 5.10). In the *Shepherd of Hermas* a certain woman named Grapte is instructed to exhort

---

[57] Two important works to consider on widows are that by Thurston, *The Widows* and Stevan L. Davies, *The Revolt of the Widows: The Social World of the Apocryphal Acts* (Carbondale: Southern Illinois University, 1980).

[58] Thurston, *The Widows*, 73. Widows in the early church will be the subject of a more detailed examination in Part 2.

widows and orphans, implying that they comprised a group, perhaps living together in the same Christian house (*Herm. Vis.* 2.4.3).

Lucian has presented us with a colourful and intriguing portrait of women and children waiting near the prison. However, as anyone who has been involved with the care of young children knows, it would be difficult to maintain organized intercessory prayer for very long! Perhaps we should look for the meaning of their presence by considering possibilities of more active service. Lucian's text itself leads to a few suggestions. While the widows and orphans wait outside, it is said that church officials penetrated the prison after bribing the guards. Might the women and children have been acting as sentries, warning of the arrival of less friendly guards? Was their visibility in a public area sanctioned by early Christians precisely because their presence would likely be ignored? Did their very invisibility in terms of the society at large contribute to their capacity to minister to those who were in prison? Was it they who were largely responsible for bringing in the elaborate meals and the sacred books? Early Christian literature provides evidence that concern for those who were in prison included practical means to provide for their needs. Tertullian, in fact, uses striking female symbolism to speak of the nature of this sustenance: 'Blessed Martyrs Designate, along with the provision which our lady mother the Church from her bountiful breasts, and each brother out of his private means, makes for your bodily wants in the prison, accept also from me some contribution to your spiritual sustenance; for it is not good that the flesh be feasted and the spirit starve . . .'[59]

Given the broad range of evidence we have been considering, it is reasonable to conclude that these widows who were accompanied by children in all likelihood acted as providers. We have noted that early church teaching calls for widows and orphans to be provided for, but this in no way would preclude these women and children using their energies to be providers in return. In fact, there is nothing in Lucian's text to imply that they are poor. Peregrinus is

---

[59] Tertullian, *Ad Martyras* 1 (*ANF* 3.693). Cited in Benko, 'Pagan Criticism', 1094 n.151. Benko here has collected interesting texts to consider.

described as having profited considerably from the gifts that Christians brought for his benefit. Of course this suggestion serves to embellish the portrait Lucian is painting of Peregrinus as a charlatan, but there seems to be no reason to doubt that Christians were able to collect significant revenue for an important cause. The group is depicted as organizing public campaigns to secure resources. In addition, as I will discuss in more detail later in this book, if we examine the evidence for the lives of widows in early Christian groups and in the Empire generally with respect to both livelihood and independent action, we encounter varying capacity for both. For example, a literal translation of the Greek phrase in 1 Timothy 5.16 (εἴ τις πιστὴ; ἔχει χήρας), 'if any believing woman has widows', implies that some women were in a strong enough position financially to support needy widows. The believing women of means are instructed to care for widows (perhaps relatives) so that the church will not be unnecessarily burdened financially and will be able to assist those who have no other source of support. It has been suggested that the believing women who are relatively well-to-do are themselves widows.[60] This combination of needy widows with widow-patrons also is reflected in Acts 9.36–42 which identifies Tabitha at the centre of a group of widows whom she supplies with clothes. The second-century apocryphal *Acts of Paul and Thecla* tells of Tryphaena, a very wealthy widow who adopts the virgin Thecla as her own daughter and provides her with all that she requires. The account of Tryphaena's actions probably reflects the benevolence of wealthy Christian women who sheltered celibate church women of limited means.[61]

In thinking about the relation between the role of provider and the description of women we find in Lucian's account, a final element of his text which has drawn little attention from past commentators is worth considering. Christians are depicted as travelling 'even from the cities of Asia' and 'at their common expense' to attend to the needs of Peregrinus. Since the Christians who are singled out for mention by Lucian include church officials, widows,

---

[60] See discussion in Martin Dibelius and Hans Conzelmann, *The Pastoral Epistles*, trans. P. Buttolph and A. Yarboro (Philadelphia: Fortress, 1972) 76. Other textual variants permit a translation as 'believing man or woman' or simply 'believing man', but 'believing woman' is generally preferred.   [61] See MacDonald, *The Legend and the Apostle*, 50–3.

and orphans we must consider women as part of the travelling group. Studies of the earliest church groups known to us, the Pauline churches, have highlighted the importance of travel in the expansion of Christianity and have sought to understand the connection between ability to travel and social stratification in the early church.[62] These studies make it clear that women were travelling. While contemporary practices in traditional Mediterranean cultures might lead us to question how women in ancient society could travel alone, there is no reason to conclude that male chaperons were always in positions of superiority. Presumably, travelling women who were well-to-do could call on the protection of their slaves. A celibate Christian woman might journey accompanied by a male co-worker, perhaps presenting their partnerhood as a marriage to the outside world when, in fact, their union was purely spiritual.[63] The most striking example of a woman traveller in the Pauline circle is Phoebe, recommended in the last chapter of Paul's letter to the Romans as a minister (διάκονον) of the church at Cenchrae who is on her way to Rome, apparently bearing Paul's letter.[64] Because of Phoebe's contribution as a patroness or protector (προστάτις) of many Christians, the Roman church members are instructed to offer her hospitality, whatever she may require. The reference to Phoebe offers significant evidence for the relationship between church leadership, wealth, and travel for the dual purpose of business ventures and church mission.

There is much in Romans 16.1–2 to suggest that Phoebe is travelling at her own expense, but there is also evidence in Pauline

[62] Two important studies should be considered here: Gerd Theissen, 'Social Stratification in the Corinthian Community' in *Social Setting*, 69–119; see especially pp. 91–6. Meeks, *Urban Christians*, 16–19, 57, 109, 230 notes 169–72.

[63] Scholars have argued that although in Paul's correspondence we may have evidence of 'spiritual marriages' (1 Cor. 7.36–8), conclusive evidence for the practice comes from later periods. However, I argue below that *Did.*, 11.11 may refer to the activities of those engaged in spiritual marriages.

[64] This is the dominant view. However, some scholars believe that Romans 16 was not originally part of the letter to the Romans but is a fragment of another Pauline letter intended for Ephesus. This issue along with other matters of interpretation relating to Phoebe are discussed in detail in Whelan, 'Amica Pauli'. It is interesting to compare Phoebe to another woman in Pauline circles who travels. Wayne Meeks has noted that Lydia, the merchant of purple goods (Acts 16.14), was from Thyatira (Asia Minor), but encountered Paul in Philippi (Macedonia). Travel for Lydia was most likely an 'occupational necessity'; see *Urban Christians*, 17.

Christianity of people travelling at someone else's expense. The members of Chloe's household who told Paul in Ephesus about Corinthian troubles were probably slaves and freedpersons who travelled as agents of their mistress (1 Cor. 1.11).[65] Thus some women were involved in financing the journeys of others. It is possible that widows who were dependent on other women were sent travelling on church missions. It has often been noted that celibacy allowed early Christian women to escape many of the responsibilities of the traditional household, but it may have also enabled women to undertake a variety of important new duties. At any rate, travelling women could count on the extension of hospitality, which by the second century became a criterion for the selection of bishops (1 Tim. 3.2; Tit. 1.8). The ancient historian, E. A. Judge, has spoken interestingly about the connection between the extension of hospitality in Christian circles and the ability of the church to mobilize individuals from poorer sectors of society: 'Security and hospitality when travelling had traditionally been the privilege of the powerful, who had relied upon a network of patronage and friendship, created by wealth. The letters of recommendation disclose the fact that these domestic advantages were now extended to the whole household of faith, who are accepted on trust, though complete strangers.'[66] Therefore, when we think of women travelling, even needy widows accompanied by orphans, we must remember that not only would church groups facilitate their efforts by financial means, but a network of hospitality was in place to offer security to even the most socially disadvantaged. The following excerpt from the *Shepherd of Hermas*, a work probably dating from the first half of the second century and of Roman provenance, speaks of the importance of hospitality and the protection of widows as duties of the bishop:

Bishops and hospitable men who at all times received the servants of God into their houses gladly and without hypocrisy; and the bishops ever ceaselessly sheltered the destitute and the widows by their ministration, and ever behaved with holiness. These then shall always be sheltered by

---

65 Meeks, *Urban Christians*, 57.
66 E. A. Judge, *The Conversion of Rome: Ancient Sources of Modern Social Tensions* (North Ryde, Australia: Macquarrie Ancient History Association, 1980) 7; cited by Meeks, p. 109.

the Lord. They who have done these things are glorious with God, and their place is already with the angels, if they continue serving the Lord unto the end.[67]

The group of women and children waiting near the prison where Peregrinus was held offers us a colourful snapshot of the lives of early Christian women. As is frequently the case with references to early Christian women, however, if we move from the point of simply observing the historical moment to interpreting its meaning, we must frame our assertions as imaginative reconstructions. In my discussion of Lucian's account and of other texts, I have aimed to contain my reconstructions within the historical limits imposed on me by the larger body of relevant evidence. In my reflections about the women as protectors and providers and in my suggestions about the possibility of travel, I have been rather bold, but I have not gone beyond what is reasonable. Nevertheless, we may ask: does Lucian's description add to our knowledge of the actual lives of early Christian women, in addition to the information it obviously provides about the way early Christian women were depicted? In other words, in what way can image be said to touch reality in this text? I am convinced that given Lucian's basic knowledge of Christianity (informed by what appears to have been a common understanding of the movement), his reference to widows offers us striking confirmation of the prominence of women in early Christianity. An outsider's view offers us a window to reality that is alternate to that provided by the group's own literature. Moreover, I contend that in order to understand early Christianity we must consider how the view of outsiders shaped the lives of believers. As we move in this book to consider how early Christian prescriptions define the lives of celibate women – widows and virgins – it will be important to bear in mind the remarks of Lucian.

Lucian's account of the imprisonment of Peregrinus also offers fruitful material to consider with respect to the questions about the relation between authority and power raised at the beginning of this book. The picture we have of church officials inside the prison

---

[67] *Herm. Sim.* 9.27.2–3; trans. K. Lake, *The Apostolic Fathers* (LCL 1913); cf. Ign. *Pol.* 4.1; Pol. *Phil.* 6.1 in the same edition.

with Peregrinus, while women and children wait attentively outside, implies that lines of authority can dictate women's removal from the centre of activity.[68] But the role these women may have had as guardians and providers reminds us that avenues of power and influence are not necessarily closed by structures of authority. Unlike the descriptions of Christianity by Marcus Cornelius Fronto and Lucius Apuleius, the comments of Lucian of Samosata do not focus upon women's involvement in the violation of the private sphere of the house by their illicit adventures in the public domain nor by their opening of the doors to dangerous outside influences. But the lines separating inside from outside nevertheless shape the existence of these women in important ways. Perhaps because they are insignificant old widows accompanied by children, women in *The Passing of Peregrinus* seem empowered to act as mediators between the interior of the prison and the world outside, a world of social networks and access to resources. Lucian's text has enabled us to raise an issue which will surface again in the course of this work. The fact that women might be ignored under certain circumstances on account of societal views about their unimportance in public affairs may have been an advantage to the early Christian movement, both in terms of its expansion and the protection of its members. However, despite what early Christian officials might have hoped, in the case of the imprisonment of Peregrinus, women and children were not ignored. Once in view, the fact that the women did not have husbands would only serve to heighten suspicion in a society which embraced the values of honour and shame. Without husbands to defend their honour, widows experienced greater risks of being viewed as shameless and, in the extreme, of being seen as sexually aggressive and dangerous.[69] As early Christians came under

---

68 The Greek phrase in *The Passing of Peregrinus*, 12 which is translated as 'their officials' is 'οἱ δὲ ἐν τέλει αὐτῶν. 'τέλει' is derived from the noun 'τέλος', meaning termination or end. In its adjectival form 'τέλειος', the term frequently refers to the expert or the accomplished one. The terminology may suit Lucian's sarcastic tone. Interestingly 'τέλειος' may also be used to refer to one initiated into mystery rites. See BAGD, 809, 811 s.v. τέλειος, τέλος. I am grateful to my research assistant, Steven Muir, for these textual observations.

69 See Malina and Neyrey, 'Honour and Shame in Luke-Acts', 44. See further discussion on widows in early Christianity Part 3, pp. 225–30.

increasing scrutiny, critics apparently looked to see if those who should have been invisible truly were invisible. The old woman who could barely be seen became a graphic image of credulity, shamelessness, and transgression.

Galen of Pergamum

Like Lucian of Samosata, Galen of Pergamum (129–199 CE) was aware of the involvement of unmarried women in early Christianity. However, unlike Lucian, he accorded these women a certain amount of respect. While Galen was critical of the lack of a rational basis for the beliefs of Christians, their rigorous devotion to abstention led him to describe their way of life as characteristic of those who are philosophers. The fact that Galen called Christianity a philosophical school and not a superstition, as other critics had done, reminds us of the acceptance that early Christians might receive within the Greco-Roman world, even within elite circles. Galen's comments are quite different in tone from those of the pagan critics we have considered so far, and he will help us to raise new questions about public opinion of early Christian women:

Most people are unable to follow any demonstrative argument consecutively; hence they need parables, and benefit from them . . .just as we now see the people called Christians drawing their faith from parables and miracles, and yet sometimes acting in the same way as those who philosophize. For their contempt of death and of its sequel is patent to us every day, and likewise their restraint in cohabitation. For they include not only men *but also women* who refrain from cohabitating all through their lives; and they also number individuals who, in self-discipline and self-control in matters of food and drink, and in their keen pursuit of justice, have attained a pitch not inferior to that of genuine philosophers.[70] (Emphasis mine)

---

[70] The text here is based on an Arabic source translated and edited by Richard Walzer, *Galen on Jews and Christians* (London: Oxford University, 1949) 15. The possibility that this description represents a later Christian interpolation cannot be completely discounted, but scholars, including Benko and Wilken, consistently treat the text as genuine. Galen makes a few other brief references to Christianity, which are not cited here because they are not directly relevant to the issue of how women figured in public opinion about the church. See *De pulsuum differentiis*, 3.3, 2.4 (and similar text from Arabic source) cited by Walzer, pp.14–15. In these brief references the teaching of Christ is compared to the

Trained in medicine in his native city of Pergamum in Asia Minor
(a city which included a Christian population, cf. Rev. 1.11), Galen
moved to Rome in 161 CE and became the personal physician of
Marcus Aurelius. Except for a brief period during which he
returned to Pergamum, he remained in Rome until his death.
Galen states that both the restraint of Christians in cohabitation
and their contempt of death could be seen on a daily basis. We do
not know how Galen formed his opinion of the early Christians. He
apparently was appointed around 158 CE as physician to the gladiators of Pergamum. Perhaps his work allowed him not only to learn
about human anatomy from the mangled bodies of gladiators,[71]
but also to encounter early Christian involvement in the games and
to witness their attitudes to death. Perhaps he had heard tales about
the stoic martyrdom around 156 CE of the famous bishop of
Smyrna, the 'blessed Polycarp' (*Mart. Pol.* 1.1), 'the teacher of Asia'
who had been teaching 'many not to sacrifice, or to worship the
gods' (*Mart. Pol.* 12.2). His time in Rome may also have offered
Galen many opportunities to increase his knowledge of Christianity, for the second century saw the growing importance of Rome as
an intellectual centre for Christianity where such important
thinkers as Justin, Valentinus, and Marcion spent some time.[72]

Scholars have seen in Galen's positive evaluation of early
Christianity a great spirit of openness to the diverse phenomena of
antique culture.[73] In relationship to his predecessors, his references
to early Christianity have been judged as factual and rooted in reliable information about early Christianity.[74] Although the references to Christians in Galen's works are few, they are considered
important because of their supposed objectivity.[75]

Behind statements professing the accuracy, objectivity, and seriousness of Galen's remarks, lies the assumption that the harsher
pagan criticisms we have examined previously are laden with
conventional marks of satire and polemic, and hence, with

teaching of Moses and hence scholars have explored Galen's tendency to discuss Judaism
and Christianity together. Wilken, for example, believes that Galen's more extensive discussion of Judaism in *De usu partium*, 11.14, including a comparison of the Greek view of
creation to Genesis, can also shed light on his treatment of early Christianity. See *The
Christians*, 83–93.   [71] Benko, *Pagan Rome*, 141–2.
[72] Wilken, *The Christians*, 71. See also Benko, *Pagan Rome*, 145.
[73] Wilken, *The Christians*, 71–2.   [74] Benko, *Pagan Rome*, 145.   [75] Ibid., p. 140.

inaccuracy and historical unreliability. In contrast, Galen's work is judged to be largely reliable.[76] Now there is no doubt that the prolific Galen was a very important intellectual in Greco-Roman society, and his more appreciative tone challenges us to rethink the shape of public opinion of early Christianity. Whether Galen's 'sober, reasoned prose',[77] however, displays less of the marks of convention than the satirical writing of Lucian of Samosata is at least a debatable point. Moreover, Galen's positive evaluation of Christian asceticism needs to be examined with respect to its implications for public opinion about Christian women. Evidence of traditional concepts of gender distinction operating in Galen's thought in particular, and in the intellectual climate of the ancient world generally, should make us cautious about assuming that Galen's reference to Christian men and women can be adequately understood in terms of modern notions of equality. We should be wary of assuming that his focus upon celibate Christian men and women who have attained the level of genuine philosophers should be read as a statement of the equal capacity of men and women to reach their full potential.

It is evident that what leads Galen to admire the early Christians and to compare them to 'those who practise philosophy' is their virtuous way of life. From Stoics to Platonists, the philosophical schools of Galen's day were not only devoted to an intellectual tradition, but were intent on propagating a manner of living.[78] Moreover, it is important to remember that Galen was keenly interested in philosophy and he was a learned critic of philosophical

[76] This is particularly true of Benko's conclusions; see notes 74 and 75 above. This is not to suggest that Benko and Wilken are unaware of points of contact between Galen and other ancient critics in terms of common themes and reflections of common opinion. Both scholars acknowledge that the argument that Christians believe things which cannot be demonstrated is one which Galen shares with his contemporaries. See Galen's references to Christianity cited in note 70 and Orig. *C.Cels.* 1.9; 6.11. See Benko, 'Pagan Criticism', 1100; *Pagan Rome*, 145; Wilken, *The Christians*, 77.

[77] This is Wilken's expression (p. 76) which he uses to contrast the tone of Galen with that of Lucian. It is interesting to note that Wilken devotes an entire chapter of his book to Galen but he only deals with the Greek satirist in passing. The length of the description of early Christianity in the works of Lucian of Samosata is comparable to that found in Galen's works, but Wilken expands the body of relevant sources for Galen to include references to Genesis; see note 70, above. I argue in this book that for the study of how women figured in public opinion about the early church, the work of Lucian is at least as historically valuable as that of Galen.   [78] Ibid., 80.

schools. He may have cast his presentation of Christianity in terms familiar to him from his study of the great traditions of the Greco-Roman world.[79] I am not suggesting that Galen had never encountered actual Christian men and women who practised strict continence, but his philosophical bent may have led him to conclude quickly what they were doing without having access to very many facts about their motivation. The materials that have come down to us from Greco-Roman moral tradition are replete with ideals of self-discipline, self-control and restraint in bodily matters, so much so that even intercourse between married couples could be said to be in need of proper decorum.[80]

One interesting example illustrates the relationship between philosophy and life-style. It concerns the circumstances under which marriage itself was desirable. While Epictetus (an early second-century writer) links marriage with the obligation of citizenship in general, his comments about the ideal Cynic philosopher call to mind Paul's observations in 1 Corinthians 7 about the anxiety that accompanies married life: 'But in such an order of things as the present, which is like that of a battle field, it is a question, perhaps, if the Cynic ought not be free from distraction, wholly devoted to the service of God . . .'[81] The connection between philosophy, moral rectitude, and sexual restraint was put to use in explaining the essence of Christianity by the apologist Justin in his petition to the Emperor Antoninus Pius in 156 CE. Having toured several philosophical schools, Justin presented Christianity as the true philosophy.[82] As in the case of Galen, Justin

---

[79] In fact, Wilken states (Ibid., p. 77) that one should recognize 'that what Galen says about the Christians could just as well be said of other schools', but he does not develop the implications of this for how one should read Galen. On Galen's interest and training in philosophy see also pp. 70–1. On the comparison of early Christianity to a philosophical school see Meeks, *Urban Christians*, 81–4.

[80] See Brown, *The Body*, 7–32; on orderly behaviour during intercourse in particular see pp. 20–1.

[81] Epictetus, *Discourses*, 3.22.69, trans. W. A. Oldfather (LCL 1926). On marriage and the responsibilities of citizenship see *Discourses*, 3.7.19–22, 25–6. Philosophers were, however, also called to marry as part of their civic responsibilities; see Brown, *The Body*, 7–8. See also the review of opinions in Greco-Roman philosophical-ethical traditions on whether marriage is desirable in O. Larry Yarbrough, *Not like the Gentiles: Marriage Rules in the Letters of Paul*, SBLDS 80, (Atlanta: Scholars 1985) 32–41.

[82] See for example, Justin, *Dialogue with Trypho*, 8 (*ANF* 1.198). On Justin see also Part 3, pp. 205–13.

depicted early Christianity as encouraging life-long continence and his language, like Galen's, reveals the sexual ideals of elite society. Marriages in Christianity are characterized by strict moral codes, but the community also includes 'virtuosos' of continence: some disciples of Christ, both men and women, remain pure from childhood to old age and Christians are proud to display their example before the whole of humanity.[83]

It is interesting to note that Justin stresses the involvement of both sexes in early Christianity, since we have seen that the pagan writers Pliny, Marcus Cornelius Fronto, and Galen have asserted the same thing. In an effort to illustrate the broad range of people involved in Christianity, Pliny insists that, 'both sexes are, and will be, brought to trial'. A similar remark is found in the text attributed to Marcus Cornelius Fronto, but the description is more elaborate; the involvement of sisters and mothers is mentioned specifically, and the credulity of women who are drawn into shameful rites is highlighted. In ancient texts the nature of the involvement of women often emerges as a telling sign of the nature of the group: women become a symbol of corporate identity. In the case of Pliny and Fronto the mention of women obviously functions to label the group negatively. But with Galen, the statement that early Christians include 'not only men, but also women' appears to strengthen his assertion that Christians are a group whose self-control and self-discipline 'is of a pitch not inferior to genuine philosophers'. In other words, the mention of women appears to define the group positively. However, as stated previously, it is nevertheless important to evaluate Galen's positive assessment critically. His assessment probably reflects cultural values which become more readily apparent when his comments are compared to a second positive assessment of ascetic women in the Greco-Roman world.

Galen's reference to 'women also' calls to mind another reference to a religious group in the ancient world that was known for its devotion to continence. Among the writings of the first-century Jewish philosopher Philo of Alexandria (20 BCE – 50 CE) is found a description of an ascetic community living on the shores of Lake

---

[83] Justin, *First Apology*, 15 (*ANF* 1.167); see discussion in Brown, *The Body*, 34.

Mareotis near Alexandria, the Therapeutic society, made up of both men (Therapeutae) and women (Therapeutrides).[84] According to Philo, the devotion of this group has as its goal the vision of the Divine. Philo describes a sacred vigil (taking place during the society's major festival) which involves the mingling of a male choir with a female choir, ritually re-enacting Israel's deliverance from Egypt. But such ritual unity is carefully limited. Apart from this festive chorus, assemblies call for segregation of the sexes. On a daily basis members live a solitary existence and follow a strict ascetic way of life which is in keeping with their dualistic vision of the world.[85] However, in Philo's description of the celibacy of the members of this group we sense none of the Pauline sensitivity, revealed by 1 Corinthians 7, about the possibility that some may lack the self-control required to remain continent. Moreover, as is to be expected given our discussion to date, when Philo speaks of sexual asceticism, he is especially concerned with the admirable behaviour of women:

The feast is shared by women also, most of them aged virgins, who have their chastity not under compulsion, like some of the Greek priestesses, but of their own free will in their ardent yearning for wisdom. Eager to have her [wisdom] for their life mate they have spurned the pleasures of the body and desire no mortal offspring but those immortal children which only the soul that is dear to God can bring to the birth unaided because the Father has sown in her spiritual rays enabling her to behold the verities of wisdom.[86]

Philo's (perhaps idealized) description of the Therapeutrides who preserve their chastity as part of their yearning for wisdom calls to

---

[84] For an excellent discussion of this group see Kraemer, *Her Share*, 113–17. See also her earlier article, 'Monastic Jewish Women in Greco-Roman Egypt: Philo on the Therapeutrides', *Signs*, 14 (1989) 342–70. A very interesting discussion is found of this group and its relationship to early Christianity in R. A. Horsley, 'Spiritual Marriage with Sophia', *VC* 33 (1979) 40–3. Scholars have suggested that the Therapeutae were members of a branch of the Essene movement. See discussion of the relationship between Therapeutae, Essenes, and Qumran in E. Schürer, *The History of the Jewish People in the Age of Jesus Christ*, vol. 2 rev. edn, G. Vermes, F. Millar, M. Black (eds.) (Edinburgh: T&T Clark, 1979) 593–7.

[85] See Philo, *Vita Cont.* 2, 12, 13, 18, 34–7, 84–5. Trans. F. H. Colson (LCL 1941). Here I am following closely my discussion in a previous article, 'Women Holy', 168–9.

[86] *Vita Cont.* 68. Here Philo is describing the society's major festival which, in Kraemer's opinion, was Shavuoth; see *Her Share*, 113.

mind Galen's description of early Christians whose devotion to continence, pursuit of justice, and general self-control is said to be of the kind associated with a philosophical school. Like the early Christians whom Galen describes, the self-discipline of the Therapeutics extends to their intake of food, presumably another potent sign of the management of desire.[87] Philo's insistence that the aged virgins are free to choose to preserve their chastity alerts us to what is also implicit in Galen's description of early church members. Those early Christian women who refrain from cohabiting all of their lives are depicted as being motivated by the loftiest of ideals and thus, are very much free to pursue a life in search of virtue. Because it is clear to Galen that a life-commitment is involved, one wonders whether he too has in mind older women. With respect to Therapeutrides, Ross Kraemer interprets the choice of pursuing a contemplative life as being within a context of privilege. Becoming a Therapeutride was an option for only a very few women in first-century Jewish society – a minority of women who were both highly educated and probably had control of significant financial resources before they had become members.[88]

In light of Philo's assertion, cited in the Introduction, about men being suited to the public, open-air life whereas the Jewish women of Alexandria 'are best suited to the indoor life which never strays from the house',[89] his favourable impression of a mixed (albeit carefully controlled) celibate community may come as somewhat of a surprise. Kraemer, however, sees no contradiction between Philo's attitude, concerning relations between husbands and wives, which endorses traditional gender distinctions, and his admiration of the Therapeutrides. In their devotion to the pursuit of knowledge, in their spiritual quest to transcend bodily pleasures and maternal desires, in their chastity and solitude, the female Therapeutics essentially had removed themselves from normal social relations.[90] They were as unusual and intriguing as the occasional individual female philosopher who emerges from the sources

---

[87] *Vita Cont.* 34–5; see *Her Share*, 230 n. 44.   [88] Kraemer, *Her Share*, 113–14.

[89] See Philo, *The Special Laws*, 3.169–75. Trans. cited from Kraemer, *Maenads*, 29–30. See Introduction pp. 32–3.

[90] See Kraemer, *Her Share*, 115. My position departs from hers slightly here.

of antiquity.[91] But we should be careful about reading Philo's comments as an unqualified endorsement of the contribution of female philosophers and of the freeing of even a privileged, heroic minority of women to achieve *equality* with men. Having pondered the influence of Platonism on Philo and his allegorical interpretation of female figures in Jewish scripture where the feminine represents the lower, sensate part of the soul and the masculine symbolizes the higher state of the soul (mind and reason), Kraemer concludes: 'For Philo, the Therapeutrides were female in form only. In other respects, like good philosophers who aspire to mystical union with the divinity, they had purged their souls of their female elements and become male and/or virgin. All this was evident in the fact that they were childless, unmarried, and probably postmenopausal.'[92]

It is interesting to consider Kraemer's conclusions in light of the discussion in the previous section about the precarious position of widows in early Christianity. When women were without male guardians, they were at a greater risk of being viewed as shameless and of being accused of acting more like men than women. In Philo's thought, however, we see the possibility of this state being turned into an opportunity for spiritual perfection when it is contained within a group of ascetic philosophers. The fact that the 'virgins' were aged and no longer fertile no doubt heightened the possibility of leaving their feminine confinement behind. At

---

[91] It is noteworthy that a number of Cynic epistles are addressed to women, including many addressed to Hipparchia, the wife of Crates, who is said to have herself lived the life of a Cynic. Note *The Epistles of Crates*, 1, 28–33 and *The Epistle of Diognetes*, 3, in Abraham J. Malherbe, *The Cynic Epistles: A Study Edition* (Missoula, MT: Scholars,1977). The first-century writings of the Stoic Musonius Rufus also are often mentioned on this question, since Musonius supported the education of women in his tract *That Women Too Should Study Philosophy*. But Musonius endorses a conventional understanding of marriage relations and he provides us with no concrete evidence for the existence of women philosophers. From Alexandria in the fourth century CE we hear of a woman, Hypatia, who actually became the head of a philosophical school, the middle-Platonic academy associated with Plotinus. This woman philosopher was, however, put to death by angry anti-pagan Christians. See discussion and bibliography in Jane M. Snyder, *The Woman and the Lyre: Women Writers in Classical Greece and Rome* (Carbondale: Southern Illinois University, 1989) 113–20. On women philosophers in the ancient world see discussion in Kraemer, *Her Share*, 89–90 and Yarbrough, *Not Like the Gentiles*, 55–6.

[92] Kraemer, *Her Share*, 114–15. On the influence of Platonism on Philo of Alexandria see also MacDonald, *No Male and Female*, 23–30.

any rate, if we consider carefully the implications of Philo's description of the Therapeutrides, we are prevented from concluding too quickly that Galen's straightforward presentation of the early Christians is simply objective and accepting. We should ask of Galen's account the same kind of question Kraemer asks of Philo's admiring description of the Therapeutrides. Could it be that a philosopher like Galen considered the women who refrained from cohabiting during their entire lives to be female in form only?

Like Philo, Galen admired a philosophical-religious group where men and women were united by a superior morality, but he also subscribed to traditional notions of gender distinction related to space. It is impossible to do justice to Galen's detailed medical treatises here, and scholars interested in the issue of gender in early Christianity should continue to mine these precious texts for the purpose of comparison.[93] However, a brief discussion at this point of Galen's views on female inferiority will help us to qualify our understanding of his attitude to early Christian women in important ways. In his *On the Usefulness of the Parts of the Body*, Galen describes everything in the male in contrast to the female. Indeed, he bases his assertion that the female is less perfect than the male on various physiological opposites: the male is warm but the female is cold, men have body parts on the outside but women have them on the inside.[94] In the following citation it is possible to observe how quickly ancient discussions of gender move between the physical and the social realms. The natural seclusion of females indoors is used to explain physical differences between the sexes:

For I have already shown many times, indeed throughout the work, that nature makes for the body a form appropriate to the character of the soul. And the female sex does not need any special covering as protection against the cold, since *for the most part women stay within doors*, yet they do need long hair for both protection and ornament, and this need they share with men. Really, however, there is another reason [χρεία, usefulness] that makes it necessary for us to have hair on both our chins and

---

[93] Brown discusses Galen in some depth in *The Body*, 10–11.
[94] Galen, *De usu partium*, 14.6; trans. Margaret Tallmadge May, *Galen on the Usefulness of the Parts of the Body* (Ithaca, New York: Cornell, 1968).

heads. For since the exhalation from the humors rises to the head, Nature makes use of its thicker residues in particular to nourish the hair, and since men have much more of these residues as they are warmer than women, she has devised for men two ways of evacuating them, from the hair of the head and from the hair of the chin.[95] (Emphasis mine)

This text offers a very good illustration of the anthropological principle that the physical body is often used to replicate the social body.[96] Despite the fact that the warmer, outside-oriented male was considered to be superior, the boundaries separating male from female were somewhat fluid in Galen's thought. In fact, one gains the impression that attributes of masculinity could be lost as quickly as a woman might be viewed as representing the antithesis of feminine virtue for violating the boundaries separating the private domain from the public sphere. For example, in his work *On the Seed* Galen identifies loss of heat during childhood as making men revert into a state of 'primary undifferentiation'.[97] Given the unmistakable presence of traditional gender distinctions in both physical and social manifestations in Galen's work, his seemingly positive reference to Christian men and women who are united by a common goal and are apparently untouched by the lines of the public, male / private, female dichotomy is remarkable. The best explanation seems to be that the philosophical and moral pursuits of early Christian women essentially have freed them to become 'male'.

In Galen's thought, and in the ancient literature of the first and second centuries generally, there is much that associates perfection with masculinity. During the second century, even some early Christians might have explained the nature of their salvation as a return to perfected masculinity. Having come from Alexandria to Rome in 138 CE, Valentinus continued to teach there until 166 and he was present in the city as one of the most important spiritual guides in the Christian community during the time when

---

[95] Galen, *De usu partium*, 11.14.

[96] The foundational work of anthropologist Mary Douglas is well known and frequently employed by biblical scholars and students of early Christianity. See, for example, *Purity and Danger: An Analysis of Concepts of Pollution and Taboo* (London: Routledge and Kegan Paul, 1966); *Natural Symbols* (London: Barrie and Rockliffe, 1970).

[97] Galen, *De semine*, 1.16; cited in Brown, *The Body*, 11.

Galen also was there.[98] The teaching associated with Valentinian circles, as well as many other fascinating gnostic texts, relies heavily on gendered images to communicate mythic systems. It is not easy to understand the implications of such imagery or even to predict how it might be related to concrete sexual practices. According to Dennis R. MacDonald, a typical consequence of the Valentinian teaching that made extensive use of gendered imagery to describe the process of fall and redemption was the performance of a baptism of re-unification, followed by a life of rigorous asceticism. MacDonald states that in Valentinian teaching, 'Insofar as one has transcended the body and reunited the sexes, one must avoid sexual relations, that is "the male with the female neither male nor female".'[99] Such language as 'making the two one' and the 'female becoming male' is associated with the quest for androgynous perfection, often imagined in the ancient world as essentially being a state of perfected masculinity.[100] The implications of the female being swallowed up into the male are startling for modern persons who value the female body and female individuality. While scholars have frequently linked social liberation with female asceticism in early Christianity, modern women surely would be repulsed by the thought of putting off the body in order to 'destroy the works of the female'.[101] It is, however, impossible to be sure how ancient women would have understood such symbolism or to predict the reaction of someone outside the group. While Galen saw female

[98] See Brown, *The Body*, 113. Valentinus' influence extended to include several pupils and scholars now generally recognize a variety of Gnostic sources as being of the Valentinian school. Brown deals in detail with Valentinus and Valentinian tradition, 103–21. On the Valentinian circle and sources associated with Valentinianism see also MacDonald, *No Male and Female*, 51–5.

[99] MacDonald, *No Male and Female*, 55. MacDonald here is explaining how a saying attributed to Jesus would have been understood by Julius Cassianus and other Valentinians. The saying contained in the Gospel of Egyptians (not to be confused with its namesake from Nag Hammadi and known to us from fragments preserved by Clement of Alexandria) is the following: 'When you trample on the robe of shame, and when the two shall be one, and the male with the female, and there is neither male nor female.' Clem. Al. *Strom.* 3.92; trans. Chadwick, *Alexandrian Christianity*; see note 45 above. On Julius Cassianus see MacDonald, *No Male and Female*, 32–3.

[100] MacDonald, *No Male and Female*, 98–9. See Philo, *Questiones et solutiones in Genesim*, 1.8. Other references are given by MacDonald, 99 n. 16.

[101] See citation of Gospel of the Egyptians in Clem. Al. *Strom.* 3.63; cf. 3.92–3. See my article, 'Women Holy', 167 n. 25.

asceticism as the pursuit of the highest form of virtue, as we will see, other equally strong voices denounced the early Christians for destroying the family.

I have placed Galen and Philo side by side because both authors illustrate the point that female ascetics in the Greco-Roman world may not always have encountered hostility. Moreover, both authors reveal to us that admiration of female ascetics, whose self-control clearly sets them apart from the usual patterns of life, does not necessarily imply an acceptance of the abrogation of traditional gender distinctions. Of course Philo cannot be considered an outside critic of the Therapeutic society in the way that Galen was a critic of the early Christians: Philo may himself once have been a member of the Therapeutic community.[102] But even Galen, by virtue of his framing the Christian movement in terms of his own philosophical interests, reminds us that we must be careful about drawing lines too firmly between insiders and outsiders. A critical voice quickly may become a curious one. Our brief discussion of Valentinian circles has enabled us to see that there is much in the world view of second-century Christianity that would suit Galen's philosophical disposition. We must remember too, that in commenting on early Christianity and at times trying to understand the movement, critics came into contact with a movement that often was extremely eager to open up the boundaries separating insider from outsider. This openness is evidensed in an account in Eusebius' *Ecclesiastical History*, which describes a group of Christians in Rome under the leadership of a certain Theodotus who sought to give Christian thought a philosophical underpinning, and incorporated the work of Galen in their teachings. Unfortunately, however, these people were designated heretics and they were excommunicated for tampering with scripture and abandoning the true faith (187–98 CE).[103]

In this section I have argued that Galen's description of early Christian women, which strikes one initially as exceptionally positive, must be evaluated in relation to a social-philosophical world

---

[102] See Kraemer, *Her Share*, 117.
[103] See Eusebius, *Historia ecclesiasticae*, 5.28.13–15. See discussions in Wilken, *The Christians*, 77–9; Benko, *Pagan Rome*, 145–7.

which understood asceticism in a particular light. Galen's comments reflect the notion that the philosophical life is one where both men and women may strive for virtue by means of asceticism. As in Philo's description of Jewish asceticism, Galen declares that the Christian group includes 'also women' and understands the female presence as especially significant. That men and women were able to live in a community without cohabiting throughout their lives indicated that unruly desires had been tamed by self-discipline and self-control. This restraint was a sure sign of the group's virtuous nature. Perhaps Galen saw the female Christian ascetics as essentially male in form. They had somehow lost their female form 'which was open, aimless, lacking in shape and direction. It stood for all that needed to be formed by being made subject to the hard, clear outlines of the male.'[104]

It is difficult to say how much the opinion of an intellectual like Galen is related to popular opinions about Christianity. In Parts 2 and 3 we will consider early Christian evidence that church members hoped to gain followers by their self-control and the stringency of their sexual ethics. Nevertheless, Galen's voice must be heard together with other less appreciative ones. His penchant for philosophical discussions, which included discussion of the desirability of marriage, must be balanced with the hard facts of living in a society where marriage laws included penalties for non-marriage and childlessness, as well as rewards for fecundity.[105] In such a society, the celibacy of women could seem especially suspect. As we move to consider our final critic of early Christianity, Celsus, we will be given an opportunity to begin to contemplate the magnitude of that suspicion.

Celsus

Very little is known about Celsus, the last and most prolific second-century critic of early Christianity. His book *The True Doctrine*, written about 170 CE, no longer exists. It is known to us

---

[104] Here Peter Brown is speaking both specifically about Valentinus and Plutarch (contemporaries of Galen), but also generally about ideas of male/female relations in the second century; *The Body*, 112. [105] See Discussion in Part 2, pp. 167–8.

only in the rebuttal composed by Origen some seventy years later, *Contra Celsum*. Origen cites Celsus at length and we are thus in a good position to recover much of what was said by Celsus, a Greek philosopher whose philosophical stance has been described as 'closest to the Platonists', but generally 'eclectic'.[106] Celsus shares Galen's interest in philosophical argumentation, but his analysis is strongly influenced by his desire to support traditional political and social institutions and to encourage the stability of society.[107]

There are three important points in Celsus' discourse where reference is made to women: the account of the birth of Jesus, the portrait of the followers of Jesus and their involvement in the inception of the resurrection belief, and the description of the sinister evangelizing tactics of the early Christians and the effect of these activities on society. I will examine each of these in turn. Note: following the standard translation of Henry Chadwick, the italicized sections here differentiate Celsus' comments (as reported by Origen) from Origen's rebuttal.

Celsus' account of the birth of Jesus

After this he [Celsus] represents the Jew as having a conversation with Jesus himself and refuting him on many charges, as he thinks: first, because *he fabricated the story of his birth from a virgin*; and he reproaches him because *he came from a Jewish village and from a poor country woman who earned her living by spinning.* He says that *she was driven out by her husband, who was a carpenter by trade, as she was convicted of adultery.* Then he says that *after she had been driven out by her husband and while she was wandering about in a disgraceful way she secretly gave birth to Jesus.* And he says that *because he was poor he hired himself out as a workman in Egypt, and there tried his hand at certain magical powers on which the Egyptians pride themselves; he returned full of conceit because of these powers, and on account of them gave himself the title of God.* [108]

---

[106] Wilken, *The Christians*, 95.   [107] Ibid.

[108] *C. Cels.* 1.28. Since the scope of my book is the first and second centuries CE I will not be discussing the mid third-century remarks of Origen to any significant extent. I am primarily interested in what intellectuals like Celsus were thinking about early Christianity in the latter half of the second century CE. For a good French translation of *Contra Celsum* see ed. Marcel Borret, S.J., *Origène. Contre Celse*, Sources Chrétiennes (Paris, 1967).

Let us return . . . to the words put into the mouth of the Jew, where *the mother of Jesus is described as having been turned out by the carpenter who was betrothed to her, as she had been convicted of adultery and had a child by a certain soldier named Panthera.* [109]

I do not think it worth while to combat an argument which he does not put forward seriously, but only as mockery: *Then was the mother of Jesus beautiful? And because she was beautiful did God have sexual intercourse with her, although by nature He cannot love a corruptible body? It is not likely that God would have fallen in love with her since she was neither wealthy nor of royal birth; for nobody knew her, not even her neighbours.* It is just ridicule also when he says: *When she was hated by the carpenter and turned out, neither divine power nor the gift of persuasion saved her. Therefore,* he says, *these things have nothing to do with the Kingdom of God.* What is the difference between this and vulgar abuse at street corners, and the talk of people who say nothing worth serious attention? [110]

There is nothing complicated about Celsus' main intent in these passages. He wishes to cast aspersions on Jesus by arguing that Jesus' origins lie in the adulterous activities of a common woman (the adulteress was treated harshly in Roman law) and in illegitimacy. While Celsus' account of the virgin birth has been described as 'the least interesting' of his historical discussions of the figure of Jesus, [111] when placed in relation to Celsus' comments as a whole, it becomes clear that this story plays an important role in one of the main lines of criticism of Christianity developed by Celsus but seldom discussed by commentators: early Christianity is the result of dubious, female initiative. Wilken estimates that Celsus' discussion of the virgin birth is especially worth noting 'because it allows him to make the larger point about Jesus' reliance on magic'. [112] However, I will argue that the circle of magic which embraces Celsus' Jesus is concentric with the circle of magic which surrounds the women associated with Christianity.

The reference to Jesus being the son of the Roman soldier Panthera (a common Greek surname of Roman soldiers in this period) has long intrigued commentators. [113] The similarity

---

[109] *C. Cels.* 1.32.   [110] *C. Cels.* 1.39. See 1.28–39, 69–70.

[111] Wilken, *The Christians*, 109. Wilken's comment illustrates that a specific interest in the topic of early Christian *women* changes what one finds 'interesting' in texts. Contrast Wilken's treatment of this text with Jane Schaberg's feminist perspective in *The Illegitimacy of Jesus: A Feminist Theological Interpretation of the Infancy Narratives* (San Francisco: Harper and Row, 1987) 165–9.   [112] Wilken, *The Christians*, 109.

[113] See for example, Chadwick, *Contra Celsum*, 31 n.3.

between this name and the Greek term for virgin (παρθένος) has been noted and it has been suggested that the term was transformed into a proper name in the context of polemical discussion about the virgin birth.[114] Patristic sources speak of a certain ancestor of Jesus called 'Panther', perhaps in an effort to create a legitimate place for the name in Christian tradition.[115] The most likely explanation for the reference to Panthera, however, seems to be that the story was circulating in Jewish circles during Celsus' time.[116] Celsus does not conduct a dialogue using his own voice, but rather chooses to have Jesus speak to a Jew. Having undertaken a detailed examination of Celsus' discussion of Jesus' birth, Jane Schaberg has argued that although the dialogue between Jesus and the Jew may be fictional and subject to exaggeration, there is good reason to see here the influence of an earlier Jewish tradition.[117] In fact, in some rabbinic texts, Jesus is referred to as the 'son of Pantera'.[118]

Despite the uncertainty which remains with respect to the origins of the story of the mother of Jesus who was *'convicted of adultery and had a child by a certain soldier named Panthera'*, it is important to recognize that a Jewish voice is implicated in the refutation of the miraculous circumstances of Jesus' birth. The dialogue between Jesus and the Jew is in keeping with the great interest in the relations between the two religions displayed by Celsus throughout the work. Celsus'

---

[114] But see arguments against this in Morton Smith, *Jesus the Magician* (San Francisco: Harper and Row, 1978) 46–7; 60–1.

[115] See Schaberg, *Illegitimacy*, 167 and 246 n.87 where she refers to Raymond Brown's collection of patristic evidence in *The Birth of the Messiah* (Garden City, N.Y.: Doubleday, 1977) 535 n.7. [116] See Wilken, *The Christians*, 110.

[117] See Schaberg, *Illegitimacy*, 245–6 n.82. More forcefully than Schaberg, Morton Smith has argued that Celsus was using an independent Jewish source in *C. Cels.* 1.28 to the end of 2. He states: 'We shall try only to pick out the traits of Jesus' life that seem to have come from it, rather than from the gospels, and supplement these with occasional remarks made by Celsus in the later sections of his work where he once or twice used data from Jewish polemic'; see *Jesus the Magician*, 59. But there has been a divergence of opinion on this question and Schaberg summarizes it in a useful manner; see 245–6 n.82.

[118] See discussion of the ben Pantera texts in the Tannaitic Period (to 200 CE) in Schaberg, *Illegitimacy*, 170–2. Schaberg concludes: 'While we have no absolutely certain evidence from the Tannaitic period (first and second centuries CE) that he [Jesus] was regarded by the rabbis of that time as illegitimate, the use of the name ben Pantera (and variants) for him is likely to be connected to the name and story found in Origen's *Against Celsus*' (p.177). See also Smith, *Jesus the Magician*, 46–7.

arguments about Christian claims to have exclusive access to the correct interpretation of Jewish scripture display an awareness of the struggles Christians faced as they both accepted and rejected Jewish heritage and law.[119] Moreover, his comments come as a reminder that it is misleading to think of the conversation between pagan Hellenism and Christianity as a simple two-way debate, since Judaism often was an active participant in this discourse.[120]

It is fascinating that Celsus is critical both of Judaism and Christianity while at the same time he uses the relationship between the two religions to argue that Christians are worse even than the Jews. Celsus takes a perceived enemy of Christianity (Judaism) and turns it into his ally in the cause of refutation of Christianity, while he carefully distances himself from both groups. Very much a man of his own time with respect to the admiration of the traditional and the ancient, Celsus offers Judaism the qualified complement: '*They observe a worship which may be very peculiar, but at least it is traditional.*'[121] Christians, on the other hand, cannot claim a tradition of their own.

Celsus criticizes both Judaism and Christianity in a manner that has much in common with other critiques of Eastern religions from the same period. Recalling the passage cited above about Jesus spending his formative years in Egypt where he '*tried his hand at certain magical powers on which the Egyptians pride themselves*', it is interesting to note that Celsus also describes the Jews as having their origins in Egypt and as having a past history of rebellion: '*The Jews were Egyptian by race, and left Egypt after revolting against the Egyptian community and despising the religious customs of Egypt.*'[122] In turn, the Christians are said to have revolted against the Jews.[123] In addition to this sedition, the Jewish scriptures (upon which Christianity also depends) contains tales of the worst type of immorality. With respect to the story of Lot and his daughters, Celsus argues that the tale is '*more iniquitous than Thyestian sins*'.[124] Making extensive use of simile, Celsus attacks the secretive yet pestilent behaviour of

---

[119] See Wilken, *The Christians*, 112–17. See for example, *C. Cels.* 2.1; 2.4; 5.25. See also the similar awareness of this argument levelled by Jews against Christians on the part of the Christian author Justin Martyr in his *Dialogue with Trypho*, 10, see *ANF* 1.199 .

[120] Ibid., 116.   [121] *C. Cels.* 5.25; cf. 5.33; 5.65. Cf.Tacitus, *Histories*, 5.5.

[122] *C. Cels.* 3.5.   [123] Ibid. 5.25.   [124] Ibid. 4.45.

Christians and Jews and their preoccupation with doctrinal controversy. They are like '*a cluster of bats or ants coming out of a nest, as frogs
holding council around a marsh, or worms assembling in some filthy corner, dis-
agreeing with one another about which of them are the worst sinners*'.[125]

When we return to the figure of Mary with an awareness of the
relationship between Judaism and Christianity in Celsus' account,
the importance of her dual role as both Jewish woman and proto-
typical Christian woman emerges. The main goal of this account
is to critique the origins of Christianity, but the Jewish interlocutor
who approaches Jesus is used to draw the attention of the reader
to the scandalous behaviour of a woman who is a member of his
own group. The accusations directed at the mother of Jesus in the
above texts are that she committed adultery and wandered about
in a disgraceful way until she secretly gave birth to Jesus (the motif
of secrecy plays an important part in many critiques of
Christianity as will be discussed below). Despite Mary's efforts to
convince 'the carpenter' (Joseph) of her innocence, she was not
saved, not even by divine power. The picture that Celsus paints
here is of a guilty, shameless woman who is driven to the streets.
She is very much like the 'whoring wife' in Lucius Apuleius'
Metamorphoses whose activities are said to have been inspired by the
worship of a god called 'only' (probably implying allegiance to
either Judaism or early Christianity). Although she lacks the deceptive powers of the woman described by Apuleius, and the carpenter lacks the naiveté of the husband whom Apuleius pities, the
mother of Jesus is accused of being guilty of the same vices. She
initiates a liaison with one who is outside the confines of her proper
domain (a poor Jewish woman has a child by a Roman soldier); she
is unfaithful and she participates in secret activities. As the mother
of an illegitimate magician, Mary's image is as negative as
Juvenal's caricature of the old Jewish beggar woman who receives
payment for her interpretation of dreams.[126]

---

[125] Ibid. 4.23.
[126] See Juvenal, *Satire*, 6 cited in Kraemer, *Maenads*, 41–2. One wonders if by saying that
Mary went away to have Jesus 'in secret', Celsus is implying that she participated in
magical rites. Jean-Jacques Aubert has collected interesting evidence illustrating how
magical practices were thought capable of interfering with the natural processes of
reproduction; see 'Threatened Wombs: Aspects of Ancient Uterine Magic', *GRBS* 30
(1989) 421–49.

Celsus apparently had a good knowledge of the relationship between Judaism and early Christianity, and he probably also was aware of the public opinion that Judaism and Christianity produced similar dangerous symptoms among women. While public opinion can by no means always be trusted to offer an accurate account of reality, one text that comes from a later period (fourth-century Antioch) suggests that for some women who joined the early church, conversion to a life in Christ did not preclude participation in Jewish rites. John Chrysostom instructed Christian men to put the Judaizing efforts of their wives to an end with language that left no room for compromise:

But now that the devil summons your wives to the Feast of Trumpets and they turn a ready ear to his call, you do not restrain them. You let them entangle themselves in accusations of ungodliness, you let them be dragged off into licentious ways. For as a rule, it is the harlots, the effeminates, and the whole chorus from the theater who rush to that festival.[127]

While the main point of this text is to halt the participation of Christian women in Jewish rites (probably Rosh Hashanah), Ross Kraemer argues that, 'it seems unlikely that Christian women would have been drawn to a festival in which Jewish women were not also actively involved'. Moreover, she notes that Chrysostom's polemical characterization of the nature of those who participate in these rites suggests that pagan women were also attracted to Jewish observances in fourth-century Antioch.[128] In the end, Chrysostom's comments prevent us from drawing the lines too sharply between Pagan, Christian, and Jew when we speak about the religious activities of women in the Roman Empire. Of course, it is precisely lines of distinction and identity that Chrysostom himself is trying to set forth, and his language about the licentious ways of women who are dragged off into Jewish rites is strikingly reminiscent of the pagan critics of the second century who labelled Christianity a religion of immorality.

---

[127] John Chrysostom, *Against Judaizing Christians*, II.4; see also II.3–6 and IV.3 cited in Kraemer, *Maenads*, 59–60. Kraemer adopts the translation by Paul Harkins in *Fathers of the Church*, 68 (Washington, DC: Catholic University of America, 1979). For discussion of this text and the nature of the feast see also Kraemer, *Her Share*, 108.

[128] Ibid., 108.

As will be evident from the discussion below, Celsus' portrayal of the mother of Jesus is consistent with his discussion of Mary Magdalene, the women around Jesus, and female members of the church. Mary is depicted not only as being shameless and immoral but also as being marginalized, essentially in a state of anomy: she is a working poor woman who is without husband, she lacks significant ancestry, she is unknown even by her neighbours! However, anthropological insights on the relationship between power and authority prevent us from accepting this picture of utter powerlessness at face value. In Celsus' focus on the body of Mary we recognize an unwitting acknowledgment of female power, albeit destructive power.

Despite his desire to depict Mary as disreputable and insignificant, Celsus must deal with the important role of Mary in the foundation of Christianity. He sets out to ridicule the notion that God would have sexual intercourse with the corruptible body of a woman: surely a god deserving of honour would not lower himself by becoming one with a poor, shameless country woman? Celsus' argument is related to the important question levelled at the early Christians during the course of his critique: 'How can a deity who is by definition immutable undergo change and alteration to live as a human being?'[129] In the following interesting text, Celsus employs the argument against the possibility of union between God and a woman to cast doubt on the nature of Jesus' body and, ultimately, upon his divine status:

And if he did wish to send down a spirit from himself, why did he have to breathe it into the womb of a woman? He already knew how to make men. He could have formed a body for this one also without having to thrust his own spirit into such foul pollution. In that case he would not have been disbelieved, had he been begotten directly from above. He said this because he did not realize that the body which was to minister to the salvation of men had a pure birth from a virgin and was not the result of any immorality.[130]

In the third century Origen defended Christians against Celsus' criticism by showing how Mary's pure virginal state redeemed Christian claims about the union of humanity and divinity in the

---

[129] Wilken, *The Christians*, 103. See *C. Cels.* 4.2–10.   [130] Ibid. 6.73.

vessel of a woman's body.[131] However, with my primary focus on Celsus' criticism within the context of the second century CE, I am concerned with what is essentially the reverse of Origen's argument. As I continue the discussion of the major points in Celsus' discourse where reference is made to women, I will point out how allegations about the corruptible nature of Mary's body set the stage for a presentation of Christianity as a religion created and sustained by corrupted women.

Women followers of Jesus and the resurrection

Origen responds to a brief citation from Celsus' work about the illicit activities of Jesus and his entourage in a manner that suggests that Celsus' original invective made reference to female followers of Jesus:

Jesus taught his disciples not to be rash, saying to them: 'If they persecute you in this city flee to another; and if they persecute you in that, flee again to yet another.' And he gave them an example of his teaching by his tranquil life; he was careful not to meet dangers unnecessarily or at the wrong time or for no good reason. This again Celsus wickedly misrepresents when his Jew says to Jesus: *You fled hither and thither with your disciples* . . . According to Celsus *Jesus went about with his disciples collecting their livelihood in a disgraceful and importunate way.* Let him declare where he got his idea of disgraceful and importunate beggary. For in the gospels certain women who had been healed from their ailments, among whom was Susanna, provided the disciples with meals out of their own substance. But what philosopher who was devoted to the benefit of his pupils did not receive from them money for his needs? Or was it proper and right for them to do this, whereas when Jesus' disciples do it, they are accused by Celsus of *collecting their means of livelihood in a disgraceful and importunate way?*[132]

While it is dangerous to draw conclusions about Celsus' original statements based on Origen's response, in this case it seems safe to assume that Origen would not mention Jesus and his disciples

---

[131] See *C. Cels.* 1.32–7; 2.69. Note, for example, the following question posed by Origen: 'And which would be more appropriate as the mother of Emmanuel, that is 'God with us', a woman who had had intercourse with a man and conceived by female passion, or a woman who was still chaste and pure and a virgin?' (*C. Cels.* 1.35).

[132] *C. Cels.* 1.65

being supported by *women* had this not been part of Celsus' original critique: there was far too much suspicion about Jesus' dubious origins from the body of a corrupted virgin to add fuel to the fire by drawing attention to women providers. Perhaps the insinuation made by Celsus was that Jesus and his followers took more than money from these women providers. It is possible that allegations of living off prostitutes were involved. This would fit well with the notions of disgraceful livelihood, charlatanism, and clandestine travel.

In a late first or early second-century Christian work (which may incorporate earlier traditions) we find concerns similar to those in Celsus, concerning the means of livelihood of Christian itinerant teachers. The *Didache* discusses limiting the visits of charismatic prophets and apostles, prohibiting the exchange of prophecy for money, and establishing community guidelines to distinguish the genuine from the fake. One intriguing extract from this work calls for the group to tolerate but not imitate certain activities of prophets: 'But no prophet who has been tried and is genuine, though he enact a worldly mystery of the Church, if he teach not others to do what he does himself, shall be judged by you: for he has his judgment with God, for so also did the prophets of old.'[133] The phrase 'worldly mystery' is enigmatic. Kirsopp Lake notes that the 'passage has never been satisfactorily explained: it probably refers to a tendency among some prophets to introduce forms of worship, or of illustration of their teaching, of doubtful propriety, if so the reference below to the prophets of old is perhaps an allusion to Hosea (Hos. 1, 2f).'[134] Hosea 1.2ff. begins with God calling Hosea to take to himself a prostitute as wife. The reserve and embarrassment one senses in this *Didache* excerpt suggests that what is not to be imitated may have been sexual in nature. Might officially 'celibate' female missionaries, who travelled with male missionaries for the sake of propriety and protection, sometimes have celebrated their spiritual union with physical union? Might itinerant teachers have sought the companionship of women in the community in order to illustrate the mysterious unity of Christ and the Church

---

[133] *Did.* 11.11; trans. K. Lake, *The Apostolic Fathers*, I (LCL 1913).   [134] Ibid., 327 n.2.

(cf. Eph. 5.21–33)?[135] Whatever the exact meaning of the text, it is clear that the *Didache* sets out to explain and control behaviour that worries some in Christian circles. The image of the charismatic ministry of Jesus and his followers which Celsus drew from scriptures was likely reinforced by what he had heard about the practices of certain Christian teachers and, in this case, these rumours probably reflected elements of what actually happened as well as embellishments.

If Celsus denounced Jesus and his followers because they were supported by women, this provides further evidence for how the theme of female initiative played an important role in Celsus' critique. Perhaps the most important allusion to female initiative is found in the following text briefly discussed in the introduction to this book. Celsus' study of Christian scripture[136] led him to focus on the intriguing figure of the woman who witnessed the resurrection, probably Mary Magdalene:

But we must examine this question whether anyone who really died ever rose again with the same body . . .But who saw this? A hysterical female, as you say, and perhaps some other one of those who were deluded by the same sorcery, who either dreamt in a certain state of mind and through wishful thinking had a hallucination due to some mistaken notion (an experience which has happened to thousands), or, which is more likely, wanted to impress others by telling this fantastic tale, and so by this cock-and-bull story to provide a chance for other beggars. [137]

At the time when he was disbelieved while in the body, he preached without restraint to all; but when he would establish a strong faith after rising from the dead, he appeared secretly to just one woman and to those of his own confraternity. But it is not true that he appeared to just one woman. In Matthew's gospel it is written that 'late on the sabbath day as it began to dawn toward the first day of the week, came Mary Magdalene and the other Mary to see the sepulchre . . .'[138]

---

[135] This text was brought to my attention in the Craigie Lecture delivered by John Dominic Crossan at the 1993 Meeting of the Canadian Society of Biblical Studies. See also his discussion of 1 Corinthians 9.5 where Paul refers to the right of an apostle to be accompanied by a 'sister wife' in *The Historical Jesus: The Life of a Mediterranean Jewish Peasant* (San Francisco: Harper 1992) 335.

[136] On Celsus' use of scripture and other traditions see Labriolle, *La Réaction Paienne*, 124–7. See also Remus, *Pagan-Christian Conflict*, 270 n. 68.

[137] *C. Cels.* 2.55. Cf. *C. Cels.* 2.59. Although in Origen's account Celsus does not explicitly identify the woman as Mary Magdalene, it is evident from Origen's response that that is how Origen understands Celsus. See also translation of this text by Remus in *Pagan-Christian Conflict*, 107.   [138] *C. Cels.* 2.70.

Celsus discusses the topic of the resurrection quite frequently, which is probably an indication of his realization of the centrality of the belief in the resurrection for the development of early Christianity.[139] While Origen corrects Celsus by pointing out contradictions and mistakes in his account concerning the details of the resurrection appearances, Origen's retorts cannot overshadow the emphasis Celsus places on the role of Mary Magdalene. The hysterical female is singled out by this pagan critic as the instigator of the Christian story of the resurrection. She is at the centre of the group which claimed to witness secret appearances of the resurrection. According to Celsus, the purpose of this fabrication was the continuation of the patterns of behaviour already begun when Jesus was alive: collecting one's livelihood in a disgraceful way, charlatanism.

In Celsus' work Mary Magdalene's role in the resurrection story denigrates its credibility, in much the same way as the role of Jesus' mother Mary casts doubt on his origins. From beginning to end, the story of Jesus' life has been shaped by the fanciful imaginings of women. In essence, it is of the type told by 'an old woman who sings a story to lull a little child to sleep'.[140] But as is also the case with the mother of Jesus, Mary Magdalene is by no means powerless in Celsus' account. As was noted previously, far from being simply deluded and immobilized by hysteria, she is an active agent, a willing participant in the business of begging and deception. Deluded by sorcery, she in turn becomes one of its main perpetrators.

Celsus' focus upon the role of Mary Magdalene may reflect second-century controversy about the importance of this woman in Jesus' circle and about the implication of this importance for leadership by women. Several apocryphal and gnostic texts provide evidence of this controversy. The *Apocryphal Gospel of Peter*, a work dating from the mid-second century CE, may reflect an effort to mute early traditions that the discovery of the empty tomb was by women (Mark 16.1–8; Matt. 28.1–8; Luke 24.1–11; John

---

[139] Wilken, *The Christians*, 104.

[140] *C. Cels.*6.34. Here Celsus is speaking generally of a series of Christian beliefs. Note that in *C. Cels.* 4.36 Celsus calls the Jewish story of the creation and temptation of Adam and Eve 'a legend which they expound to old women'.

20.1–8); by the time Mary Magdalene, a woman disciple of the Lord, and her companions discover the empty tomb in the *Gospel of Peter*, it has already been observed by a group of men.[141] In other texts, however, Mary's role is trumpeted. For example, Mary is granted the title 'companion' of Jesus in the gnostic *Gospel of Philip*, a work dating from the second, or possibly the third century CE.[142] Other texts convey ambivalence about Mary's role. The second-century *Gospel of Mary* portrays Mary in competition with Peter for a leadership role. The challenge to Mary's position has been evaluated as an indication of tensions between 'the existing fact of women's leadership in Christian communities and traditional Greco-Roman views about gender roles'.[143] Whether or not Celsus was aware of controversy surrounding Mary Magdalene's role in early Christian circles, I will demonstrate below that he clearly knew about female participation in evangelization and probably had heard of female teachers and leaders in church groups. From Jesus' birth to Celsus' own time, Christianity is understood by Celsus as a religion born of female initiative.

In order to appreciate the force of the role ascribed to Mary Magdalene in Celsus' account, it is important to examine the notion of sorcery. Celsus calls Jesus a sorcerer. He argues that the miracles of Jesus are on the same level as:

> the works of sorcerers who profess to do wonderful miracles, and the accomplishments of those who are taught by the Egyptians, who for a few obols make known their sacred lore in the middle of the market-place and drive daemons out of men and blow away diseases and invoke the souls of heroes, displaying expensive banquets and dining tables and cakes and dishes which are non-existent, and who make things move as though they were alive although they are not really so, but only appear as such in the imagination. [144]

[141] *Gospel of Peter*, 12.50–4; cf. 9.35–13.57, trans. E. Maurer, *NTApoc*, 1: 179–87. See discussion by Kraemer in *Her Share*, 234, n.15. On the history of traditions concerning Mary Magdalene and women's discovery of the tomb see John Dominic Crossan, *Four Other Gospels: Shadows on the Contours of the Canon* (Minneapolis: Winston, 1985) 157–64.

[142] *Gospel of Philip*, 59.6–11; 63.32–6, trans. Wesley W. Isenberg, *NHL*. On Mary Magdalene in the *Gospel of Philip* see Jorunn Jacobsen Buckley, '"The Holy Spirit is a Double Name": Holy Spirit, Mary, and Sophia in the Gospel of Philip', Karen L. King, ed., *Images of the Feminine in Gnosticism* (Philadelphia: Fortress, 1988) 214–17.

[143] Karen Jo Torjesen, *When Women were Priests*, 36. See *Gospel of Mary* 17, *NHL*, 470–4.

[144] *C. Cels.* 1.68.

A typical person of his age, Celsus believes in magic and the treachery of demons.[145] Celsus does not deny that Jesus has miraculous powers; rather, he asserts that since Jesus was not alone in manifesting miraculous powers, there is no logical basis for concluding that he is the son of God: '*Since these men do these wonders, ought we to think them sons of God? Ought we to say that they are the practices of wicked men possessed by an evil daemon?*' [146] The sentiment Celsus expresses is very much in keeping with the critical voice echoed in the Gospels: 'He casts out demons by the prince of demons' (Matt. 9.34).[147]

The Greek word for sorcerer employed by Celsus to label Jesus is γόης. According to Morton Smith, by New Testament times this term usually had an abusive ring: 'The word had lower-class connotations and was widely used of political orators and the like to mean approximately 'spellbinder', or just plain 'fraud'.[148] Smith sees in Celsus' depiction of Jesus a caricature of the common, lower-class magician: 'a miracle worker whose wonders are illusory, transient, produced by tricks or by the help of demons controlled by spells, sacrifices, and magical paraphernalia. Such a man is primarily an entertainer whose feats are trivial, performed for money, and of no practical value.'[149]

We will need to keep this picture of marketplace trickery in mind when we consider subsequent depictions of early Christian women. But first we must explore the relationship between Jesus as sorcerer and the one who is deluded by sorcery.

Women were described as victims of sorcerers in the ancient world. The critic of Christianity considered previously, Lucius

---

145 On this world view see Peter Brown, 'Sorcery, Demons, and the Rise of Christianity from Late Antiquity into the Middle Ages', in Mary Douglas (ed.), *Witchcraft, Confessions and Accusations* (New York: Tavistock, 1970) 17–45; see especially pp. 20, 28; see also Smith, *Jesus the Magician*, 68–9. According to Remus, Celsus reflects a common tendency for philosophers of the day to embody 'a tension between popular and critical thought in regard to the extraordinary'; see *Pagan-Christian Conflict*, 104; see pp. 104–5.

146 *C. Cels*.1.68. On Jesus accused of being a wicked sorcerer who performed miracles by magic see also *C. Cels*. 1.6; 1.71; 2.32; 2.49. On Jesus as sorcerer see Wilken, *The Christians*, 98–101; Smith, *Jesus the Magician*, 57–60; Eugene V. Gallagher, *Divine Man or Magician? Celsus and Origen on Jesus*, SBLDS 64 (Chico, CA: Scholars, 1982).

147 On this pattern of argumentation in the Gospels see Smith, *Jesus the Magician*, 32–6.

148 Smith, *Jesus the Magician*, 70. See also Smith's discussion of the related, but often less derogatory, concepts of 'magus' and 'divine man', 71–5.

149 Ibid., 83; see pp. 82–4.

Apuleius, was himself charged with such a crime. He married a rich older widow, Pudentilla, and was accused by her relatives of winning her by sorcery for her money.[150] Women, however, were also the performers of magical rites. The following excerpt from the early third-century work, *The Martyrdom of Saints Perpetua and Felicitas*, implies that the jailers of these early Christian women tortured them in order to incapacitate their magical powers which could be used in an escape: 'The military tribune had treated them with extraordinary severity because on the information of certain very foolish people he became afraid that they would be spirited out of the prison by magical spells.'[151] In response to the outsiders who accused them of sorcery, early Christians stressed that they performed genuine miracles. Expulsions of demons and healings were accomplished by prayers, not by magical arts. Yet early Christians were also willing to accuse heretics of engaging in such magical practices.[152] Early Christian awareness of how some activities such as exorcism might become wedded with the tricks of the sorcerer is revealed, for example, by the Pseudo-Clementine, *De Virginitate*, probably composed in the first half of the third century. Here, under the pretense of exorcism, impostors are said to 'gad about among the houses of virgin brethren and sisters . . . [and] make merchandise of the name of Christ'.[153]

Accusations of sorcery often raise suspicions about the person involved (the sorcerer) as is implied by Celsus' question: '*Ought we to say that they are the practices of wicked men possessed by an evil daemon?*' Anthropologists who study witchcraft accusations have argued that, in many cultures, the line between the one who has the power to control demons and the one possessed by demons is a fluid one.[154]

---

[150] Apuleius' defence against this charge is recorded in a work called *Apologia*. See Benko, *Pagan Rome*, 104–5.

[151] *The Martyrdoms of Saints Perpetua and Felicitas* 16; cited in Kraemer, *Maenads*, 104. The translation adopted by Kraemer is by H. Musurillo, *Acts of the Christian Martyrs* (Oxford: Clarendon, 1972). For interesting discussion of women practitioners of magic in the ancient world see Kraemer, *Her Share*, 90; 108–9. See collection of evidence on the role of the sorceress in the ancient world in Portefaix, *Sisters Rejoice*, 56–8. See also, Aubert, 'Threatened Wombs', 421–49.   [152] See Benko, *Pagan Rome*, 114–16.

[153] *De Virginitate* 1.10, *ANF* 8.58 (2 Epistles Concerning Virginity); cited in Benko, *Pagan Rome*, 116; cf. 116–17.

[154] See discussion in Smith, *Jesus the Magician*, 77 where he cites Mircea Eliade. See also Crossan, *Historical Jesus*, 315–20.

In trying to understand the relationship in Celsus' argument between the one deluded by sorcery and the sorcerer we can see this fluidity: the possessed becomes the possessor. In Celsus' account, the followers of Jesus are implicated in Jesus' activities. It is difficult, however, to estimate the impact of Celsus' singling out of a woman (Mary Magdalene) as one deluded by sorcery. Does this heighten the aura of sorcery and trickery that surrounds Jesus and his followers? Modern research on women consumers and practitioners of magic in antiquity is in its infancy, and whether such evidence as the Greek Magical Papyri might shed light on the religious leadership of women in the Greco-Roman world remains to be seen.[155] What is clear is that the description of a hysterical female deluded by sorcery is consistent with the tendency in antiquity to see women as susceptible to religious madness, inclined towards excesses in religious activities, and suspiciously talented as religious practitioners.

It may be that Celsus said more about Mary Magdalene and women followers of Jesus than Origen discloses. For example, one wonders if Celsus had discussed Mary as one 'from whom seven demons had gone out' (Luke 8.2). The text of Luke 8.1–3, which speaks of women healed of 'evil spirits and infirmities' providing for Jesus and the twelve out of their means, is cited by Origen in response to the accusation that Jesus and his disciples collected their livelihood in a disgraceful and importunate way.[156] It is easy to imagine that such possessed women became obvious targets for Celsus' criticism, and that he portrayed them as willing compatriots for a sorcerer who cast out demons by the prince of demons. As we move on to consider Celsus' depiction of women in the early Christian movement we will gain a greater sense of the social consequences of female initiative and involvement which surfaces throughout his critique.

The evangelizing tactics of the early Christians and society

In the last series of texts to be examined from Celsus' account, women are depicted as the focus of early Christian evangelizing

---

155 See Kraemer, *Her Share*, 90.
156 De Labriolle in *La réaction* argues that Celsus knew the Gospel of Luke; see p.125.

tactics, involved in missionary efforts, and are even presented as prominent leaders of early Christian groups.

Then after this Celsus quotes what is entirely contrary to Jesus' teaching, and is maintained only by a few people who are supposed to be Christians, not, as he thinks, by *the more intelligent*, but by the most ignorant. He says: *Their injunctions are like this. 'Let no one educated, no one wise, no one sensible draw near. For these abilities are thought by us to be evils. But as for anyone ignorant, anyone stupid, anyone uneducated, anyone who is a child, let him come boldly.'* By the fact that they themselves admit that these people are worthy of their God, they show that they want and are able to convince only the foolish, dishonourable and stupid, and only slaves, women and little children.*[157]

Moreover, we see that those who display their secret lore in the market-places and go about begging would never enter a gathering of intelligent men, nor would they dare to reveal their noble beliefs in their presence; but whenever they see adolescent boys and a crowd of slaves and a company of fools they push themselves in and show off.[158]

In private houses also we see wool-workers, cobblers, laundry-workers, and the most illiterate and bucolic yokels, who would not dare to say anything at all in front of their elders and more intelligent masters. But whenever they get hold of children in private and some stupid women with them, they let out some astounding statements as, for example, that they must not pay any attention to their father and school-teachers, but must obey them; they say that these talk nonsense and have no understanding, and that in reality they neither know nor are able to do anything good, but are taken up with mere empty chatter. But they alone they say, know the right way to live, and if the children would believe them, they would become happy and make their home happy as well. And if just as they are speaking they see one of the school-teachers coming, or some intelligent person, or even the father himself, the more cautious of them flee in all directions; but the more reckless urge the children on to rebel. They whisper to them that in the presence of their father and their schoolmasters they do not feel able to explain anything to the children. But, if they like, they should leave father and their schoolmasters, and go along with the women and little children who are playfellows to the wooldresser's shop, or the cobbler's or the washerwoman's shop, that they may learn perfection. And by saying this they persuade them.[159]

In these texts Celsus criticizes early church members for the effect they have on the wider social order. Evangelists are said to direct their energies exclusively towards inconsequential and impressionable members of society: '*the foolish, dishonourable and stupid, and only slaves, women and little children*'. Like the tactics of the sorcerer Jesus, the activities of the early Christian evangelists are clandestine. They peddle their 'secret lore' (magical arts) in the marketplace

---

[157] *C. Cels.* 3.44.   [158] Ibid., 3.50.   [159] Ibid., 3.55.

and go about begging, but they choose their audiences carefully, avoiding intelligent men at all costs. They are especially skilful at entrapping children and 'stupid women' in private places. Their teaching is revolutionary; it encourages disobedience of fathers and schoolteachers and it proposes an alternative way of life.

It is clear that Celsus believes that women make up a considerable part of the early Christian population. But if one reads attentively the third text cited above, it becomes evident that women are not merely followers of the early Christian evangelists, but they are also actively involved in the missionary enterprise. Early church teachers are said to encourage prospective members to go along with women and little children to various shops in order to 'attain perfection' (presumably to receive further instruction and initiation). Scholars have argued that the workshop may have been an important locus of missionary activity among early Christians.[160] In addition, the shops that are listed by Celsus as the sites for early church meetings are ones where women may have worked.[161] Of particular significance is the reference to the γυναικωνῖτις. The English translation as 'wooldresser's shop' does not capture the clearly feminine connotations: the term may also be translated literally as 'women's apartments'.[162] Whatever the translation, there is an unmistakable connection in Celsus' text between women's crafts and their domain. In fact, Celsus alternates between references to private homes and workshops in such a way as to suggest the extended households of antiquity that sometimes included

---

[160] See especially Ronald F. Hock, *The Social Context of Paul's Ministry: Tentmaking and Apostleship* (Philadelphia: Fortress, 1980) 37–42.

[161] On women and work see S. Pomeroy, *Goddesses, Whores, Wives and Slaves* (New York: Schocken, 1975) 198–202.

[162] The translation offered by Roberts and Donaldson in *ANF* 4.486 (1885) is 'women's apartments'. Chadwick prefers 'wooldresser's shop' following W. den Boer, 'Gynaeconitis, a Centre of Christian Propaganda' *VC* 4 (1950) 61–4. However, one of the main arguments used by den Boer would not be considered valid today not only because it does not do justice to the female initiative implied by the text, but also because it is not in keeping with our current understanding of the involvement of women in the missionary enterprise: 'it can never have been the intention of these male missionaries to compromise their work of instruction by having it take place in the women's quarters which to them were out of bounds' (p.63). On the importance of the term 'γυναικωνῖτις' in defining the cultural expectations of male, public and female, private spheres and the actual living arrangements of women see the detailed treatment by Neyrey, 'What's Wrong With this Picture?', 79–80.

shops.[163] Perhaps he has in mind the activities of female slaves or former slaves, who now work for the head of the household as wooldressers.[164] Whatever the precise circumstances may be, it is clear that Celsus thinks that the authority of the head of the household is violated by what goes on in these private household-shops.

Given the symbolic association in antiquity of women with the private sphere and men with the public domain it is interesting to see Celsus link early Christianity with women's spaces while at the same time characterizing the movement as a secretive, revolutionary group. Christianity seems to have challenged Celsus' fundamental belief that respectable religion should be associated with the public institutions of cities and nations; the nature of Christianity's threat lies in the 'privatizing' of religion.[165] If we allow the discussion of honour and shame in the Introduction to inform our analysis, it becomes quickly apparent that the movement into the private/female domain by early Christians threatens the honour of the elders, masters, fathers, and teachers who are said to be actively disobeyed. While Celsus stresses that the church draws its membership from the inconsequential members of society, including the dishonourable, the stupid, women, and little children, the harsh polemic may well conceal an awareness that some (previously) honourable men are also among the adherents. Moreover, the adolescent boys who are presented as members of the easily-duped Christian audience will, after all, become men. In the Introduction, it was noted that anthropologists have gathered information about the shaming that occurs in Mediterranean societies when men are viewed as being 'too much of the house'.[166] This is precisely the sentiment behind Celsus' declaration that early Christianity is a religion of women's spaces. Religion which should properly be tied to the public domain of men has become privatized and feminized. Church groups are offensive because in them the public sphere is swallowed up by the private and women

---

[163] See Meeks, *Urban Christians*, 30.   [164] See Roberts and Donaldson, *ANF* 4.486, n.4.
[165] Wilken, *The Christians*, 125. Wilken has also spoken of the 'privatizing' of religion, but not with respect to the values of honour and shame as in this volume. On privatization as a broad societal trend during the third and fourth centuries CE see Ramsay MacMullen, *Corruption and the Decline of Rome* (New Haven and London: Yale University, 1988).   [166] See Introduction, pp. 29–30.

play a major role in defining the new ethos. The true purpose of the home is negated when it shelters church meetings and male responsibilities in public affairs are ignored or subverted.

Scholars working on early Christian texts have drawn attention to aspects of this privatization when studying how Christianity made its way through the Mediterranean world. There has been considerable interest, for example, in how the structure of the Greco-Roman household facilitated the winning of new church members, and a great deal of attention has been given to the importance of the household for defining church life in general. While there is caricature and exaggeration in Celsus' account of activities in the private houses of early Christians, Celsus does discuss what scholars believe were actual evangelizing practices. We are, however, only beginning to understand what the privatizing of religion that occurred within early Christianity meant for the lives of early Christian women. We need to reflect more about the specific challenges faced by women who joined a group which had a distinct ethos and traditions that were often perceived by larger society as a revolutionary challenge to the stability of the state and the household (a microcosm of the state).[167] For example, we need to consider the circumstances of many early Christian women who became church members without the support or even knowledge of their husbands. While this is the subject of a subsequent chapter, it is worth citing at this point one particularly intriguing piece of evidence which points to the suspicion that early Christian women practised magic. In a work addressed to his wife, Tertullian described the problems faced by a Christian woman married to a non-believing husband. His account puts us in touch with the concrete difficulties of everyday Christian life:

Shall you escape notice when you sign your bed, or your body; when you blow away some impurity; when even by night you rise to pray? Will you not be thought to be engaged in some work of magic? Will not your husband know what it is which you secretly taste before taking any food?

---

[167] Discussions of the household codes in the New Testament have highlighted the importance of the topos 'concerning household management' in Greco-Roman society and have aimed to understand how early Christian household ethics responded to criticisms about the church threatening household and state. See for example, Balch, *Let Wives*.

And if he knows it to be bread, does he not believe it to be that bread which he said it to be? And will every husband, ignorant of the reason of these things, simply endure them, without murmuring, without suspicion whether it be bread or poison?[168]

As we examine more early Christian sources in subsequent chapters it will become even clearer that in his focus on the secret activities of women, Celsus was touching upon an important element of their lives.

My main purpose in this section has been to highlight a critique of Christianity developed by Celsus but seldom discussed by commentators: early Christianity is the result of dubious, female initiative. Unfortunately, however, some of Celsus' most important statements concerning female involvement in early Christianity probably have been lost. We are left with only an impression, based on a list of teacher-leaders of early Christian groups which include a majority of women, some of whom are featured prominently in early Christian gnostic and apocryphal sources: Helena, Marcellina, Salome, Mariamme, and Martha.[169] Celsus also refers to early Christian belief in '*a power flowing from a certain virgin Prunicus*'.[170] Moreover, Celsus notes that some early Christians are Sybillists. In response, Origen is quick to distance the early Christians from the Sybil, a prophetess of obscure origin known to us from Jewish and pagan sources, but also mentioned in early Christian literature.[171] Although there is no detailed and explicit critique recorded by Origen that early Christian groups have female teacher-leaders, one wonders if such a criticism was part of Celsus' original work. Had Celsus encountered early Christian groups in the second century where women had prominent roles? Certainly such groups existed.[172] In his response, Origen misses no

---

[168] Tertullian, *Ad uxorem*, 2.5, *ANF* 4.46–7 (To His Wife); cited in Benko, *Pagan Rome*, 126.

[169] *C. Cels.* 5.62. Chadwick offers a thorough collection of references to these women in early Christian literature; see 312 notes 4, 7, 8, 9. On Celsus and Gnostics see Remus, *Pagan-Christian Conflict*, 119–35.

[170] *C. Cels.* 6.34. Origen replies that 'Prunicus' is the name given to Sophia (Wisdom) by the Valentinians who saw an allegory of her in the gospel story of the woman who had an issue of blood. See *C. Cels.* 6.35. For other references see Chadwick, 350 n.1.

[171] See *Herm. Vis.* 2.4.1. On Sybil see Introduction, p. 4.

[172] See for example the discussion of women's prominence in second-century Christianity in Asia Minor in MacDonald, *The Legend and the Apostle*, 38–40.

opportunity to denigrate the involvement of women in pagan religiosity, for example:

> If the Pythian priestess is out of her senses and has not control of her faculties when she prophesies, what sort of spirit must we think it which poured darkness upon her mind and rational thinking? Its character must be like that of the race of daemons which many Christians drive out of people who suffer from them, without any curious magical art or sorcerer's device, but with prayer alone and very simple adjurations and formulas such as the simplest person could use.[173]

Origen's arguments about the oracle of the Pythian priestess echo the suspicions of sorcery and hysteria in Celsus' depiction of early Christian women. We cannot be sure if Origen's response is an attempt to rebut Celsus' charges about a preponderant number of female teachers in early Christian circles, but the vigour with which Origen attacks the roles of pagan priestesses certainly suggests that this was the case.

Witchcraft accusations, female power, and social definition

In an attempt to analyse the significance of the place given to female involvement in Celsus' critique and by way of conclusion to this discussion, it is useful to return to the theme of sorcery. Accusations of demon possession, witchcraft and sorcery are investigated by anthropologists under the rubric of 'witchcraft accusations'.[174] The extensive work on witchcraft by anthropologist Mary Douglas (which includes the results of her own field work in African societies and a synthesis of the studies of other scholars) is being employed as a useful analytical tool by scholars of early

---

[173] *C. Cels.* 7.4. See also 7.3–6 where Origen argues that the use of women prophets casts doubt on the validity of the prophecy. For Celsus' original argument where he mentions the predictions of several priestesses, see *C. Cels.* 7.3.

[174] Sometimes the following distinction is made: 'witchcraft' refers to internal psychic powers to harm, and 'sorcery' refers to bewitching by means of external symbols (spells, charms, or potions). See Mary Douglas, 'Introduction: Thirty Years after Witchcraft, Oracles and Magic' in Douglas (ed.), *Witchcraft, Confessions, & Accusations* (New York: Tavistock, 1970) xxxvi n.1. Peter Brown has placed the emergence of the 'witch in the full sense as a person who either is born with or achieves an inherent character of evil' in the context of the transition from late antiquity to the middle ages. See Brown, 'Sorcery, Demons', 35–6.

Christianity.[175] Douglas identifies specific characteristics of witch-craft societies and she offers theoretical reflections on the societal function of witchcraft accusations. Some of Douglas' analytical insights suggest new ways to understand the impact of Celsus' focus on women in his critique of early Christianity.

I have already discussed the relationship between the depiction of women in Celsus' critique and the presentation of Jesus as sorcerer. We have seen that Jesus' entourage, and indeed many early Christians, are tainted by the suspicion of sorcery in Celsus' account. Citations of the activities of women apparently heighten this suspicion. While it is obvious that we must study how these witchcraft accusations function in the specific context of *The True Doctrine*, it is important also to keep in mind how they fit within the overall relationship between church and society in the second century CE, a relationship that was often tense. As Mary Douglas puts it, when investigating witchcraft beliefs, 'there are always two levels of analysis, the individual and the community'.[176] She notes that individuals accuse others of witchcraft where social relations are ambiguous. Such ambiguity is the result of relations which are 'competitive and unregulated' and may also be the result of individuals assuming an 'anomalous position of advantage or disadvantage so that the umbrella of community protection is withdrawn from them'.[177] Moreover, Douglas identifies close human interaction as a necessary factor that contributes to the development of witchcraft-dominated cosmologies. She argues that where 'social interaction is intense and ill-defined, there we may expect to find witchcraft beliefs. Where human relations are sparse and diffuse, or where roles are very fully ascribed, we would not expect to find witchcraft accusations.'[178] The categories of ambiguity, competition, intimate human contact, and anomaly are

---

[175] See Brown, 'Sorcery, Demons', 17–45; Margaret Pamment, 'Witch-hunt', *Theology* 84 (1981) 98–106; Jerome H. Neyrey, 'Bewitched in Galatia: Paul and Cultural Anthropology', *CBQ* 50 (1988) 72–100; Neyrey, *Paul in Other Words*; Philip F. Esler, *The First Christians in their Social World: Social-Scientific Approaches to New Testament Interpretation* (London and New York: Routledge, 1994) 131–46. For useful summaries of Douglas' insights see the introduction to the collection of essays cited in note 174 and Douglas, *Natural Symbols*.

[176] Douglas, 'Introduction', xxiv.   [177] Ibid., xxv.

[178] Ibid., xxxv. Douglas is aware of the fact that she is creating models and explains that not all social groups will 'fit'. She warns against 'too rigid social determinism' (p.xxxvi).

useful when trying to understand the background to Celsus' accusations of sorcery. When we consider how Celsus' comments may have operated at the social or community level, it is valuable to keep Douglas' statement in mind: 'witchcraft beliefs are essentially a means of clarifying and affirming social relations'.[179]

In order to understand the situation which fostered sorcery accusations in pagan critique of early Christianity, it is useful to recall the social-scientific theory on the difference between power and authority, discussed in the Introduction to this book. We have seen that while women often are prevented from occupying positions of authority, this does not exhaust their avenues for power. We have observed in Celsus' arguments, and in those of the other critics we have been studying, depictions of early Christian women exercising power, albeit of a destructive kind. Witchcraft accusations often occur when this illegitimate power is perceived to be a threat to those who possess legitimate positions of authority. The threat is especially strong when the origin of illegitimate power seems particularly intangible and its advantages seem particularly imponderable.[180] Sorcery accusations may reflect this kind of societal clash, and they may be signs of competition and ill-defined but intense social relations. In *The True Doctrine*, Celsus' linkage of early Christian women with sorcery labels church members as outsiders and it reaffirms the group boundaries of a stable Roman society.[181]

As Christianity spread through the urban world of the Roman Empire, it made its way through houses, shops, and marketplaces, areas where privacy was rare. Housing was crowded and much of daily existence took place on the streets.[182] News travelled rapidly from neighbour to neighbour and suspicions could flare up quickly. A good illustration of how this atmosphere of 'everybody is watching' shaped the interaction between pagans and Christians can be seen in texts which refer to witnessing and even spying on religious rites. In *Alexander the False Prophet*, Lucian of Samosata records

---

[179] Ibid., xxv.

[180] Brown has spoken in a similar way of sorcery accusations being the result of a clash between articulate and inarticulate power; see 'Sorcery, Demons', 21–2.

[181] It is interesting to compare Celsus' treatment of early Christian women to the reference to Jezebel in Rev. 2:20. Esler believes that the description of Jezebel functions as a sorcery accusation in order to label her as a deviant in the name of community values. See *First Christians*, 143.   [182] Meeks, *Urban Christians*, 29; see 28–9.

Alexander's proclamation that atheists, Christians, and Epicureans who come to spy on his services should be expelled.[183] While Lucian's text may reflect Alexander's fear that Christians will expose him as a fraud, 'it is also possible that Alexander's fear of the Christians was based on his knowledge that Christians were well-known exorcists, and so their presence at meetings might have "broken the spell"'.[184] In contrast to the pagan fear of Christians penetrating and disrupting their group, it is interesting to consider Celsus' criticism that Christians invite sinners to their services while the mysteries properly exclude them.[185] This kind of accusation calls to mind Paul's apparent endorsement of practices that allowed non-believers to observe early church rites in the hope that they might be converted (1 Cor. 14.23–5). Yet from New Testament times onwards Christians displayed ambivalence towards outsiders; they maintained a certain distance from non-members, yet they also encouraged new membership. Celsus' criticism of the early Christians may, in fact, reflect this tension. His point about Christians inviting sinners to gatherings must be read in conjunction with his accusation that Christians are secretive and choose their audiences very carefully. Some Christian texts simply do not display the openness to all people for which Celsus chided early Christians. A striking example of this suspicion of outsiders comes from the writings of Cyprian in the third century. A pagan woman who secretly participated in a Christian eucharist is said to have had terrible pains, like those which follow the ingestion of poison.[186]

Such texts underline the competition and close associations between various religious groups in antiquity and they highlight the difficulty of keeping religious matters quiet. In terms of Douglas' analysis, within the urban environment where Christianity developed, conditions were ripe for witchcraft accusations. Amid the intense and crowded interactions of city life, Christians were visible, but were nevertheless accused of being

---

[183] Lucian, *Alexander the False Prophet*, 38; trans. A. M. Harmon (LCL 1913). Cited in Benko, *Pagan Rome*, 112. This work was addressed to Celsus who may be the same author who wrote *The True Doctrine*; see Benko, p.108.   [184] Benko, *Pagan Rome*, 112–13.

[185] *C. Cels.* 3.59; see Benko, *Pagan Rome*, 112.

[186] Cyprian, *De lapsis* 25–6 (*ANF* 5.444); cited in Benko, *Pagan Rome*, 125.

evasive. It was precisely the Christian determination for secrecy, and their efforts to hide from view what normally was in the public eye, that infuriated Celsus. According to Celsus, Christians moved their activities from the streets to the more secluded domains of houses, shops, and women's apartments. Previously I noted that at the heart of Celsus' critique of early Christianity is the notion of the privatizing of religion. Celsus accuses early Christians of severing the usual ties between religion, tradition, and the public institutions of cities and nations. Celsus' extensive critique of early Christianity and his focus on their evangelizing tactics makes it clear that this anomalous group, which seemed to have little regard for the public domain and which even encouraged members to ignore fathers and schoolteachers, was perceived as a disruptive and competitive menace to society. Peter Brown's description of a society which engages in the hunting down of the sorcerer offers an excellent insight into Celsus' world view:

The society, or the group within the society that actually acts on its fears is usually the society that feels challenged, through conflict, to uphold an image of itself in which everything that happens, happens through articulate channels only – where power springs from vested authority, where admiration is gained by conforming to recognized norms of behaviour, where the gods are worshipped in public, and where wisdom is the exclusive preserve of the traditional educational machine.[187]

In Celsus' *The True Doctrine*, women are used to draw negative attention to a group where power is exercised in illegitimate clandestine ways, where norms of behaviour are violated, where God is worshipped in private and where the only 'wisdom' comes from magical lore. Women are assigned major responsibility for the group's influence and, as we shall see as we move on to discuss a selection of early Christian texts, there is good reason to believe that early Christian women were in fact often successful evangelists. In essence, the women of Celsus' account are witches. They are 'attackers and deceivers'. They use 'what is impure and potent to harm what is pure and helpless'.[188] Little children are carried off to women's quarters, away from the influence of legitimate figures

---

[187] Brown, 'Sorcery, Demons', 22.
[188] See discussion of characteristics of a witch in Douglas, 'Introduction', xxvi.

of authority. In implicating women in the general charge of sorcery throughout his work, Celsus is reaffirming the group boundaries and solidarity of legitimate society and he is firmly labelling the early Christians as outsiders. Celsus knew well what would convince an ancient audience. He spoke to a world that perceived a strong connection between societal immorality, female degeneracy, and the illegitimate religious activities of women.[189]

Conclusion

Throughout this discussion of how women figured in pagan critique of early Christianity I have examined the relationship between image and reality: the interplay between the world of historical events and the social construction of reality including impression, rumour, and stereotype. When analysing public opinion of early Christianity, it is evident that image and reality both are operative, and they may never fully be separated despite the most conscientious attempts at scholarly dissection. We are forever the recipients of accounts which have been shaped by cultural codes embedded in language itself. While this is true for all historical evidence, and the search to recover pure historical fact now is recognized by historians to be an illusory aspiration, the material we have been considering offers especially vivid illustrations of how image *shapes* reality. It is not only the case that image shapes reality in the sense that all communication about historical happenings is affected by the priorities, beliefs, and norms embedded in the symbol systems of particular cultures; rather, we must also be aware that image shapes reality in the sense that during any given historical moment the *actors themselves* will experience and react to a reality that is profoundly shaped by such symbol systems.[190] With respect to the evidence discussed above, we must remember that what was being said of early Christian women had

---

[189] See MacDonald, 'Women Holy', 178. See Pomeroy, *Goddesses*, 212; Balsdon, *Roman Women*, 14, 241–2; Mary R. Lefkowitz, 'Influential Women', in Averil Cameron and Amélie Kuhrt (eds.), *Images of Women in Antiquity* (London & Canberra: Croom Helm, 1983) 59–60.

[190] Here I have been influenced by the treatise on the sociology of knowledge by P. L. Berger and T. Luckmann, *The Social Construction of Reality* (Garden City, N. Y.: Doubleday and Company, 1967).

real consequences for their lives. I have suggested throughout this section (and I will argue further in Part 2) that even assessments of early Christian women that had little to do with their actual activities nevertheless influenced their lives in important ways.

While scholarly caution is always necessary, the fact that there is a constant tension between image and reality in Greco-Roman critique of early Christianity does not mean that it is impossible to make any assertions about historical events. Throughout this discussion I have sought to discover whether a given pagan author's description of early Christianity may add something to our knowledge of how early Christian women actually lived, in addition to the information it provides about how early Christian women were depicted. The importance of public opinion of early Christianity for our understanding of the lives of early church women will become even clearer in Part 2 of this book, but it is possible at this point to summarize some of the observations made in Part 1 that will receive further treatment in the next section. By way of general comment, it is important to note that sometimes our picture of early Christian women based on Christian sources is confirmed by outsiders' critiques of early Christianity. Lucian, for example, attests to the importance of the ministry of widows in the second century CE. His comments suggest that we should expand our concept of widows' active service to include travel and the role of benefactor and protector of prisoners. Similarly, in Celsus' critique of early Christianity we find support for the growing scholarly consensus that the household-workshop was an important arena for conversion in early Christianity. Furthermore, through Celsus we gain insight into how this arena facilitated the work of women evangelists. Early church sources also speak about these women, but frequently in barely audible tones. When early Christian and pagan sources thus converge, we may be confident of touching historical reality quite firmly.

It also is the case that when pagan opinion and early Christian sources diverge, we may want to revise our assessment of history. Pliny's letter to the Emperor Trajan offers surprising information about the prominence of female ministers who were also slaves, during a period of church history when Christian writings such as the Pastoral Epistles defined church leadership roles in terms of the structures of the Greco-Roman household. Another example of divergence emerges when we consider the portrait of widows with children in Lucian's *Passing of Peregrinus*. As I will discuss further, scholars have thought that the sanctioning of orders of widows and virgins in early Christianity created new avenues for women to remain free of the burdens of the patriarchal household that were imposed on married early Christian women. Lucian's reference to widows accompanied by children leads us to rethink the relationship between the lives of married and unmarried women in early Christianity.

A central aspect of the historical experience of early Christian women which I examine in this book is how their behaviour was interpreted in relation to idealized images of women in Greco-Roman society and how such interpretations affected their lives. Most obviously, the material we have been analysing points to the fact that by joining the early Christian group, women violated what was thought to be religious activities appropriate to their sex. Celsus offers a good example of how outsiders may have understood the close relationship between two religions which were seen as causing problems in the Roman Empire, Judaism, and Christianity. It is clear from his arguments that both religions cause revolution and immorality. His detailed description of the involvement of women in early Christianity is in keeping with the tendency to depict Judaism and Christianity, along with other illicit Eastern religions, as having a seditious effect on women. For Celsus, the very origin of Christianity lies in the adulterous behaviour of a disreputable peasant woman. In Fronto's polemic we also hear the charge that Christianity produces immorality among women: women and children are depicted as engaging in promiscuous rites and violating the appropriate order of society. Another example of how early Christian women may have been understood as embodying the antithesis of feminine virtue is offered by Lucius Apuleius. A long list of vices embodying everything from drunkenness to obstinacy culminates in the charge of infidelity, expressed in dramatic terms as the violation of the husband's house and bed, an assault upon the very essence of his honour. Studies by cultural anthropologists working on Mediterranean society of the symbolic association of women with the household have led us to a greater understanding of how the image of the 'whoring' Christian wife may have been fed by activities of women that had little to do with sexual adventure. If a woman left the home unexpectedly and without explanation to attend a mysterious religious rite, rumours would quickly erupt about her basic moral nature and the charge of adultery could have very serious consequences for a wife in Greco-Roman society.

In general, references to women in pagan descriptions of early Christianity are an important means of signifying the nature of the group. The focus on women in Celsus, for example, heightens the suspicion of sorcery that embraces Jesus and Christianity. The tendency to associate women with clandestine acts of magic and charlatanism is no doubt related to the tendency in antiquity to imagine women as susceptible to religious madness, inclined towards excesses in religious activities, and yet suspiciously talented as religious practitioners. In the next section we will explore how such perceptions may have shaped Christian prescriptions concerning female behaviour. One of the most interesting (but difficult to weigh historically) insights we take away from this review of references to women in the earliest descriptions of Christianity by outsiders might be expressed as follows: even if they behaved in a manner that was quite conventional and might otherwise have won them approval, early Christian women could be characterized in the most negative way as whores, witches, and enemies of the state.

With the aid of social-scientific analysis of the relationship between power and authority, we have learned that negative characterizations of early Christian women should not be taken at face value. These assessments often reveal as much about the influence of women in the new religion as the seemingly more factual references to specific events involving early Christian women, such as Pliny's description of the torture of two female deacons. Apuleius' picture of the wicked woman who worships a god called 'only' is clearly a caricature created in the interests of satire. However, this caricature, which extends to include a depiction of a pitiful husband who is incapable of thwarting his wife's activities, might also be understood as a cultural acknowledgment of the woman's power, even if it is clearly illegitimate power according to those who are in positions of authority. As I will illustrate in Part 3 of this book, Apuleius' account sheds light upon references in Christian literature to early church women married to unbelievers.

Related to the notion that authority structures do not exhaust the avenues for power available to women is a second point that will also receive further development in the next section. Lucian of Samosata's description of the activities of widows has drawn our attention to the possibility that the limited authority of women in public affairs may have contributed to their usefulness as ministers in the early Christian movement. The portrait of widows and children waiting near the prison, probably praying, but in all likelihood also standing guard and caring for the various needs of the prisoner, is significant. It suggests that convictions about the relative unimportance of women in the public arena (i.e. they were more likely to be ignored) served the early Christian movement in various ways. Celsus also focused on the role of women and children in Christianity, and he was critical of their subversion of public institutions by such clandestine acts as conducting the church's important business in 'private' women's quarters. Despite the care taken by Celsus to locate the origins of Christianity in the activities of a poor and disreputable woman and to illustrate the continued popularity of the movement among such unfortunates, he inadvertently pointed to the influence of gullible, 'bucolic yokels' in the creation and development of a new religion. The hysterical female, Mary Magdalene, fits the image of the woman susceptible to bizarre religious impulses that emerges from ancient literature. Yet, she is by no means a silent victim of Jesus' magic. Although she is deluded by sorcery, Mary Magdalene also becomes one of its main perpetrators. She is an active witness, a creator of the Christian belief in the resurrection.

The result of this collection of references to women in second-century critiques of early Christianity is a surprising array of impressions. Although the degree of diatribe varies, and the genre ranges from letter to satire to philosophical treatise, there are many similarities among the texts. At the same time, Galen's treatment of the Christians reminds us that we should not think in terms of a single, uniform reaction to early Christian women. When Galen's admiration of the virtuous way of life of Christian ascetics is compared to other references to early Christian women, it becomes especially clear that variations in opinion were possible even among the elite circle of government officials and intellectuals that recorded their reactions to early Christianity during the second century. In Part 2 of this book I will argue that early Christian women embraced celibacy with zeal, and that this practice contributed to the perception that the church was harmful to household and society; however, Galen's comments indicate that the ascetic efforts of women sometimes may have contributed to Christianity's appeal. Nevertheless, both positive and negative reactions to early Christian women must be viewed critically. Galen understood the philosophical life as one where both men and women tamed their desires through self-discipline and self-control, but his comments probably also reveal a world view where women achieve such virtue only by becoming essentially male. In the ancient world, admiration of female asceticism in no way necessarily implies openness to social liberation as understood in modern terms. Such admiration can occur without any interest in transforming societal gender distinctions. A final point on the significance of Galen's positive reaction to the behaviour of early Christian women needs to be considered. While the strongly negative critiques of early Christianity which form the majority of our collection tend to reinforce the impression of a firm division between insiders and outsiders, Galen's description of the early Christian movement in terms of his own philosophical interests warns us against drawing lines too firmly between insiders and outsiders, and between criticism and curious inquiry. In the next section we will study evidence suggesting that early church members hoped to attract followers through their self-control and the stringency of their sexual ethics.

An important contention of this book is that the history of early Christian women includes the record of public reaction to their lives. In the next section we will move on to search for indications in early Christian texts of a desire to respond to this public reaction and we will consider how the view of outsiders shaped the lives of believing women. Part 1 has been devoted to uncovering a perception shared by several critics of early Christianity about the influence of women in the birth of a new religion – a perception that might be succinctly expressed as 'the power of the hysterical woman'. By concentrating on early Christian sources in the next sections we will gain a greater awareness of how this aspect of pagan opinion stood in relation to the actual shape of the power exercised by women in early church circles.

Concern expressed in early Christian texts about the respectability of women, and even generally about their behaviour, is seen in a new light when one appreciates that critics understood the behaviour of early church women as a reflection of the nature of the group as a whole. The use of the involvement of women in early Christianity to articulate the identity of the religion is shown most dramatically in Celsus' determination to illustrate that women were central figures in the religion's inception, leadership, and expansion efforts. In Celsus, emphasis on female initiative functions in conjunction with sorcery accusations to communicate why Christianity is such a menace in Greco-Roman society. The focus on women is to draw attention to the essence of a group where power is exercised in dangerous, illegitimate ways, where the norms of household order are subverted, where traditional male control of house and school is compromised, where the public practices of religion are ignored in favour of a god who is worshipped in private, and where the only wisdom comes from magical lore. Of all the figures that have been analysed in this section, *Celsus* should be singled out as exceptionally important, but heretofore largely neglected, for the study of early Christian women. During the course of the following discussion of early Christian material, the magnitude of his views for understanding how women were both central actors and signifiers in the tense relationship between the church and Greco-Roman society will become even more apparent.

PART TWO

Celibacy, women, and early church responses to public opinion

The main goal of Part 1 of this book was to illustrate that women figured prominently in descriptions of Christianity by non-Christians in the second century CE. New Testament evidence indicates, moreover, that outsiders also critiqued the early church in the first century. The challenge involved in studying such evidence is that the comments of outsiders are only available to us as they are communicated through early church voices. These Christian writings express public opinion indirectly, frequently couching it in language which is intended to exhort community members towards appropriate behaviour for life in the church. As we move on in Part 2 to look at the impact of public opinion on the lives of early Christian women, non-Christian reactions to the church will be compared to indirect expressions of public opinion found in several early Christian texts. Unlike the remarks of the observers examined in the previous section, the indirect expressions of public opinion cannot be analysed on their own terms; they must be studied in light of early church concerns for social respectability and the desire to respond to public opinion.

Some New Testament texts explicitly discuss church communities having been burdened by slanderous rumours (e.g. 1 Pet. 2.12; 3.15–16; 1 Tim. 3.6–7, 5.14). Even if the public reactions which triggered these early church responses lack the depth of the challenging questions posed to Christianity by an intellectual like Celsus, we must not underestimate their importance in the establishment of community values of prestige and failure. Gossip is far more than a minor aggravation to an emerging religious community; it is an extremely important conveyer of public opinion.[1] Paul Veyne has spoken about the power of rumours in the Roman Empire in a manner that reminds us that even before early Christianity received systematic attention from intellectuals, church members were subject to the dangerous consequences of gossip in Roman society: 'Those who braved public opinion faced ridicule. Insulting songs (*carmen famosum*) were quietly circulated, and pamphlets (*libelli*) passed from hand to hand, heaping obscene insults and sarcasm upon the deviant in order to demonstrate that public opinion was stronger than any man.'[2] It seems that such rumour-circulating devices may have been instrumental in bringing Christians to the attention of government officials in Pontus-Bythinia at the beginning of the second century. The correspondence between Pliny and Trajan that we considered in Part 1 includes the Emperor Trajan's instruction to Pliny to disregard anonymous pamphlets accusing Christians, because they set a very bad precedent and were not in keeping with the civilization of that age.[3]

In addition to the suffering that might be the result of negative public reaction, encounters with hostility or even misunderstanding threatened to thwart the early church's hope of winning the world. Christian communities of the period we are discussing no doubt varied in the level of missionary activities. In an effort to remain separate from the polluting influences of the world outside, some groups stressed their identity as the elect, set apart from the world. In order to explore the ambivalence that can be detected in certain early church texts (openness to the outside, yet a strong desire to remain distinct from the world) some New Testament scholars have employed sociologist Bryan Wilson's analysis of religious sects. They have often found useful Wilson's description of the 'conversionist' response to the world, exhibited by some contemporary religious sects.[4] Pressure to accept new members (who may not be fully socialized to group values) means that in conver-

---

[1] See Campbell, *Honour, Family, and Patronage*, 190–1, 306–15.

[2] Paul Veyne, 'The Roman Empire', in Veyne (ed.), *A History of Private Life*, vol. 1.: *From Pagan Rome to Byzantium* (Cambridge, MA and London: Belknap Press of Harvard University, 1987) 5–234, esp. 172.

[3] Pliny, *Epistles*, 10.97; cf. 10.96. See Part 1, pp. 51–9.

[4] B. Wilson's work on sects includes a seven-part typology based on various responses to the world. *See Magic and the Millennium* (New York: Harper and Row, 1973) 18–26. On the

sionist sects, accommodation to external, worldly values is always a danger. The conversionist sect, with its strong interest in evangelism, has conditions particularly likely to lead to the sect's transformation into a denomination (a new level of institutionalization involving accommodation to the standards of the world and increased formalism in worship and group organization).[5] Work on conversionist sects by Bryan Wilson has been suggestive not only for charting degrees of isolation from, and engagement of, the world in early church communities; but also in identifying the circumstances under which community teaching and practices are institutionalized. In this study a typical feature of conversionist religious sects – concern for social respectability – will be shown to be of paramount importance for analysing the institutionalization of church teaching on women and for understanding the constraints that were placed on their lives.

Paul's teaching on marriage as a 'conversionist' response to the world

Wilson and his collaborators have noted that marriage practices constitute one of the most important ways by which contemporary sects set themselves apart from the world. In particular, they have studied rules of endogamy (prescriptions that marriage should take place within the group).[6] Scholars have noted that endogamy practices vary within modern religious sects. Sometimes a sect will exhibit special concern to control the leaders' choice of wives.[7] Sometimes a great deal of energy will be devoted to asserting that

---

use of Wilson's findings for the study of early Christianity see for example, MacDonald, *Pauline Churches*, 34–42; MacDonald, 'The Ideal of the Christian Couple', 105–25; Elliott, *A Home*, 73–8; H. O. Maier, 'The Charismatic Authority of Ignatius of Antioch', *SR* 18 (1989) 185–99. While the use of the Wilson's work on sects for the study of early Christianity has not escaped criticism, it has generally been accepted as being very valuable for the study of early church attitudes towards the world. For an evaluation of the use of Wilson's work on sects by New Testament scholars see Holmberg, *Sociology and the New Testament,* 77–117; see also my response to Holmberg in 'The Ideal of the Christian Couple', p.108 n.16.

[5] See B. Wilson, 'An Analysis of Sect Development', in Wilson (ed.), *Patterns of Sectarianism* (London: Heinemann, 1967) 36–42. See also MacDonald, 'The Ideal of the Christian Couple', 108. [6] Wilson, 'An Analysis', 37.

[7] See B. Wilson, 'The Pentecostal Minister', in Wilson (ed.), *Patterns*, 152–3.

the sect's marriage practices differ substantially from those of the outside world. Marriage here becomes a symbol of social protest.[8] In turn, the marriage practices of the group may become a touchstone, determining society's reaction as tolerant or hostile.[9]

Even in the earliest stages of Pauline Christianity, how one married was understood as an indicator of separation from an evil world. In 1 Thessalonians 4.4–5 members are instructed to take wives 'in holiness and honour, not in the passion of lust like the Gentiles who do not know God' (cf. Eph. 2.3; 4.22; Col. 3.5). While the traditional features of Paul's teaching have frequently been noted – especially the similarity between this text and instructions which served to distinguish the Jewish community of the Diaspora from the Gentile world – the important point is that Paul expects the Thessalonians to behave in a distinctive manner, pleasing to God and rooted in the Lord Jesus (1 Thess. 4.1–3). In other words, how one marries is understood as vital in establishing the distinction between 'us' and 'them'.[10]

While it is perhaps expressed somewhat more indirectly, an interest in the boundary between believers and unbelievers, between the church and the world, also is expressed in 1 Corinthians 7. In 1 Cor. 7.2 immorality ($\pi o \rho v \varepsilon i \alpha$) is viewed as a threat to the lives of the unmarried, those who do not possess the special gift of celibacy. The power of immorality looming over Corinth has already become evident in the community, as Paul's discussion of the incest case in 1 Corinthians 5 makes clear: a man is living with his stepmother.[11] For Paul, this act has transferred the member into the evil

---

[8] See E. Isichei, 'From Sect to Denomination among English Quakers', in Wilson (ed.), *Patterns*, 169–70.

[9] R. Robertson, 'The Salvation Army: The Persistence of Sectarianism', in Wilson (ed.), *Patterns*, 86.

[10] For similar Jewish teaching during the Hellenistic period see Tobit 4.12–13; *Testament of Levi*, 9.10. O. Larry Yarbrough also notes that some Hellenistic moralists call for an attitude similar to Paul's condemnation of the 'passion of lust'. See his discussion in *Not like the Gentiles*, 65–87. Yarbrough believes that it is important to understand Paul's teaching on marriage in Thessalonians within the setting of vv.1–12 which clearly displays an interest in relations with outsiders (v. 12). See discussion of issues involved in translating 1 Thessalonians 4.3–8, pp. 68–76.

[11] See full discussion of this text in Andrew D. Clarke, *Secular and Christian Leadership in Corinth: A Socio-Historical and Exegetical Study of 1 Corinthians 1–6* (Leiden, New York, Köln: Brill, 1993) 73–88. A study of the social and legal background to first-century society in Corinth leads Clarke to suggest that the community's tolerance of the relationship may

and immoral outside world. The seriousness of the events in Corinth are conveyed by Paul by means of a dramatic comparison: such immorality (πορνεία) is worse even than that found among pagans! (1 Cor. 5.1; cf. 1 Thess. 4.5). Here Paul uses the sexual behaviour of outsiders as a point of reference for setting the ethical standards for those within the church group. It appears that one effect of Paul's teaching in 1 Corinthians 7 is to put into place the insulating features of endogamy prescriptions. A system of marriage between believers, in which divorce is prohibited, is a means of containing immorality (1 Cor. 7.1–7, 9, 39).[12] While it is impossible to be certain, it is likely that when Paul instructs widows to remarry 'only in the Lord', he means that new marriages (marriages undertaken after entry into the church and in contrast to those in view in 1 Cor. 7.12–16) must take place between believers (1 Cor. 7.39).[13] As will become clear in Part 3, Paul's teaching sets the stage for the further development of endogamy rules. At the beginning of the second century, the Bishop of Antioch pronounces that marriages should take place only with the permission of the bishop (Ign. Pol. 5.1–2).

In describing the capacity for groups to maintain their 'sectarian' quality, Bryan Wilson notes the importance of strict, clearly defined marriage practices.[14] Throughout 1 Corinthians 7 we sense an implicit acknowledgment of the value of marriage between believers for keeping the evil world at bay. However, the

---

have had to do with the social status of the couple and the role of the man as patron. The offence was so serious, however, that Paul was not willing to make any exceptions on the basis of social privilege.

[12] On marriage as containment in 1 Corinthians 7 see Jouette M. Bassler, '1 Corinthians', in Carol A. Newsom and Sharon H. Ringe (eds.), *The Women's Bible Commentary* (Louisville Kentucky: Westminster/John Knox, 1992) 323–4.

[13] This is how B. Malina reads the passage in *The New Testament World*, 116. Another interesting text to consider here is 2 Corinthians 6.14–7.1 which instructs believers to avoid being mismated with unbelievers. Doubt has been expressed about the authenticity of these verses, and scholars generally feel that they are out of place where they stand. Michael Newton, however, notes that this text is consistent with Paul's teaching about the church as the Temple of God made up of sanctified believers (cf. 1 Cor. 3.16; 6.19). See *The Concept of Purity at Qumran and in the Letters of Paul*, SNTSMS 53 (Cambridge University Press, 1985) 110–14, cf. 105–6. While 2 Corinthians 6.14–7.1 may be taken as contradicting Paul's apparent allowance of mixed marriages in 1 Corinthians 7.12–16, the text may also be understood as a warning against entry into a new mixed marriage and, therefore, would be consistent with 1 Corinthians 7.39.

[14] See Wilson, 'An Analysis', 44.

exhortation concerning mixed marriage in 1 Corinthians 7.12–16 also illustrates how a 'world-accommodating' teaching on marriage creates ambiguity with respect to the boundaries of the saved community. In Part 3 I examine at length how 1 Corinthians 7.12–16 shapes the lives of early Christian women who were married to non-believers, but it is possible here briefly to outline the weight of Paul's main argument. In essence, Paul qualifies the notion that the dissolution of marriages between believers and non-believers is acceptable. The non-believing partner is the only one who may initiate separation. As I will illustrate, Paul's interest clearly is evangelical. But in the hope that the non-believer may be saved, Paul exposes the church member to risks that come from intimate contact with the outside world. Is it not likely that believers married to non-believers would be especially susceptible to doubting and double-mindedness, displaying the kind of behaviour that leads the author of James (Jas. 1.6–8; cf. *Herm. Mand.* 9–10; *Sim.* 8.8) to compare some believers to a wave that is driven and tossed by the wind? Would not life in such close proximity to the outside world increase the chance that a believer would leave the church?[15] Concerning the group as a whole, would not the continuation of mixed marriages make inevitable certain compromises on church principles? For example, a woman who was worried about eating idolatrous food might be required to set her conscience aside and partake of her pagan husband's table.[16]

In Paul's writings the desire to remain separate from the world is in constant tension with the desire to engage the world in the hope of winning it. In this section, my main concern is to illustrate how the issue of women's asceticism in Pauline communities, from the time of Paul's ministry to the middle of second century CE, was especially significant in demarcating the boundaries between

---

[15] At the beginning of the second century CE, Pliny's interrogations led him to discover those who had once been Christians, but who were so no longer. See Pliny, *Epistles*, 10.96.

[16] The tension resulting from a simultaneous interest in evangelizing and avoiding outsiders clearly is evident in 1 Corinthians 8 and 1 Corinthians 10, where Paul deals with the problem of food sacrificed to idols (cf. Rom. 14.20–3). See my discussion in *The Pauline Churches*, 41–2. Like the teaching concerning mixed marriage, these exhortations are ambiguous regarding relations with outsiders. On the connection between sexual intimacy and the sharing of food in the context of mixed marriage, see Justin Martyr's account of believing woman with the unchaste husband in Justin, *Second Apology*, 2 to be discussed in detail in Part 3.

the church and the world. In 1 Corinthians 7 the celibacy of women functions as an important means of setting the church apart from the world, both in terms of religious identity and with respect to the social consequences of behaviour. The celibate women of Corinth who were holy in body and spirit took on a special significance in a community living in a world that was thought to be passing away. However, even in these earliest stages of church development, the behaviour of these women could act as an irritant to Greco-Roman society. When Paul exhorted these women, he endorsed their lifestyle of undivided devotion to the Lord, expressing his preference that women choose this way of life whenever possible. Yet already in 1 Corinthians 7 Paul also reveals a concern for stability and social respectability that is typical of groups intent on evangelization. The result, as we shall see, was that some women were called to set aside the choice of celibacy.

Paul's focus on women holy in body and spirit in 1 Corinthians 7

A quick reading of 1 Corinthians 7 immediately reveals two dominant elements of the text: (1) a preference for celibacy, expressed by such apparently unambiguous judgments as 'the widow is better off if she remains unmarried' (1 Cor. 7.40); and (2) an almost monotonous series of parallel statements about the mutual obligations of men and women, a style consistent with Paul's approach in 1 Corinthians 11.2–16. Yet in recent years scholars have called for a critical examination of these two tendencies, and it is now possible to speak of a growing scholarly consensus: Paul's qualified preference for celibacy seeks to balance more extremist ascetic tendencies in Corinth.[17] Moreover, it is becoming increasingly

---

[17] A key text is 1 Corinthians 7.1b where Paul proclaims: 'It is well for a man not to touch a woman.' However, Jouette M. Bassler has spoken of 'a growing consensus that these words do not represent Paul's own opinion but are a quotation from the Corinthians' letter'. Bassler notes that the *NRSV* now encloses the words in quotation marks to indicate that Paul is quoting an ascetic slogan. See '1 Corinthians', 323. For the debate on the meaning of 1 Corinthians 7.1b see discussion in R. Scroggs, 'Paul and the Eschatological Woman', *JAAR* 40 (1972) 281–303, esp. 294–7. The issue is complicated by the fact that libertinism (1 Cor. 5–6) and asceticism (1 Cor. 7) seem both to have been alive in the Corinthian community. See discussion in MacDonald, *There is No Male and Female*, 69–72, esp. p. 70.

accepted that Paul's parallelism actually masks a particular concern for the behaviour of women, which can be detected at several points in the text.[18]

One place where these elements emerge boldly is 1 Corinthians 7.32–4. Here, in balanced references to men and women, Paul communicates the need for a community in which members are free of anxiety (μεριμνάω). The Apostle is often understood here as contrasting marriage which involves worldly, negative anxiety (anxiety to please one's spouse) with the unmarried life which allows for a positive type of anxiety (anxiety to please only the Lord). In other words, the teaching seems at first glance to be a strong endorsement of celibacy as the preferred way of life. But, the use of the word 'anxiety' is actually quite ambiguous in the text; it is possible that Paul may view anxiety to please the Lord in somewhat negative terms, as standing in the way of proper devotion to the Lord.[19]

In order to appreciate fully how the notion of anxiety functions to temper ascetic enthusiasm in Corinth and to perceive how this tempering is related to women's lives, we must study the parallelism in the text carefully. If we examine the language used in 1 Corinthians 7.32–4, it becomes clear that the attempt to make parallel statements addressing married men and married women, unmarried men and unmarried women, is interrupted by the unusual and intriguing language used in the case of the unmarried women. First, it is important to note that in 1 Corinthians 7.32 Paul speaks simply of the unmarried man (ὁ ἄγαμος), but in 1 Corinthians 7.34 he speaks of both the unmarried woman and 'the virgin' (ἡ γυνὴ ἡ ἄγαμος καὶ ἡ παρθένος).[20] It is impossible to determine conclusively what Paul meant when he used these two categories. If he were trying to distinguish virgins from other unmarried women such as widows, it is difficult to understand why

---

[18] My article, 'Women Holy', 161–81, illustrates how 1 Corinthians 7 reveals a special concern for the behaviour of women. See also Antoinette Clark Wire, *Corinthian Women Prophets*, 82–90. Wire argues that Paul makes use of a rhetoric of equality, particularly in 1 Corinthians 7.1–7 to attract women to his position (p.82).

[19] See discussion in C. K. Barrett, *A Commentary on the First Epistle to the Corinthians* (London: Adam and Charles Black, 1968) 179.

[20] But note that the manuscript tradition includes a number of variant readings of 1 Corinthians 7.34. See discussion in Hans Conzelmann, *A Commentary on the First Epistle to the Corinthians*, trans. J. Leitch (Philadelphia: Fortress, 1975) 130–1 n. 4 who nevertheless prefers the reading used here.

he did not use more precise terminology (cf. 1 Cor. 7.39–40).[21]
Perhaps the best explanation is that Paul was clarifying the term
'unmarried' in order to ensure that his audience knew that he was
addressing a specific problem in their community. In essence, Paul
was saying: 'by "unmarried", yes I mean the virgins, those who
strive to be holy in body and spirit' (1 Cor. 7.34).[22]

This reading of 1 Corinthians 7.34 gains support from the
importance of the term 'virgin' as a means of identifying women
in 1 Corinthians 7. Although there is nothing to indicate gender in
the first reference to virgins in (1 Cor. 7.25), the other uses of
'παρθένος' here all clearly refer to women (1 Cor. 7.28, 34, 36, 37,
38).[23] In particular, the special use of the term in 1 Corinthians
7.36–8 implies that the virginity of women was of central significance in Corinth, probably especially among those who shared
strong ascetic fervour. Scholars have long puzzled over the precise
meaning of Paul's instructions to the man who feels he is not
behaving properly towards his virgin, where Paul advises marriage
'if it has to be'. It is not certain whether this passage refers to the
case of an engaged couple, to the relationship between father and
daughter, or possibly even to 'spiritual marriages' (couples living
together without physical union).[24] Yet, however one chooses to

---

[21] See discussion of possible meanings in Barrett, *First Epistle to the Corinthians*, 180–1.

[22] Ibid., 180. Antoinette Clark Wire reads this text somewhat differently: 'Paul refers to the
consecrated women as those "not married" as well as "virgins" (7:34), indicating a cross-
generational group that would provide mutual support among consecrated women.' See
Corinthian Women Prophets, 92. But Wire's explanation does not account for Paul's lack of
specific terminology. Another possibility is that by employing the category 'unmarried'
Paul is referring to women who do not qualify either as virgins or widows: the text of
1 Corinthians 7 points to the presence of women who were separated from their husbands
(7.10–11) and to those who had been abandoned by unbelieving husbands (7.12–16).

[23] Note that παρθένος referring to male virgins is found in Revelation 14.4, but this appears
to be the only such reference in the church literature of the first century. The importance
of this term in 1 Corinthians 7 is to a certain extent masked by the tendency to adopt
various English translations of the term. For example, the *RSV* employs three different
English translations of the Greek word in these texts: unmarried (v. 25), girl (vv. 28, 34),
betrothed (vv. 36, 37, 38). The *NRSV* seeks to rectify this problem.

[24] Against the 'spiritual marriage' interpretation, however, is the fact that we have no other
evidence for this phenomenon from this early period. It is difficult to harmonize Paul's
alleged approval of the practice in 1 Corinthians 7.36–8 with 1 Corinthians 7.2–5 where
he rejects perpetual celibacy within marriage, unless 1 Corinthians 7.36–8 refers to
cohabitation in marriages which have never been consummated. In 1 Corinthians 9.5
Paul refers to a 'sister wife' (ἀδελφὴν γυναῖκα) and some scholars have taken this to be a
reference to spiritual marriage. On the history of interpretation of this text and its

translate this text, it is evident that 'what to do with one's virgin' was understood by Paul as a crucial issue for members of the Corinthian community.

To return to the parallelism of 1 Corinthians 7.32–4, it is important to note that it is interrupted not only by the terminology concerning unmarried women, but also by the notion of a desire attributed to the unmarried woman or virgin: she is anxious about the affairs of the Lord and how to be holy in body and spirit (1 Cor. 7.34). Paul compares this anxiety to an attempt to please (ἀρέσκω) in all his balanced references to married and unmarried men and women, except for his statements about the unmarried woman or virgin. As in the case of the labelling of the unmarried woman as a virgin, this is probably an indication that Paul has a specific problem in mind. Instead of stating that the unmarried woman or virgin is anxious about the affairs of the Lord and how to please the Lord, Paul states that she is anxious about the affairs of the Lord and how to be holy in body and spirit. Her goal is personal holiness, not pleasing the Lord; and Paul critiques this position. Since in other places in Paul's letters, holiness is an attribute of the married state (1 Thess. 4.4; 1 Cor. 7.14), it is unlikely that 1 Corinthians 7.34 should be read as a straightforward contrast of the holiness of the unmarried woman with the worldliness of the married woman. Rather than being a statement of the ideal motives of the unmarried woman or virgin, C. K. Barrett has argued convincingly that 'she may be holy in body and spirit' are words quoted from the ideology of the Corinthian ascetic party, which Paul seeks to refute.[25] In light of their extremist tendencies, Paul is worried that those who seek to remain unmarried and are not naturally gifted with continence might become so anxious in their efforts that the result will be distraction from devotion to the Lord, and even perhaps immorality (cf. 1 Cor. 7.1–7). In other words, while married life can be subject to anxiety, anxiety also can result from an attempt to be holy that is motivated primarily out of a rigid preference for celibacy.

notoriously difficult problems of translation see Bassler, '1 Corinthians', 325; Wire, *Corinthian Women Prophets*, 224–5; Conzelmann, *1 Corinthians*, 134–6; J. C. Hurd, *The Origin of 1 Corinthians* (London: SPCK, 1965) 169–75; J. Duncan M. Derrett, 'The Disposal of Virgins', in Derrett, *Studies in the New Testament*, vol.1 (Leiden: E. J. Brill, 1977) 184–91.
25 Barrett, *First Epistle to the Corinthians*, 181.

One of the most intriguing aspects of the special concern for unmarried women or virgins we see in 1 Corinthians 7.32–4 is that Paul categorizes the goal of these women as an active devotion to holiness in body and spirit. Moreover, there are other subtle indications of the initiative of ascetic women in 1 Corinthians 7. Once again, interruption of the rhetorical parallelism signals Paul's focus on a particular community concern. In 1 Corinthians 7.10–11 Paul applies the command of the Lord against divorce equally to believing men and women. But in a surprising manner, he admits parenthetically that some women have separated from their husbands and he instructs that they should either become reconciled to their husbands or remain unmarried. Given that the exhortation concerning women is longer and precedes the corresponding instruction concerning men (where no mention is made of them initiating divorces), it is likely that women were the main instigators of separation.[26] If they were especially fervent to be ascetic, they may have sought to dissolve unions with believing husbands because sex desecrated their holiness. Abstinence within marriage would not be enough (cf. 1 Cor. 7.5) if the husband did not share the wife's passion for celibacy and found the temptation of living with her too great or perhaps even had sought sexual fulfilment elsewhere.

Evidence of female initiative also surfaces in the exhortation concerning widows. Given the later concern about the actions of widows expressed by the author of 1 Timothy (composed about the beginning of the second century CE), it is not surprising that even in a much earlier period widows are the subject of special instruction without reference to male counterparts (1 Cor. 7.39–40; cf. 1 Cor. 7.8). Widows in Greco-Roman society might find themselves in desperate economic situations, and from an early period the church offered them support (cf. Acts 6.1; 1 Tim. 5.16). But widows also could demonstrate considerable autonomy,

---

[26] Note that Paul uses the terms 'to separate' (χωρίζω) and to 'divorce, send away' (ἀφίημι) interchangeably in 1 Corinthians 7.10–16. See Jerome Murphy-O'Connor, 'The Divorced Woman in 1 Corinthians 7.10–11', *JBL* 100 (1981) 601–6, esp. 605. Murphy-O'Connor believes that men were the main instigators of the separation here; arguing that, contrary to the usual reading, 1 Corinthians 7.10b should be translated as 'the wife should not allow herself to be separated from her husband' (pp.601–3). But see convincing arguments against this hypothesis by Yarbrough in *Not Like the Gentiles*, 111, n. 67.

especially if they were financially independent. They could be in a position to make a substantial contribution to leadership in the church (cf. Acts 9.36–43; 1 Tim. 5.3–16).[27] An indication of the power and resolve of widows is revealed by Paul's expectation that his position may be challenged on the basis of some spiritual authority (1 Cor. 7.40; cf. 7.25). While it is sometimes masked by some modern translations which eliminate the term 'also', a more literal translation of the Greek text reveals a rejoinder to antici-pated resistance: 'I think that I also (κἀγώ) have the Spirit of God.'[28] Some widows who were inspired by their interpretations of their experiences of the Spirit may have sought to impose their understanding of holiness on women who found the possibility of remaining unmarried unattractive and/or financially impossible. In an effort to counter extremism, Paul agrees that a widow is better off if she remains unmarried, but admits that this might not always be possible. In contrast to the author of the Pastoral Epistles, Paul does not explicitly set out restrictions concerning who might remain a widow in the church. Paul thus sanctions a variety of possibilities for the involvement, service, and leadership of women. But in a manner that prepares the way for his later interpreter, he clearly opposes mandatory celibacy for widows.

That 1 Corinthians 7 is intended to qualify a rigid preference for celibacy which may have been strong among women is implied by the passage that follows immediately after the reference in 1 Corinthians 7.32–4 to the unmarried women or virgins who strive to be holy in body and spirit. 1 Corinthians 7.35 offers what may well be the strongest expression of Paul's intention, not only in 1 Corinthians 7.32–5 but also throughout 1 Corinthians 7 as a whole. Here Paul states that he does not want to restrain the

[27] Augustus' legislation, which will be examined in detail below, encouraged widows and divorced women to remarry. But this legislation does not seem to have thwarted the activ-ities of some wealthy widows who chose to remain in control of their affairs and were praised for remaining faithful to the memory of their dead husbands. See Pomeroy, *Goddesses*, 149–50, 158, 161; Balsdon, *Roman Women*, 76–7, 89–90, 220–2; Jo Ann McNamara, *A New Song: Celibate Women in the First Three Christian Centuries* (New York: The Haworth Press, Inc., 1983) 59; MacDonald, *Pauline Churches*, 185–7.

[28] Both Barrett and Conzelmann opt for this more literal translation. Conzelmann, for example, suggests that the closing might be 'a subtle thrust at the pneumatics'. See *1 Corinthians*, 136. See also Barrett, *First Epistle to the Corinthians*, 186. In contrast to some earlier translations, the *NRSV* includes the word 'too' (also).

Corinthians with firm regulations. With respect to marriage and celibacy he wishes them to do what is expedient in relation to their own circumstances and gifts (cf. 1 Cor. 7.6–7). If 1 Corinthians 7.32–4 did constitute a straightforward description of celibacy as conducive to pleasing the Lord and a condemnation of marriage as necessarily being worldly, it would be difficult to accept Paul's claim in 1 Corinthians 7.35 about not laying restraint upon the Corinthians. Rather, Paul seems to be warning community members of the anxiety that can engulf both ways of life; as elsewhere in 1 Corinthians 7, his intention seems to be to temper ascetic tendencies.

1 Corinthians 7.35 also states that Paul wishes to promote good order and desires that the community wait upon the Lord without hindrance. His attempt to ensure that community members remain focused on the Lord and act in a seemly fashion, coupled with his desire to reduce anxiety, is frequently understood as Paul's effort to instil a sense of eschatological reservation within the Corinthian community – a sense of 'not yet'.[29] The eschatological language of 1 Corinthians 7 indicates that Paul believed that the world was on the verge of transformation, and that the celibacy of men and women was an important sign of this transformation. But Paul could not agree with members of the Corinthian community who seemed to have believed that the old universe had already been replaced with a world purely spiritual in nature (1 Cor. 4.8; 15.12) and who therefore sought to enact their spiritual perfection in a celibate way of life.[30] Paul understood the conditions of the old world as still somewhat binding to a certain extent, since the kingdom of God had not yet been perfectly realized. Ironically, immorality remained a real threat, even among those who attempted sexual abstinence as the route to spiritual perfection.

Paul's call for seemliness and undivided devotion to the Lord acts as an effective means of addressing the concerns of a

[29] On eschatological reservation see D. R. Cartlidge, '1 Corinthians 7 as a Foundation for a Christian Sex Ethic', *JR* 55 (1975) 220–34.

[30] The belief system of Paul's opponents in 1 Corinthians has often been described as 'realized eschatology'. See Wayne Meeks, 'The Image of Androgyne: Some uses of a Symbol in Earliest Christianity', *HR* 13 (1974) 202–3. The question of the identity of Paul's opponents is beyond the scope of this chapter, but see my discussion in 'Women Holy', 162–70. See also MacDonald, *No Male and Female*, 69–72, 110.

community living in a world on the brink of transformation. It enables him to balance a legitimate quest to live as though one were no longer fundamentally bound by the limits of the old world (1 Cor. 7.31), with the warning that the immorality which governed the old world could still lead community members astray (1 Cor. 7.2–7). It enables him to balance exhortations to both the married and the unmarried to remain as they are (1 Cor. 7.27), with a teaching which accepts that sometimes virgins and widows should marry (1 Cor. 7.36–40), and an acknowledgment that divorces do take place (1 Cor. 7.10–16). 1 Corinthians 7.35 serves to subordinate both the advice to 'remain as one is' and the identification of situations where this might not be possible, to the priority of undistracted devotion to the Lord. Promoting seemliness obviously acts as a means of discouraging the social disruption that might occur from abrupt changes in status and/or the adoption of a way of life which is not compatible with one's particular gifts; such disruption, no matter how sincere the intentions, could distract community members from their true focus on the Lord.

Because seemliness is so closely associated with the priority of undivided devotion to the Lord in 1 Corinthians 7.35, we should probe the meaning of this quality beyond its obvious role in avoiding social disruption. In fact by examining the importance Paul attributes to good order in this text, we will see that his focus on women in 1 Corinthians 7 involves more than the immediately apparent reason that they seem to have been especially enthusiastic proponents of ascetic teaching. As was the case with the earliest critics of early Christian women, exhortations in the early church concerning women were shaped not only by women's concrete actions, but also by the symbolic significance of their presence.

Whether one chooses to translate 'τὸ εὔσχημον' in 1 Corinthians 7.35 as 'seemliness' or as 'good order', it reveals a concern for propriety or social respectability.[31] A reflection of this

---

[31] Perhaps on account of a tendency to explain authorial intent in terms of religious doctrine, commentators frequently have failed to appreciate cultural concerns – in this case, a desire to promote seemliness. Recent social-scientific analysis of New Testament texts critiques such explanations which focus only on narrowly defined religious concerns and ignore cultural ones. For a broader definition of religion see for example, Malina, *New Testament World*, 27.

concern also is found in 1 Corinthians 7.36, where a cognate of 'εὐσχήμων' appears (cf. 1 Thess. 4.12; 1 Cor. 14.40). This is the text mentioned above where Paul gives instructions about the one who feels that he is not behaving properly (ἀσχημονεῖν) towards his virgin, and he recommends marriage if necessary (1 Cor. 7.36–8). The notoriously difficult problems of translating this text mean that we must evaluate the call for propriety in relation to various possible scenarios. If the 'father-daughter' translation of 1 Corinthians 7.36 is chosen, then Paul is acknowledging the pressures of social respectability on a household where a woman is passing the reasonable age of marriage.[32] If the 'engaged couple' translation is preferred,[33] the problem involves the incompatibility of unbridled desire (1 Cor. 7.36, 37) with the image of a pure *ekklesia* that needs to be projected to the outside world (cf. 1 Cor. 5.1). Similarly, if Paul has in mind spiritual marriages without physical union, then lapses or lack of self-control may lead one to become part once again of the immoral outside world. In Part 1 we considered evidence from the *Didache* suggesting that embarrassment for the church sometimes ensued from improprieties among lapsing celibate missionary couples.[34] Whatever the precise circumstances in view in 1 Corinthians 7.36–8, it is evident that the passage deals with the potent issues that arise when asceticism confronts the institution of marriage. In a family-centred society such as the first-century Mediterranean world, decisions to remain unmarried or to marry are influenced by group factors. This influence occurs to a greater extent than in modern western society with its emphasis on the individual's autonomy.[35] Controversy would inevitably result from the challenge an ascetic group would pose to the household and its head. For example, how would the

---

[32] On the involvement of parents in arranging marriages for their children in Greco-Roman society see Balsdon, *Roman Women*, 173–7; on the role of the paterfamilias in relation to his daughter see P. E. Corbett, *The Roman Law of Marriage* (Oxford: Clarendon, 1930) 1–6.

[33] On betrothal in the Roman world see Corbett, *Law of Marriage*, 1–23; Balsdon, *Roman Women*, 177–9; on betrothal and Augustan legislation see Pomeroy, *Goddesses*, 166.

[34] See *Did* 11.11 See discussion in Part 1, pp. 103–4. For a collection of evidence on spiritual marriages see Elizabeth Castelli, 'Virginity and its Meaning for Women's Sexuality in Early Christianity', *JFSR* 2 (1986) 61–88, esp. 80.

[35] See discussion of family-centredness by Mark McVann in Pilch and Malina (eds.), *Biblical Social Values and Their Meaning*, 70–3.

struggling celibate man explain his reluctance to marry a virgin to her non-believing father?

While Paul does not explicitly state in 1 Corinthians 7 that he is concerned about how the community's sexual or marriage practices will be perceived by outsiders, there are indications in 1 Corinthians and in other Pauline works that we should understand the desire in 1 Corinthians 7 to promote seemliness in this light. A useful comparative text to consider is 1 Corinthians 14.23–5, where Paul expresses worry that outsiders who watch the worship of the Corinthians and witness the confusion of tongues will conclude that members of the early church are mad rather than worshipping God. Scholars have suggested that tongues, like celibacy, may have been viewed as a potent sign of the community's perfected state in light of the arrival of the eschaton; hence, those who possessed the gift of tongues were inclined to adopt an elitist stance which Paul appears to be counterbalancing throughout 1 Corinthians 14.[36] One of the explanations Paul offers, in the hope of setting the priorities of the Corinthians straight, indirectly exposes us to a very early example of public opinion concerning the early church. Paul fears that outsiders will conclude that worshipping Corinthians are mad (μαίνομαι), and there seems to be no good reason for doubting that this impression was based on Paul's actual experiences in attempting to win the world. The book of Acts in fact recounts the reaction of the Roman procurator Festus to the Apostle's preaching as: 'Paul you are mad!' (Acts 26.24). The relationship between 1 Corinthians 14 and 1 Corinthians 7 is further reinforced by the conclusion to Paul's discussion of worship in 1 Corinthians 14.40, where he calls for all things to be done in a seemly manner (εὐσχημόνως) and in order. The same language appears in 1 Thessalonians 4.12 where Paul instructs community members to 'walk becomingly towards' (command the respect of) outsiders.

An examination of the concern for seemly behaviour in 1 Corinthians 7.35, in relation to other key Pauline texts where the same concern is expressed, reveals a correlation existing between seemly behaviour, the goal of evangelism, the church's encounter

---

[36] See Meeks, *Urban Christians*, 121; Yarbrough, *Not Like the Gentiles*, 118–20.

with public opinion, and an interest in social respectability. The discussion of the model of the conversionist sect at the beginning of this section highlighted the inevitable tension between social respectability and separation from the world that has been observed in sectarian groups with a mission to save the world. An understanding of this tension can help explain why a preference for celibacy becomes tempered by an acknowledgment of the need for caution when living on the margins of a world dominated by immorality. The broad effect of Paul's teaching in 1 Corinthians 7, with its special interest in the lives of unmarried women, is to accept celibacy as a potent sign of a transformed community, but also to warn that celibacy might not always be possible. There is a constraining of women's choices that results from Paul's teaching in 1 Corinthians 7. Presumably the father who experienced social pressure might require his virgin daughter (or the widowed or divorced daughter who remained under his control) to marry despite her wishes to the contrary.[37] Likewise, the woman who persisted in her determination to remain in the state in which she was called would need to sacrifice her freedom from worldly trouble, if the man to whom she was engaged was troubled by sexual desire. The Pauline movement was unavoidably caught up in a dialogue with a world where marriage arrangements were largely in the hands of men, and where the celibacy of women inevitably would come to challenge male prerogatives.[38] As numbers grew and time passed in the generations that followed the death of Paul, the increasing visibility of female celibates would cause greater concern in a church that was appearing more and more subversive to curious onlookers and learned critics. As we consider texts from the Deutero-Pauline authors and Apostolic Fathers we will witness greater circumspection in relation to the marriage-free life, a greater insistence on the importance of the believing woman's subjection to

---

[37] On the complicated question of Roman law on marriage in relation to the role of the father see Pomeroy, *Goddesses*, 150–63; S. B. Pomeroy, 'The Relationship of the Married Woman to her Blood Relatives in Rome,' *Ancient Society* 7 (1976) 215–27; David C. Verner, *The Household of God: The Social World of the Pastoral Epistles*, SBLDS 71 (Chico, Calif.: Scholars, 1983) 39–40; J. Carcopino, *Daily Life in Ancient Rome* (New Haven and London: Yale University, 1940) 76–100.

[38] On the power of husbands and fathers in marriage in the Greco-Roman world and the limited possibilities for female initiative see Clark, 'Roman Women', 193–212, esp. 205.

her husband, and a more pronounced association of early church women's lives with the desire to promote social respectability.

But before we treat the special concern for the behaviour of non-married women that occurs in 1 Timothy, we need to examine how Paul's focus on women in 1 Corinthians 7 is related to the values he holds as a Mediterranean male and the values shared by the members of the Corinthian community.[39] In order to accomplish this it is useful for us for the moment to set aside our sociological perspective with its interest in the construction of institutions (such as the development of the sect) and to draw from the findings of cultural anthropologists on human behaviour.[40] We will discover that our findings about how early church teachings on marriage and sexuality were shaped by the tension between social respectability and withdrawal from the world are complemented by a greater understanding of first and second-century societal expectations concerning the proper actions and qualities for human beings.

A focus on women in light of the values of honour and shame

The notoriously complicated text of 1 Corinthians 11.2–11 on veiling makes it clear that Paul was concerned over practices involving the abandonment of physical barriers that separated men from women.[41] That the consequences of these practices are

---

[39] In *Biblical Social Values and Their Meaning*, Pilch and Malina define the word 'value' as 'some general quality and direction of life that human beings are expected to embody in their behaviour. A value is a general, normative orientation of action in a social system. It is an emotionally anchored commitment to pursue and support certain directions or types of actions' (p.xiii).

[40] The perspectives of sociology and cultural anthropology (social anthropology in Britain) are closely related, so it often is difficult to distinguish between the two. See Cyril S. Rodd, 'Sociology and Social Anthropology' in R. J. Coggins & J. L. Houlden (eds.), *A Dictionary of Biblical Interpretation* (London: SCM, 1990) 635–9. John H. Elliott has recently commented on the distinction: 'Sociology focuses on interpersonal rather than intrapersonal phenomena, on groups rather than individuals. Sociologists, in contrast to anthropologists, tend to focus predominantly but not exclusively on complex, modern, industrial societies' (p. 134). See his definitions of anthropology and sociology in *What is Social-Scientific Criticism?* 127, 134. See also Tolbert, 'Social, Sociological and Anthropological Methods', 256–7.

[41] On how veils replicated the walls or barriers which spacially seclude women see Neyrey, 'What's Wrong With This Picture?', 80.

144

understood by Paul in terms of the values of honour and shame is made clear by the language he uses to describe what happens when men and women adopt inappropriate head covering. The man who prays or prophesies with his head covered 'shames' (καταισχύνει) his head. The woman who prays or prophesies with her head uncovered 'shames' (καταισχύνει) her head. The uncovered woman is like a shaved, shameful (αἰσχρός) woman, and should consequently be veiled (1 Cor. 11.4–6).[42]

I believe that whatever the precise shape of the events that led to 1 Corinthians 11.2–16, Paul's impassioned response must be understood in light of his obvious sensitivity to the public visibility of Christian ritual (cf. 1 Cor. 14.23–5).[43] One of the many issues that has puzzled scholars about this text is why it calls for a return to hierarchical patterns that had been transformed or abandoned in the family-centred setting of the house-church. While it is likely that the prayer and prophecy of women that Paul understands as being 'out of control' in Corinth takes place in the 'private' world of the house-church, 1 Corinthians 14 makes it clear that Paul understands the rituals of community gathering to be publicly visible, undoubtedly subject to the evaluations of curious neighbours, and circulated by means of gossip networks.[44] Paul's teaching must be understood as a response to behaviour which takes place on the boundary between the private and the public, the house-church, and the outside world.

In the gender-divided Greco-Roman society, a concern with boundaries often leads to attention on female deportment.

---

[42] On 1 Corinthians 11 reflecting the values of honour and shame see Plevnik, 'Honour/Shame', in Pilch and Malina (eds.), *Biblical Social Values*, 100.

[43] One might also consider 1 Corinthians 14.34–5 where Paul says that it is shameful (αἰσχρός) for women to speak in church. However, many scholars believe that these verses represent a marginal gloss, perhaps inserted to harmonize Paul's teaching with similar exhortation in 1 Timothy 2.11–12. Brief discussion of 1 Corinthians 14.35–6 will occur in the section on the Pastoral Epistles below. For a full discussion of the issues see Bassler, '1 Corinthians', 327–8; Wire, *Corinthian Women Prophets*, 149–52.

[44] A similar, though, not identical interpretation has been proposed by Wire in *Corinthian Women Prophets*, 183. On the notion of a 'gossip-network' see Neyrey, 'What's Wrong With This Picture', 81 where it is defined as 'a technical term used by anthropologists to describe the spread of information in a media-less world'. He refers to Deborah Jones, 'Gossip: Notes on Women's Oral Culture', *Women's Studies International Quarterly* 3 (1980) 193–8; Don Handelman, 'Gossip in Encounters: The Transmission of Information in a Bounded Social Setting', *Man* 8 (1973) 210–27.

Scholarly consensus is that, despite his deliberate attempt to make parallel statements about men and women (cf. 1 Cor. 7), in 1 Corinthians 11.2–16 Paul is primarily concerned with the behaviour of women. Paul's focus on women may have as much to do with the general concept that women in Mediterranean society embody community concern for reputation, as it does with their specific actions. In fact, the women's actions may have been based on ideas which Paul inspired, or with which Paul fundamentally agreed, concerning the transformation that occurs when one 'puts on Christ' (Gal. 3.28), even though he disagreed with the nature of the symbolic performance that occurred in the midst of prayer and prophecy.[45] Behaviour that might be judged by the outside world as shameful for women could dishonour men and bring disgrace on the whole community. With an understanding of the honour and shame syndrome in Mediterranean society, it becomes much easier to comprehend why a cultural concern for a loss of manliness becomes superimposed on a discussion of women removing their head covering in the midst of the *ekklesia*.

While scholars have explored a possible relationship between women's asceticism reflected in 1 Corinthians 7 and the activities of women during prayer and prophecy reflected in 1 Corinthians 11.2–16,[46] what interests us here is how values of honour and shame frame the exhortations in both texts. Our brief examination of 1 Corinthians 11.2–16 enables us to see what is somewhat less explicit in 1 Corinthians 7. The general concern with good order in 1 Corinthians 7.35 and with the case of the man who is not behaving in a seemly manner towards his virgin in 1 Corinthians 7.36 broadly reflect the values of honour and shame.[47] We have

---

[45] It is beyond the scope of this study to discuss in detail the women's theological position 1 Corinthians 11.2–16 or other complicated issues related to the text. Two very good recent discussions are Wire, *Corinthian Women Prophets*, 116–34; Kraemer, *Her Share*, 146–9.

[46] See for example, MacDonald, 'Women Holy', 162–73; Wire, *Corinthian Women Prophets*, 183.

[47] Malina and Neyrey have argued that we should relate the values of honour and shame in the New Testament to a variety of concepts: '*honour*: nouns such as glory, blamelessness, repute, fame, and verbs such as to honour, to glorify, to spread the fame of, to choose, to find acceptable, to be pleased with; *shame*: nouns such as disgrace, and dishonour, and verbs such as to shame, to be ashamed, to feel ashamed' See 'Honour and Shame in Luke-Acts', 46. On terms for honour and shame in 1 Corinthians see Wire, *Corinthian Women Prophets*, 19–21.

seen that the desire to promote seemliness in 1 Corinthians 7 is related to the conferral of public esteem upon the community; the honour of the community in relation to the outside world is at stake. The attempt to ensure that the man behaves in a proper manner towards his virgin offers us an example of how the values of honour and shame are enacted at the level of community relations. 1 Corinthians 7.36 can be translated as: 'if anyone thinks that he is behaving dishonourably (ἀσχημονέω)[48] towards his virgin', or in other words, 'if anyone thinks he is "shaming" his virgin'. While, as noted above, it may be impossible to determine the precise circumstances which led to Paul's response in this text, an examination of the text in light of the use of a cognate of the verb 'ἀσχημονέω' and other honour/shame language in 1 Corinthians 12.23–4 will lead to a greater appreciation of what is at stake.

In the midst of his argument in 1 Corinthians 12 in which he is trying to inspire proper attitudes towards charismatic gifts and relations between community members that reflect the harmonious workings of the body, Paul speaks of the need to protect shameful parts of the body. Dishonourable (ἀτιμότερα) parts require investment of greater honour (τιμή) and unseemly parts (ἀσχήμων) need to be treated with a seemliness (εὐσχημοσύνη), which the more seemly (εὐσχήμων) parts do not require (1 Cor. 12.23–4; cf. Rom. 1.27). Jerome Neyrey sees here an example of a characteristic link in biblical texts between shame and nudity. In the ancient Mediterranean world the public nudity of women was a strong conveyor of shame: it was an obvious sign that their chastity had been compromised.[49] The exposure of the unveiled woman in 1 Corinthians 11 immediately comes to mind. But such considerations probably also shape the teaching on virgins in 1 Corinthians 7. Whatever the precise nature of the man's improper or dishonourable actions (whether he be fiancé, father, or spiritual spouse) in 1 Corinthians 7.36, he is clearly in danger of forfeiting his responsibilities as an honourable community member towards the woman. Somehow the virgin's chastity is threatened. Instead of

---

[48] See BAGD 119.
[49] See Jerome H. Neyrey, 'Nudity', in Pilch and Malina (eds.), *Biblical Social Values*, 120.

protecting his most valuable resource he is in danger of stripping her naked, exposing her tauntingly to the male members of the community and, ultimately, to the world outside. If her virtue is violated (even against her wishes) she will be reduced to the level of the adulteress.

Given that so much attention has been devoted in this chapter to understanding Paul's special focus in 1 Corinthians 7 on the lives of unmarried women and with identifying indications of women's interest in ascetic teaching, it is surprising that we are still confronted with such a blatant endorsement of male prerogatives regarding marriage arrangements (1 Cor. 7.36; cf. 1 Cor. 7.28).[50] Paul's teaching recognizes the male role of defender of the chastity of women and protector of this most precious resource, in a manner consistent with the classic Mediterranean model of honour and shame. The importance of these values in the Corinthian context is made clear by the Corinthian slogan which underlines male initiative and the apparently passive role of the woman whose chastity must be safeguarded against male sexuality: 'It is well for a man not to touch a woman' (1 Cor. 7.1). We have seen that Paul qualifies this statement in order to prevent community members from adopting a stance of ascetic absolutism, but we should also consider how this statement reflects the cultural values Paul shares with the members of the community and, to some degree, with Greco-Roman society in general. Given a first-century cultural setting, it is probable that the celibate efforts of women, traditionally subordinate members of the household, would require the blessing of males if the community was to continue as a mixed group. But we should not think that such arrangements preclude the possibility that the impulse for celibacy often originated with women. As noted above, a close reading of the text reveals two things: interruptions in rhetorical parallels which express special concerns with female behaviour, and indications that Paul expected to be contradicted by the women in the community. Behind 1 Corinthians 7.36–8 (if the 'engaged couple' translation is preferred) may be the voice of a woman who is reminding a man that

---

[50] On Paul acknowledging male authority see Barrett, *1 Corinthians*, 176; see also discussion in Wire, *Corinthian Women Prophets*, 88–9.

she is doing far more for his sanctity by remaining his virgin than by becoming his bride. In response to the man's hesitancy, Paul cautions that if there is danger that he will shame his virgin – violate her virtue – then he is free to marry. If a man is to marry a woman at all, she should undoubtedly be the pure vessel of 1 Thessalonians 4.4: a wife taken in holiness and honour (τιμή), not in the passion of lust like the pagans who do not know God.

1 Corinthians 7 reveals patterns of behaviour that are in keeping with the honour and shame syndrome that has been observed in Mediterranean societies, both modern and ancient. The Corinthian slogan 'it is well for a man not to touch a woman' clearly relates the man's standing in the community to the chastity of the woman. Her sexual purity becomes inextricably linked with his sanctity, and it is the means by which honour and shame are maintained.[51] The correspondence between textual evidence and the honour/shame model developed from anthropological studies is significant, but even more interesting is how the values of honour and shame are enacted within the setting of first-century Pauline Christianity. In fact, our attempt to see what is particular about the Corinthian context is in keeping with recent methodological reflection about honour and shame among anthropologists which calls for attention to rich ethnographic diversity.[52]

In order to appreciate fully how the Corinthian values are played out at the level of community interaction, we should recall the methodological issues discussed at the beginning of this book about power and authority, and the gender division in Mediterranean society in terms of public and private space. First, although the Corinthian slogan and Paul's teaching in 1 Corinthians 7 make it clear that authority structures which place

---

[51] John J. Pilch defines purity as 'a means value because it facilitates the realization of the core values of honour and shame'. See 'Purity', in Pilch and Malina (eds.), *Biblical Social Values*, 151.

[52] There are various issues at stake here: the degree to which honour and shame are linked, whether these concepts are always in opposition, and the association of honour with men and shame with women. See Gilmore, 'Introduction: The Shame of Dishonour', 5–8; Stanley Brandes, 'Reflections on Honour and Shame in the Mediterranean', in Gilmore (ed.), *Honour and Shame*, 122–3; J. G. Peristiany and Julian Pitt-Rivers, 'Introduction', in Peristiany and Pitt-Rivers (eds.), *Honour and Grace in Anthropology* (Cambridge University Press, 1992) 6; Moxnes, 'Honour, Shame, and the Outside World', 209.

ultimate authority for marriage arrangements in the hands of men are as much at work in the church community as they are in society at large, we must be cautious about concluding that women lack power. Rather, through complying with a system that places that much importance on women's sexual purity, female community members actually may attain influence. They may exercise power by pressing even harder for stricter protection of their chastity. Moreover, they may celebrate the purity of their bodies as the best representation of the sanctity of the community and the best protection against pollution from the immoral world outside. They may even, to Paul's dismay, make special claims about possessing the Spirit of God (1 Cor. 7.40).

The connection between the sanctity of women and corporate identity is a phenomenon which has frequently been observed by anthropologists. Carol Delaney, in discussing how endogamy practices (marriage within the group) function to ensure control of female chastity in a Turkish village, notes:

Because of the practice of endogamy for generations, villagers see the village as an interrelated and integrated group, as one body in relation to all others and symbolically female. Access to it is limited and under surveillance. The village, like a woman, is perceived as *kapalı* (closed, covered) and *temiz* (clean and pure), as opposed to the cities (as well as Europe and America) which are *açik* (open), *pis* (dirty) and *bulasik* (tainted, contaminated). Those who protect and represent the honour and integrity of the village are men. In other words, the notions of honour and shame, grounded in the sexual nature of male and female, also apply to the way the house, village, and even the nation are perceived. A transgression against the boundaries of any of these culturally discrete but homologous entities is an affront to the sense of honour of those whose duty it is to protect them.[53]

The special language to describe the virgins or unmarried women as holy in body and spirit in 1 Corinthians 7, and other indications of a strong interest in female purity in the community, point towards the symbolic significance of the chastity of women as an expression of corporate identity. Delaney's remarks about how the female body becomes a symbol for a village which stands in oppo-

---

[53] Carol Delaney, 'Seeds of Honour, Fields of Shame', in Gilmore (ed.), *Honour and Shame*, 44.

sition to the evil world, calls to mind the sectarian response exhibited by Pauline Christianity.[54] In the Corinthian community the woman's body is a powerful indicator of what is wrong with a tainted society. Although Paul aims to moderate this response in 1 Corinthians 7, the woman who is not to be touched may offer an apt representation of the process of leaving an immoral world behind. But, as I noted in the introductory discussion of the gendered division between public and private space in Mediterranean society, when women become symbolically associated with a 'closed' space such as a house, it is important not to exaggerate the static nature of their lives. Women's bodies may symbolize the closed space that male honour must defend in relation to the wide-open public world, but their bodies also represent the boundaries that mark the transition from inside to outside. This is especially clearly visible in the use of the symbol of 'the woman church' (cf. Eph. 5.26–7), a subject which will be explored in Part 3. In the case of Pauline Christianity, the attempt to demarcate these boundaries is always to a certain extent elusive, for the community is constantly reaching out to embrace the world outside. Even the pure church wife may remain dangerously close to the immoral world outside by her marriage to the unbeliever, if by doing so, he too may be brought into the holy community (1 Cor. 7.12–16).

It is interesting to observe how the values of honour and shame are enacted in a community which is characterized by an interest in evangelism and a fervent eschatological expectation. There is clearly a connection between the focus on celibate women in 1 Corinthians 7 and the chastity of women as the means by which shame (concern for reputation) is demonstrated in the Mediterranean world. But the critique of the value of family-centredness and of the need for procreation (implicit in the asceticism encouraged in 1 Cor. 7) means that there is also a sense in which the old basis for honour is rejected in favour of a new standard.[55]

---

[54] How the honour and shame syndrome defines boundaries between insiders and outsiders in Pauline Christianity has also been discussed by Halvor Moxnes, but his interests differ somewhat from mine here. See 'Honour, Shame and the Outside World', 215.

[55] On family-centredness as a part of honour see McVann, 'Family-Centredness', in Pilch and Malina (eds.), *Biblical Social Values*, 70–1; on new standards for honour in Paul's teaching see Plevnik, 'Honour/Shame', in Pilch and Malina (eds.), *Biblical Social Values*, 99–100.

The connection drawn by Delaney between male attitudes to individual female bodies and the role of men in protecting and representing the honour and integrity of the (symbolically female) village receives important qualification in Corinth. This is clearly visible in the exhortation concerning the widow (1 Cor. 7.39–40). By approving of the widow's choice to remain unmarried, Paul is sanctioning a life where the woman is removed from the immediate protection of a male and is responsible for representing her own honour and the honour of her community to the outside world. Without a male guardian, however, the widow risks being viewed as shameless. Like divorcées, widows who remain unmarried find themselves in a precarious position; they are viewed 'more like males than females, therefore sexually predatory, aggressive, hence dangerous'.[56] The church seems to have offered a haven to such vulnerable women (Acts 6.1; 1 Tim. 5.16). As will be discussed further below, by legislating remarriage, Roman law sought to ensure the re-integration of women into the normal social structures of the household. Yet, there were unmarried women who were free of male tutelage, who were in control of significant economic resources and who had considerable influence in societal affairs in the Greco-Roman world.[57] What is remarkable about Paul's exhortation in 1 Corinthians 7.39 is that it is so unqualified; it does not limit the choice to remain unmarried only to widows of a certain age, with a certain number of progeny or of a certain economic stature. At a later date in the Pauline movement, the approach to such honourable women would be far more cautious (cf. 1 Tim. 5.3–16).

To give unmarried women in the community responsibility for defending their own honour and the honour of the community is a remarkable gesture within the context of first-century society. In a subsequent section we will make an effort to gain a greater understanding of how public reaction would have shaped the lives of the women holy in body and spirit who, unprotected by fathers and husbands, stood as representatives of the community. We will recall what was said about early Christian women by the

---

[56] Malina and Neyrey, 'Honour and Shame in Luke-Acts', 44.
[57] See discussion in McNamara, *A New Song*, 59.

earliest critics of Christianity and will strive for a better understanding of how women who remained unmarried would have
fared in Greco-Roman society. But at this point it is important to
try to understand the encounter between public opinion and a
community which exhibits transformed values of honour and
shame on the basis of the internal evidence in 1 Corinthians. By
approaching this text with two social-scientific models we have
been able to appreciate the importance of public opinion for the
church community. To be able to see the Mediterranean values of
honour and shame at work in 1 Corinthians, with their close association to sexuality and gender distinctions, sheds light on this
text's special focus on women. Given the cultural context of Paul's
churches we would expect a special interest in chastity of women
since it is the women of the community who embody concern for
reputation. If the community is under scrutiny, we would expect
that the chastity of women would be guarded and scrutinized
ever more closely. I believe that 1 Corinthians gives us clear indications that, even at this early stage of community development,
the values of honour and shame are taking on a heightened
importance because of expressions of public opinion. We have
seen that Paul is clearly worried about how outsiders will view the
rituals of the community; he states explicitly that he fears that
outsiders will conclude that the Corinthians are mad! Moreover,
the special concern for the behaviour of women in 1 Corinthians
7 and 11 probably indicates that there have been disapproving
expressions of public opinion. At the very least, we may say that
Paul is cautious with respect to the behaviour of women that
might lead to misunderstanding and be judged negatively by the
public.

There is a great deal of theoretical usefulness to be gained by
drawing upon both the honour/shame model from cultural
anthropology and the model of the conversionist religious sect
from sociology of religion for analysing Paul's teaching concerning
unmarried women. Both these models address the issue of community reaction to public opinion, with the conversionist sect
model giving us insight into the tensions related to the place of a
religious group within a broad societal context, and the honour
and shame model allowing for more intense focus on the nature of

specific community interaction. By drawing upon the sociological model of the conversionist sect we are able to see what happens when a community's desire to escape from an evil world is combined with a strong interest in evangelism and a concomitant concern with public opinion. The presence of the values of honour and shame in the community means that there is a strong inclination to communicate concern for reputation by presenting the women of the community as the embodiments of its shame. Under the scrutiny of hostile eyes there is a tendency for the woman to remain indoors, be shrouded by veils, and to guard her chastity carefully. The community remains private, meets discreetly in the household, and makes claims concerning exclusivity. But a strong interest in winning the world for Christ means that community members cannot remain hidden for very long and the doors of the house are constantly opening. The urgency of life in a world whose form is quickly passing away means that the celibate woman, a potent symbol of the transformation, is allowed to stand dangerously close to the boundary between the church and the world. The protection of her reputation is to a certain extent guaranteed by the private nature of daily interactions in a household setting. But she is never only associated with the private world of her own house and house-church, for she must always have arms outstretched towards the world outside. The teaching she receives from community leaders includes an ambiguous mix of elements of inward and outward orientation, and she is called to transform her life on the basis of the results of the fiery encounter between community priorities and cultural values. As we shall see, when the public opinion that judges her and her community heats up, her life will become more dangerous, more circumscribed, but on occasion, also more powerful as she becomes an instrument of evangelization.

1 Timothy 5.3–16 – second-century celibate women under public scrutiny

The Pastoral Epistles of 1 Timothy, 2 Timothy, and Titus offer evidence that a strong desire to save the world was carried into the early decades of the second century by Pauline Christianity (e.g. 1

Tim. 2.1–4; Tit. 2.11; Tit. 3.1–2).[58] In fact, these documents, probably written by an unknown author who desired to bring Paul's
authority to bear upon the changed circumstances of church life,
reflect the life of a community where the balance between isolation and engagement of the world has shifted towards greater
engagement. In these texts we find exhortation to avoid false teachers and those responsible for division in the community, who both
may be seen as representatives of the unbelieving world. However,
in the Pastorals (cf. Tit. 1.10–16; 2 Tim. 3.1–9; 1 Tim. 5.8; Tit.
3.10), there is a virtual absence of the kind of encouragement
towards separation from past associations and patterns of life that
is visible in Paul's letters.[59] The conversionist sect model predicts
that a response of such openness will precipitate new levels of institutionalization in community life, and increased institutionalization of community roles is indeed reflected in the Pastoral Epistles.
In comparison to earlier Pauline writings, the Pastorals are striking
for the evidence they provide for established church offices (e.g.
1 Tim. 3.1–7).[60] In addition, they clearly display an effort to establish rules to govern the lives of women in the community, to limit
their involvement in certain ministerial roles, and to ensure that
they remain faithful to their duties as wives in a Greco-Roman
household (1 Tim. 2.11–15; 1 Tim. 5.3–15; Tit. 2.1–8). The community's experience of negative expressions of public opinion may
have been a catalyst in creating conditions where accommodation
to the standards of the world accompanied a tightening of church
structures. The critics of the early church community apparently
had a great deal to say about early Christian women.

It is interesting to compare Paul's concern in 1 Corinthians
14.23–5 about Corinthian Christian ritual leading to damage of
the community's reputation with 1 Timothy 3.7, where the author
instructs that the bishop must be 'well thought of by outsiders'
(μαρτυρίαν καλὴν ἔχειν ἀπὸ; τῶν ἔξωθεν) or he may fall into

---

[58] I have discussed the general attitude of openness towards Greco-Roman society and
interest in evangelism exhibited by the Pastoral Epistles at length in *Pauline Churches*,
167–70. On dating the Pastorals and the issue of pseudonymity see Joanna Dewey,
'1 Timothy', in Newsom and Ringe (eds.), *Women's Bible Commentary*, 353.

[59] MacDonald, *Pauline Churches*, 165–6.

[60] On the transformed nature of the community of the Pastorals and the process of institutionalization in the Pauline movement, ibid., 163–5.

reproach (ὀνειδισμὸν) and the 'snare of the devil' or slanderer (παγίδα τοῦ διαβόλου). Both 1 Corinthians 14.23–5 and 1 Timothy 3.7 exhibit a concern for social respectability; the difference between the texts lies primarily in the fact that Paul expresses concern in relation to particular community problems, whereas the author of the Pastorals sets in place a general social structure designed to prevent mishaps from occurring. The exhortation to choose a leader who has won the approval of outsiders seems a curious priority, but it becomes more understandable when one considers it in light of the cultural value of honour (cf. 1 Tim. 5.10; 1 Clem. 44.3). The bishop who is viewed as honourable by outsiders defends the honour of the community in relation to the external world. His role becomes especially important if the community is being challenged and scrutinized. 1 Timothy 3.6–7 in fact refers to the danger of being shamed through the agency of a slanderer (διάβολος). Although this term may also be rendered as 'devil' (cf. 2 Tim. 2.26), such a translation blurs the relationship between evil expressed as the work of the devil and the disaster caused by the actions of human slanderers (cf. 1 Tim. 3.11; 2 Tim. 3.3).[61] The reference to reviling or reproach also highlights the fear of being shamed and the ruination of reputation.

If we examine the injunctions about church offices in the Pastorals, norms associated with the household repeatedly emerge. Qualifications for church officials include a strong interest in household or family relationships (1 Tim. 3.2, 4–5; 3.11–12; 5.4; Tit. 1.6). There is a connection between traditional roles in the household and roles in the church which are modelled on the household. The man chosen as bishop will only be able to care properly for God's church if he knows how to manage his own household well (1 Tim. 3.4). The church is referred to as the household of God (1 Tim. 3.15).[62] The close association of church offices with traditional household roles, coupled with the obvious link

---

[61] See ibid., 167 where I respond to Dibelius/Conzelmann's preference of the translation of 'devil' in both 1 Timothy 3.6 and 3.7. See Dibelius and Conzelmann, *The Pastoral Epistles*, 54.

[62] On the close association between the development of ministerial roles and the household in the Pastoral Epistles, the work of David Verner is especially useful. See *Household of God*, 83–111, 147–60.

between the nature of the household and church identity, calls to mind the male role as protector of honour both in the household and the house-church discussed previously. The bishop is leader of a community in danger of experiencing slander, and as the head of this household he has the crucial role of embodying its standing in society. In light of language which suggests hostile reaction to the church, the strong endorsement of traditional manly virtues[63] we see in 1 Timothy 3.1–7 are an indication that the male leader's protective role involves a strong defence. In order to gain a sense of why such a defensive stance was seen as necessary, we should consider 1 Timothy 5.3–16. It, like 1 Timothy 3.1–7, reflects a heightened concern for the honour of the community, but it also offers a clear indication of what those who wished to shame the community were saying.

1 Timothy 5.11–15 offers valuable insight into the nature of public opinion concerning the early Christians. Here, community members are told to refuse to enrol younger widows in the office of widows.[64] There are two main reasons offered for this. First, they are described as having violated their 'first pledge' when they desire to marry (1 Tim. 5.11–12). This pledge was likely a celibacy oath taken when widows were first enrolled in the order.[65] That more than a simple desire to marry was sometimes involved is suggested by the announcement that some young widows have already followed Satan (1 Tim. 5.15). Secondly, we are told that some young widows are idle gossips and busybodies. They are gadabouts: they go from house to house saying what should not be said (1 Tim. 5.13). They are perhaps contributing to rumours about the early church by spreading information which is meant to remain inside the house-church.

There is a remarkable correspondence between the depiction in the Pastoral Epistles of inappropriate behaviour of young early

---

63 We should not assume, as has often been done in the past, that the inclusion of traditional virtues in exhortations means that the content is not relevant for current situations of the community. See my discussion in *Pauline Churches*, 160–3. See also Verner, *Household of God*, 112–25.

64 On the Pastoral Epistles offering evidence for an official order of widows which includes ministerial roles in the community see Verner, *Household of God*, 163–5; Thurston, *The Widows*, 36–55.   65 Verner, *Household of God*, 165.

church widows and what we discovered during our survey of outsiders' opinions concerning early church women in the second century. Lucius Apuleius' tale of the wife who sneaks outside of the house at night with seditious and immoral intentions comes immediately to mind. She is depicted as neglectful of household duties and extravagant in expenses. Similarly, a certain amount of economic security is implied in the Pastorals' charge that the young widows are idle! Celsus' description of the clandestine behaviour of early Christians in households and women's quarters is in keeping with what we hear of the roamings of the young widows in the Pastoral Epistles. While the author of the Pastorals depicts the visits as frivolous and lacking in ministerial purpose, we should not assume that the young widows themselves understood their activities this way.

Through their deeds, the widows may have confirmed the suspicion of critics that early Christianity largely involved female initiative. The fact that it is the behaviour of women who have some type of ministry in the community[66] which is censured by the deutero-Pauline author is also interesting to consider, in light of what we know of pagan impressions of early Christian women. With respect to both the accounts of early Christianity by Pliny and by Lucian of Samosata considered in Part 1, we discussed the visibility of female ministers in early Christianity. Pliny organized the interrogation and torture of two female slave ministers who had come to his attention. From Lucian of Samosata we hear of the visits of widows to imprisoned Christians.

1 Timothy 5.14 confirms that the description of the young widows as gadabouts and busybodies in 1 Timothy 5.13 not only expresses an internal impression of certain community members, but also is tied to the community's experience of public opinion. Here, the author of the Pastorals offers a solution to the problem of the inappropriate behaviour of young widows: they are to marry and assume traditional responsibilities in the household. Consequently, the adversary (ἀντικείμενος) will have no reason to contribute to the reviling or shaming (λοιδορία) of the community.

---

[66] It is difficult to determine precisely the type of ministry undertaken by the women who were part of the 'order of widows' in the early second century CE. This issue will be discussed in Part 3.

The reference to young widows already following Satan in 1 Timothy 5.15, which comes after the reference to the contact with an adversary (cf. 1 Cor. 16.9; Phil. 1.28), stresses the close connection between being attacked by an earthly opponent and the evil supernatural powers that grip the unbelieving world. Whatever the precise nature of the events that shape the lives of the young widows, the author of the Pastorals feels that they are causing these women to transfer their allegiance outside the church. The term for reviling (λοιδορία) and its cognates are employed in the New Testament to refer to an aggressive challenge (cf. 1 Pet. 2.23; 3.9; Jn 9.28; Acts 23.4; 1 Cor. 4.12). What is at stake is the shaming of the community by an external opponent, and this is an attack that seriously threatens the bonds of membership. The fear expressed here is the same as that in the exhortation concerning the selection of the bishop in 1 Timothy 3.7: it relates to the slander of the community by outsiders. The defensive strategy includes strong male leadership and exemplary behaviour of women in the household. Men protect honour, and women embody shame.

As I discussed in Part 1, it is quite common to find early Christian authors expressing criticism of internal factional groups in language and concepts drawn from conflicts between early church members and non-believers. In the case of the Pastoral Epistles it seems that what outsiders are saying about early Christian women is being internalized and transformed into a teaching about the behaviour of women. Such a phenomenon may, of course, not be a conscious process. However, it is one that is clearly observable in the Pastorals, especially when we consider the more tightly controlled behaviour of celibate women in comparison to the early stages of the Pauline movement. What we see in the Pastoral Epistles amounts to a reapplication in Pauline churches of previously relaxed social norms concerning women's behaviour in the household and in religion.

While the author of the Pastorals explicitly links the dangers of the young widows gadding about with the reviling of an external opponent, there also is good reason to suspect that the author understands the behaviour of the young widows as originating in a teaching which has penetrated to the heart of the community. The effect of 1 Timothy 5.3–16 is to encourage the remarriage of most widows: only widows sixty years and over who have been the wife of one husband are eligible to be enrolled in the office of widows (1 Tim. 5.9). To a far greater extent than Paul, the author of the Pastorals aims to restrict the number of women who remain celibate. This circumscription of the role of widows in the church is probably related to the ascetic false teaching condemned by the author of the Pastorals. False teachers are said to forbid marriage and enjoin abstinence from foods which God created to be received with thanksgiving (1 Tim. 4.3).[67] 2 Timothy 3.6 enables us to draw a firm connection between the false teaching that is threatening the community and the activities of church women. Among the false teachers are those who creep into households and capture 'silly women' (γυναικάρια) who are burdened by sin, and are being led by various lusts. These women are further depicted as being intellectually weak: capable of being swayed by anybody, they can never arrive at a knowledge of the truth. As in 1 Timothy 5.13 we have here references to clandestine movement between houses, and illegitimate activity taking place in the private domain. But, perhaps to an even greater extent than with what is said about the roving widows in 1 Timothy 5.13, in 2 Timothy 3.6 we have correspondence between general opinion about the effect of illegitimate religion on Greco-Roman women and church teaching concerning the inappropriate religious inclinations of women. Just as Greco-Roman women were understood as vulnerable to the dubious tactics of early Christian teaching, church women are depicted as vulnerable to the despicable tactics of false teachers who are described not only as conceited and lovers of money, but interestingly, also as slanderers (διάβολοι) (2 Tim. 3.2–3).

A final text that links women with false teaching and reflects popular notions of female vice is 1 Timothy 4.7. In this text community members are instructed to avoid profane and 'old-woman-ish' (γραώδεις) tales. Although the Greek term has often been translated innocuously as 'silly', some scholars are now in favour of preserving a more literal translation, suggesting that the Pastoral Epistles are written in response to the stories told by old women or

---

[67] On the nature of the false teaching threatening the community see my discussion in *Pauline Churches*, 178–9.

widows, stories such as those contained in the *Acts of Paul and Thecla*.[68] Derogatory references to old women and their story-telling were found among the pagan impressions collected at the beginning of this book. It was with a certain amount of jeering that Lucian of Samosata referred to the 'old women called widows' waiting near the prison of the Christian. The story-telling of early Christian women also emerged as an important jibe in the work of Celsus. Mary Magdalene was depicted as the creator of the fantastic tale of the resurrection. But Celsus also dismissed Christian beliefs in general by comparing them to the efforts of 'an old woman who sings a story to lull a little child to sleep'.[69]

While there are several texts indicating that unmarried early church women figured in the intersecting problems of false teaching and criticism of the church by outsiders, it is important not to rule out the involvement of men in the tangled circumstances of community life. In fact, the passage which speaks about the infiltration of false teachers into households to capture weak women suggests male initiative (2 Timothy 3.6–9). But as I argued with respect to 1 Corinthians 7, given the importance of the cultural values of honour and shame and the importance of female chastity in maintaining those values in the ancient Mediterranean context, it is probable that among the false teachers denounced by the author of the Pastorals were men who understood female celibacy as a special reflection of their own identity. The initiative of the young widows who travelled from house to house may have been bolstered by men who saw in young celibate women a vivid representation of their own male status in a transformed community. While it is impossible to draw a straightforward connection between the situation reflected in the Pastoral Epistles and that reflected in 1 Corinthians, there is much to suggest a general correlation. Like 1 Corinthians 7, 1 Timothy 5.11–15 reveals strong ascetic tendencies among women, refers to the problem of

---

68 The relationship between the *Acts of Paul and Thecla* and the Pastoral Epistles is discussed below. The foundational work on the subject is by Dennis R. MacDonald, *The Legend and the Apostle*; see 'The Pastoral Epistles Against "Old-Wives' Tales"', 54–77; 'Introduction', 13–15. See also Virginia Burrus, *Chastity as Autonomy: Women in the Stories of the Apocryphal Acts* (Lewiston/Queenston: Edwin Mellen, 1987) 68–72. On the term 'old-womanish' see Dibelius/Conzelmann, *Pastoral Epistles*, 68. 69 *C. Cels.* 6.34; cf. *C. Cels.* 4.36.

misguided ascetic efforts leading to immorality, and reveals an interest in social respectability. Moreover, as with the Corinthian letter, in the Pastorals we find evidence to suggest that ascetic tendencies were related to the belief that one had already transcended the boundaries of the world; false teachers proclaimed that the resurrection had already happened (2 Tim. 2.18; cf. 1 Cor. 4.8; 1 Cor. 15.12).[70]

We have seen that recognizing the influence of the cultural values of honour and shame in Paul's world sheds light on the special focus on women in 1 Corinthians 7. At times, such as is the case with respect to marriage of one's virgin (1 Cor. 7.36), texts mirror traditional values. Aspects of the Apostle's teaching in 1 Corinthians 7, however, also point to notions of honour and shame that have been transformed with respect to society at large. The usual means of protecting honour in the household and community has to a certain extent been abandoned under Paul's leadership. While men continue to view chaste women as a special reflection of the shame of household and community, they no longer seek to ensure that the chastity of women is guaranteed only in light of marriage (by means of the male guardianship of virgin daughters before marriage or of faithful brides married once or several times). There is now an ideal of female chastity that exists outside of marriage. Widows in particular are recognized as having a choice as to whether or not to remarry, and they are made responsible for protecting their own honour and demonstrating it to the community (1 Cor. 7.39–40).

In the Pastoral Epistles there is a shift back towards traditional patterns for maintaining values of honour and shame. Only widows who are well past the child-bearing age may become members of the order of widows (1 Tim. 5.9). There are obviously many widows who are turning to the community for support, but the author of the Pastorals seeks to ensure that as many as possible are supported by their own families (1 Tim. 5.3–8, 16). The community is to honour (τίμα) widows who are real widows (1 Tim. 5.3). Real widows are women who are utterly dependent on the

---

[70] On the affinity between this kind of teaching and later gnostic systems see MacDonald, *Pauline Churches*, 178–9.

church for support, and to honour them means to help them in their need.[71] But there is also a sense in which honouring these women means conferring respect on women who exemplify model piety and feminine virtue. In contrast to the wife who was wasteful in sumptuous expenses satirized by Lucius Apuleius, they are not self-indulgent (1 Tim. 5.6). Like the bishop exhorted in 1 Timothy 3.2, they are above reproach (ἀνεπίλημπτος); they live honourable lives which are exemplary even by the standards of the most demanding public scrutiny. Likewise, the women who are members of the order of widows and who seem to be a distinct group from the 'real widows' (but who nevertheless may have included some of these needy women)[72] are well-attested (μαρτυρέω) for their good deeds which include such home-based virtues as hospitality, bringing up children, and relief of suffering (cf. Tit. 2.4–5). The focus is once again on the public demonstration of the fine reputation of these women. In short, language reflecting the values of honour and shame abounds in 1 Timothy 5.3–16.

Elsewhere in the Pastorals where women are in view, we also see interest in maintaining these values. Both the reference to women who may be either wives of deacons or female ministers in 1 Timothy 3.11, and the exhortation to older women in Titus 2.3 include the command that these women must not be slanderers (διαβόλους). Titus 2.4–5 is especially interesting to consider as an expression of how older women may protect the reputation of the community. They are to teach the younger women to be model wives and mothers, and be subject to their husbands in order that the word of God not be blasphemed (βλασφημῆται). In this way the community's honour will not be defamed (cf. 1 Tim. 6.1). Here, it is clear that a very important responsibility is being given to older women. The guidance they are to give to younger women is in keeping with the roles recommended for the younger widows in 1 Timothy 5.14 who, in the author's opinion, have already contributed to the defamation of the community on account of their behaviour.

---

[71] See Verner, *Household of God*, 161.
[72] See discussion in MacDonald, *Pauline Churches*, 184–6.

The encouragement of women's traditional household roles also is central to the infamous call for women's submission in 1 Timothy 2.11–15, which culminates in the pronouncement that a woman will be saved by her childbearing. In this text, concerns about the public visibility of women are intertwined with definitions of what constitutes female religiosity. Men and women are assigned appropriate roles for ritual settings involving prayer and teaching. The prohibition in 1 Timothy 2.12 against women teaching is especially intriguing, given the fact that teaching has a very public dimension in the Pastoral Epistles.[73] Gender distinctions involving public and private space clearly are in view. The silence and modest attire of women act as an appropriate barrier between honourable men and chaste women during attention-drawing acts of worship. But what is appropriate during ritual in the household of God is inseparable from what takes place in marriage (cf. 1 Cor. 14.34–5). The worshipping woman's reverence is defined by her subordinate status in the household and role as a child bearer. It is interesting to consider how similar lines of thought operate in 1 Corinthians 14.34–5, a text which many scholars believe was not composed by Paul but by a later interpolator in order to bring the teaching in 1 Corinthians in harmony with 1 Timothy.[74] Here, in the midst of concerns about ritual, we have a call for women to remain silent and to ask questions of their husbands at home (in private). The text culminates in a proclamation that is significant when one is aware of the importance of the division between private and public as a means of maintaining the values of honour and shame: It is shameful (αἰσχρόν) for a woman to speak in church!

By considering evidence for the influence of the values of honour and shame in early Christianity, we have been able to trace a shift in perspective concerning unmarried women from Paul's day to the time of the Pastoral Epistles. We have noted that both the presence of strongly ascetic teaching in the community and increasing public scrutiny were catalysts for this change of per-

[73] See discussion in Part 1, pp. 62–4.
[74] See Bassler, '1 Corinthians', in Newsom and Ringe (eds.), *Women's Bible Commentary*, 327–8.

spective, which manifests itself in a return to traditional patterns for maintaining the values of honour and shame. In the next section we will gain further understanding of the historical circumstances related to the changed place of celibate women in certain Pauline communities, as we consider additional evidence for how an unmarried person would have been perceived in Greco-Roman society. At this point it is important to recognize, however, that the shift in perspective is one revealed by the author of the Pastorals. It is not necessarily shared by all members of his communities. The young widows may have continued in their determination to live a chaste life, despite the Pastoral author's insistence that they marry. In the *Acts of Paul and Thecla* we find evidence that the values of honour and shame that we see transformed under Paul's guidance in 1 Corinthians 7 continued to evolve in Pauline circles in ways that were diametrically opposed to values promoted by the author of the Pastoral Epistles. By focusing on the relationship between social contexts revealed by the Pastorals and the *Acts of Paul and Thecla* we will gain greater insight into what was at stake for the young widows who travelled from house to house, as well as for the other unmarried women who braved public visibility. These women all were intent on living out the gospel with their holy bodies, removed from the worldly hazards that accompanied contact with male sexuality.

When the private becomes public – contacts between 1 Timothy 5.3–16 and the *Acts of Paul and Thecla*

One of the major conclusions emerging from the discussion in Part 1 of the reaction of outsiders to the birth of Christianity was that the church was offensive because it 'privatized' religion. By promoting an ultimate loyalty to one god worshipped in intimate household settings, it severed the connection between religion and public matters of the state. From the perspective of the second-century pagan critics of the early church, in Christianity the public had become dangerously private. In contrast, the author of the Pastorals in 1 Timothy 5.3–16 appears to have been concerned that the private had become dangerously public. Young widows were said to be imprudently wandering from house to house, telling what should not be told, and the result was slander towards the community. In the second century, activities that might have gone unnoticed in the first generation of Christianity became the object of public scrutiny.

A suspicious outsider who looked inside an early Christian house at the beginning of the second century did not expect to find there the microcosm of the well-ordered state that had been described so often by the philosophers and moralists of the time. The outsider would have been primed to discover rituals where the lady of the house was engaged in a strange act of prophecy during which she symbolically became male. The critical onlooker would have paid careful attention to the reluctance of the daughters of the house to marry. In turn, the early Christian would need to confront the common assumption that new religious groups upset the equilibrium of the hierarchically structured household and led to immoral activities among women who were inherently vulnerable to their influences. Slander and ostracism, which stripped an individual of all honour, were dangers that loomed ominously outside early Christian houses. In addition, when the prominence of asceticism among women became known, the early church member risked confrontation with violence that could be the result of a perceived threat to the social order.

Experiments with sexual abstinence were not unknown in the period before, and contemporary with, the birth of the church. The remarks of both Philo and Galen, discussed previously, illustrate that under certain circumstances the celibacy of women could be admired greatly. There is good reason to believe that in many cases female asceticism may have contributed to Christianity's growth and popularity.[75] Strong endorsements of marriage in Greco-Roman society were sometimes countered with philosophical arguments and practical considerations.[76] In fact, Will Deming has recently interpreted 1 Corinthians 7 against the background of the Stoic-Cynic debate concerning the desirability

---

[75] Aline Rousselle has argued that 'the pagan experiments with sexual abstinence . . . prepared the way for Christian asceticism'. See *Porneia: On Desire and the Body in Antiquity* (Oxford: Basil Blackwell, 1983) 131.

[76] See full discussion in Yarbrough, *Not Like the Gentiles*, 31–63.

of marriage.[77] There is no doubt that the question of whether or not to marry remained a controversial issue. If a group was already under suspicion for illicit activities, the presence of celibate women in their circle could be used as further evidence for classifying Christianity as a social irritant. The Roman state made firm efforts to ensure that inclinations to remain unmarried and/or childless were thwarted by a legal system of rewards and penalties. Legislation promulgated by Augustus and his successors penalized unmarried women twenty to fifty years of age 'including widows who had not remarried within a year (later two years) and divorcées not remarried within six months (later eighteen)'.[78] A woman who remained unmarried and childless during the period we are discussing could face restrictions on her inheritance and the denial of her privileges of legal independence. Noblewomen who bore three children, and freedwomen who bore four children were granted freedom from tutelage; they could arrange their own legal affairs without a male guardian acting as the intermediary.[79] There is even evidence to suggest that the bearing of children was related to how quickly slaves were manumitted and released from obliga-

[77] Will Deming, *Paul on Marriage and Celibacy: The Hellenistic background of 1 Corinthians 7*, SNTSMS 83 (Cambridge University Press, 1995). This book offers a convincing illustration of the importance of measuring Pauline theology against the ideologies current in Greco-Roman society. Deming argues that 1 Corinthians 7 'represents an example of Stoic morality as adapted for use in a non-Stoic system of thought, thereby further documenting the popularization of Stoicism in the period of the Empire' (p. 214). His study sheds greater light, however, on the nature of Paul's response to community concerns than on the nature of the concerns themselves and the priorities of his audience. Part of the problem in interpreting 1 Corinthians 7 lies in the fact that beyond the level of intellectual discourse about the desirability of marriage for philosophers we have so little evidence in Greco-Roman society for celibacy being embraced to a significant degree by a community of men and women in the way that seems to be the case in the Corinthian church (but see discussion in Part 1 of this book, pp. 86–91). In order to understand the particular issues that gave rise to questions about marriage in Corinth we need to continue to reflect upon the relationship between intellectual traditions, ideologies, and cultural values such as honour and shame.

[78] On the details of the Augustan legislation of 18 BCE and 9 CE (*lex Julia et Papia*) in general see Gardner, *Women in Roman Law and Society*, 77; see pp. 77–8. See also Yarbrough, *Not Like the Gentiles*, 45–6, n.78; Balsdon, *Roman Women*, 75–9, 89–90, 202, 230; Corbett, *Law of Marriage*, 119–21; McNamara, *A New Song*, 45; Clarke, *Secular and Christian Leadership*, 82–5. On the enforcement of the legislation during the course of the first three centuries CE see Pomeroy, *Goddesses*, 166; E. Fantham, H. Peet Foley, N. Boymel Kampen, S. B. Pomeroy, H. A. Shapiro, *Women in the Classical World: Image and Text* (New York and Oxford: Oxford University, 1994) 302–6.

[79] McNamara, *A New Song*, 45; Gardner, *Women in Roman Law and Society*, 19–20.

tions to their former owners.[80] Clearly, Pauline teaching in 1 Corinthians 7, which encouraged women of all ages and of varying social status to remain unmarried if possible went against the tenor of Augustus' marriage legislation.

It is difficult, however, for the modern historian to evaluate the effectiveness of these laws and to judge whether and to what extent they would have affected women at various echelons of society and in different areas of the Empire. One scholar has argued that the frequent attempts to enforce Augustus' laws by his successors suggest that the legislation was not very successful.[81] Even if these laws were difficult to enforce, they offer valuable insight into the concern among government officials about the deterioration of households in the Empire. Such unease is expressed succinctly in a speech attributed to Tiberius (Emperor 14–37 CE) where he responds negatively to a plea to repeal the legislation concerning the unmarried and the childless: 'How can the State be preserved, if we neither marry nor have children?'[82]

In addition to social illness, the celibacy of women could elicit fear about physical illness in the Greco-Roman world. Aline Rousselle has collected interesting evidence from Greek literature which draws a connection between female continence and disease of the womb, 'ὑστερικός'. Involuntary continence among women was thought to lead to the disease whose symptoms included apnoea, fainting, hallucinations, and convulsions and whose cure was marriage followed by pregnancy.[83] Given the prominence of widows in early Christian circles, it is intriguing to hear Galen associate the disease particularly with them:

---

[80] See Balsdon, *Roman Women*, 230; Pomeroy, *Goddesses*, 195–8; P. A. Brunt, *Italian Manpower 225 B.C–A.D. 14* (Oxford: Clarendon, 1971) 563–6.

[81] See McNamara, *A New Song*, 45.

[82] Dio Cassius, *Roman History*, 56.7,4; see 56.1–10 (trans. E. Cary; LCL). See also Polybius, *Histories*, 36.17, 5–10 (trans. W. R. Paton, LCL 1927).

[83] See *Porneia*, 67–9. The literal meaning of ὑστερικός is 'suffering in the womb' and it is the term from which the modern English word hysteria is derived. The Greek term is related to, but should not be confused with, the term employed by Celsus to characterize the deranged behaviour of Mary Magdalene, πάροιστρος (translated as hysterical or frenzied in this book); see discussion in Introduction, pp. 2–4. Among the most important sources treated by Rousselle is the second-century Greek physician Galen who, as discussed earlier, admired early Christian women for their continence. In contrast to the women with the disease of the womb, the exceptional early Christian women were chaste according to their own will.

It is generally agreed upon that this disease mostly affects widows, and particularly those who previously menstruated regularly, had been pregnant and were eager to have intercourse, but were now deprived of all this. Is there a more likely conclusion from these facts than that in these patients the retention of the menstrual flow or of semen causes the so-called uterine condition . . . by which some women become apnoic, suffocated or spastic? And possibly, this affliction is made worse by the retention of semen. The female semen is a burden to them; in a similar manner they are used, I believe, to regard the elimination of stool and urine as a natural act. [84]

Thus, the early Christian woman who remained unmarried was likely to be evaluated in terms of several converging lines of public opinion. We have seen that illicit religious groups were accused of causing 'hysterical' behaviour among women. The fact that early Christianity encouraged women to remain unmarried and childless would only serve to strengthen convictions about the derangement of early Christian women; their bizarre behaviour would cease only with marriage, sex, and children. It is true that a few individuals of the mind-set of Philo or Galen might see in the early Christian celibate woman a perfect representation of the ideals of self-control and chastity. But it is also probable that early Christian women who remained unmarried would be understood by many as displaying symptoms of disease caused 'celibacy under compulsion'. Such negatively appraised women would include virgin daughters in Christian households who remained at home beyond the normal age of marriage, widows whose vow of continence in the church was their only guarantee of sustenance, and celibate women like Thecla who were believed to have been forced into an unnatural state under the bewitchment of a clever teacher like Paul. Moreover, early Christian celibate women would be subject to public scrutiny not only because they failed to produce the children that the Empire craved,[85] but also because they were, in their chaste state, understood as being particularly vulnerable to corruption. As we have seen in examining the critique of early Christian women by outsiders, the accusation of adulteress was

---

[84] Galen, *On the Affected Parts* 6.5; trans. Siegel. Galen's position should be compared to that of Soranus, who argues that permanent virginity for women is healthful, but acknowledges that this is a subject of great debate; see *Gynecology*, 1.7.30–2, trans. Temkin.

[85] On Roman concern about a falling birthrate see Balsdon, *Roman Women*, 14, 78–9, 190–7.

never far removed from even the purest of early Christian women.[86] In short, the early Christian woman who remained unmarried inevitably collided with cultural values linking popular morality and female degeneracy.[87]

The behaviour of the young widows of the Pastoral Epistles who embraced ascetic teaching would often have been interpreted as a challenge to Greco-Roman society. The reaction of the author of the Pastoral Epistles was to stress the public dimension of ministry, to emphasize woman's place in the private domain of the household, and to enforce traditional structures to protect the values of honour and shame. In essence, the author of the Pastorals strove to ensure that the ethical standards of early Christianity should, as much as possible, conform to what was publicly acceptable. The *Acts of Paul and Thecla*, however, provide evidence that other segments of the Pauline movement countered outside hostility with an increased determination to persevere in their publicly unacceptable way of life. Dennis R. MacDonald has thoroughly explored the intriguing points of contact between these two works, and he has argued that the Pastoral Epistles were written in response to the kind of teaching found in the *Apocryphal Acts of Paul and Thecla*.[88] Identifying second-century Asia Minor as the probable setting for these documents, MacDonald notes that even if in their current form the *Acts* come from a generation later than the Pastoral Epistles, the stories they contain may have been circulating orally at an earlier time. In describing the origins of the *Acts*, he points to the story-telling of celibate women who sought to be faithful to Paul's instructions in 1 Corinthians 7 about remaining unmarried.[89] An oblique reference to their stories may even be contained

---

[86] The vulnerability of early Christian virgins was recognized even within early Christian circles. See Castelli, 'Women's Sexuality', 87–8.

[87] The following remarks of Sarah Pomeroy, concerning the efforts of one first-century emperor to respond to the sickness he saw in society, illustrate the strength of the association between popular morality and female degeneracy, and the serious consequences which might await those who would challenge this morality: 'Domitian's campaign for virtue included the enforcement of the Augustan marriage legislation and the restoration of the shrine of Plebeian Chastity. He also made public examples of the Vestals by holding capital trials of Vestals and their lovers.' See Pomeroy, *Goddesses*, 212.

[88] See MacDonald, *The Legend and the Apostle*, 54–77. On MacDonald's work see Kraemer, *Her Share*, 151–4 and M. Y. MacDonald, *Pauline Churches*, 181–7.

[89] See MacDonald, *The Legend and the Apostle*, 17–53.

in 1 Timothy 4.7 which exhorts the community to avoid profane and 'old-womanish' tales.[90] In light of several factors – the accusation against false teachers making their way into houses to capture women in 2 Timothy 3.6, the concern expressed in 1 Timothy 5. 13 about widows travelling from house to house, and a general interest in public ministry and public perception in the Pastoral Epistles – the movement of women in and out of houses recounted in the *Acts* is remarkable. The *Acts* have been judged to be especially important for interpreting the Pastoral Epistles because of the information they provide about the shape of the strong ascetic teaching which seems to have been popular among the widows exhorted in 1 Timothy 5.3–16.

Many interesting lines of inquiry with respect to the relationship between the *Acts of Paul and Thecla* and the Pastoral Epistles have been pursued by Dennis R. MacDonald and others.[91] However, what interests us primarily here is what the relationship between these texts reveals about why early church women who remained unmarried could be viewed as offensive, and what it reveals about the nature of the opposing early church reactions to criticism. The key to unlocking the interplay between public opinion and early church response in these works is to be found by focusing on how the categories of public and private operate in the stories and exhortations.

We have seen that the Pastoral Epistles display a strong interest in the structures of the household, and in the church understood in terms of the model of the household. Moreover, we have observed that because the household served as the nucleus of early Christian organization, the distinction between what is private and what is public often becomes blurred. It is apparent that for the author of the Pastoral Epistles there is no doubt that the Christian household acts as the public manifestation of church identity. The hope is that a Christian household (and therefore the church) will exhibit the kind of order and discipline that will put to rest any slanderous accusations concerning impropriety and immorality

---

[90] There are many characters in the *Acts* who are also mentioned in the Pastoral Epistles; see MacDonald, *Pauline Churches*, p. 264, n. 72.

[91] In addition to the works mentioned in note 88 above see Burrus, *Chastity as Autonomy*, 22–3, 70–1.

among church women. The aim is to end any suspicious activities among widows in private quarters which might lead to a public condemnation of community life.

As with the Pastoral Epistles, the household is prominent in the early church life described in the *Acts of Paul and Thecla*. In keeping with typical New Testament patterns, the church meets in households, and conversion is clearly a household affair (3.2, 7, 23).[92] In contrast to the Pastorals, however, the movement of women in and out of houses in the *Acts* is celebrated. For example, the virgin Thecla rests in the house of the wealthy widow Tryphaena for eight days, instructing her in the word of the Lord. Thecla's evangelical teaching clearly spans the hierarchy of household relationships, for we are told that the maidservants also believed and there was great joy in the house (3.39). Thecla's failure to meet her own household responsibilities, her travels outside of her home, and her ministerial efforts are judged by the non-believers in the *Acts* to be an assault on the Greco-Roman household. Her activities are inspired by an encounter with Paul's teaching of 'fearing one single God only and living chastely' (3.9, cf. 3.12). Her refusal to go through with her marriage is interpreted by hostile outsiders as a rejection of her pre-determined role as wife, mother and mistress of maidservants. It is a rejection of precisely the role the author of the Pastorals seeks to encourage (3.10; cf. 3.20). The forfeiture of her traditional household responsibilities takes on proportions which are unmistakably public, for she becomes an ascetic teacher independent of Paul (3.41). Hostility at the hands of outsiders turns to violence, for on several occasions throughout the *Acts* people try to kill Thecla.

Due to its legend-like quality, it is more difficult to draw conclusions about life-directives from the *Acts of Paul and Thecla* than from the ethical exhortations of the Pastoral Epistles. However, it is evident that the *Acts* envisions a response to the hostile reactions of Greco-Roman society opposite to that recommended by the author of the Pastoral Epistles. There is no attempt to limit the

---

[92] The translation of the *Apocryphal Acts of Paul and Thecla* is by W. Schneelmelcher, in Hennecke and Schneemelcher (eds.), *NT Apoc.*: 2. See Schneemelcher's notes, 322–51 and *Acts of Paul*, 352–87 (including *Acts of Paul and Thecla*, 353–64).

activities of celibate women; in fact, celibacy is fundamental to salvation, and it seems to be Thecla's chaste state that empowers her to confront the most insidious societal menace. Instead of discretion and apology, the stance adopted is one of bold confrontation. While this confrontation is clearly due to Thecla's blatant disregard for society's laws and norms which would see her become a married woman, a close reading of the work reveals that hostility results from her public bravado. Her celibacy offers dramatic proof of this daring. From the perspective of a non-believer, Thecla lacks shame.

In the *Acts of Paul and Thecla* it is possible to detect the celibate woman moving outside her own home into the dangerous world of the public realm, where she gains periodic shelter in the private sphere of women. It is critical to note, however, that when Thecla leaves her own home, her life becomes vulnerable and transient. The story of her encounter with Paul begins with her sitting by a window listening to Paul but unable to see him. She is on a threshold, in a transient state between enclosure in a house and movement on the outside. This position is likely a symbol of the process of conversion from membership in a household of unbelievers to the entrance into a community whose way of life demands confrontation with society. Thecla's mother interprets her daughter's position at the window and her longing to have contact with Paul as bewitchment, and she interprets Thecla's behaviour as a kind of infidelity:

For indeed for three days and three nights Thecla has not arisen from the window either to eat or to drink, but gazing steadily as if on some joyful spectacle she so devotes herself to a strange man who teaches deceptive and subtle words that I wonder how a maiden of such modesty as she is can be so sorely troubled (3.8; cf. 3.9).

The confusion and the mourning in the household for a lost daughter and would-be bride in no way interferes with Thecla's devotion: She 'did not turn away, but gave her whole attention to Paul's word' (3.10).

Eventually, Thecla secretly leaves her house at night to visit Paul in prison. The visit of the widows to the imprisoned Christian described by Lucian of Samosata is an obvious parallel, as is the description by Lucius Apuleius of the wife who secretly left her

home to participate in illicit religious rites. When Thecla's clandestine voyage is discovered by the members of her household and
her fiancé, her activities are considered highly suspect and are
reported to the authorities: 'they . . . found her, so to speak, bound
with him in affection. And they went out thence, rallied the crowd
about them, and disclosed to the governor what had happened'
(3.19). The non-believers' perception, indirectly communicated
here, is that sexual impropriety has taken place. Later in the story
Thecla's sexual purity is directly challenged.[93] Thecla's move into
the public sphere involves her refusal to marry her fiancé Thamyris
'according to the law of the Iconians' (3.20). She is sentenced to
death, but escapes and begins her life on the road which culminates
in her role as early Christian teacher.

Virginia Burrus has noted a pattern that characterizes the
behaviour of women in several stories contained in the
Apocryphal Acts of the Apostles. She has drawn attention to the
tendency for the women of these accounts to transgress the conventional boundaries of the woman's sphere. In particular when a
woman 'leaves the house she is crossing the boundaries, intruding
into the male world and provoking disapproval, hostility and suspicion of infidelity'.[94] The aura of promiscuity seems to surround
Thecla as she assumes her life outside of her family's home: her
purity comes very close to being violated. As she travels with Paul
into Antioch she is grabbed by a Syrian named Alexander:

[He] being a powerful man, embraced her on the open street; she
however would not endure it, but looked about for Paul and cried out bit-
terly, saying: 'Force not the stranger, force not the handmaid of God!
Among the Iconians I am one of the first, and because I did not wish to
marry Thamyris I have been cast out of the city.' And taking hold of
Alexander she ripped his cloak, took off the crown from his head, and
made him a laughing-stock. But he, partly out of love for her and partly

---

[93] Due to Thecla's perseverence in remaining a virgin, the eroticism that seems to characterize her relationship with Paul frequently has been of interest to commentators. The
probability that women who became involved with early Christian teachers risked accusations of sexual immorality may partially explain this phenomenon.

[94] Burrus, *Chastity as Autonomy*, 90; see pp. 87–93. On the relationship between the *Acts of
Paul and Thecla* and other stories contained in the *Apocryphal Acts* see also Kraemer, *Her
Share*, 154–5; Kraemer, 'The Conversion of Women', 298–307; Davies, *The Revolt of the
Widows*.

in shame at what had befallen him, brought her before the governor; and when she confessed that she had done these things, he condemned her to the beasts . . .(3.26–7)

The examination in Part 1 of references to early Christian women by outsiders made use of anthropological studies of the symbolic association of the women with the house. We saw how quickly suspicious religious activities outside the house might be cast as sexual immorality. Alexander's public embrace of Thecla probably reflects this aspect of public opinion. But the text is also significant because it offers a good illustration of how the suspicion that early Christian celibate women were sexually immoral was tied to the core cultural values of honour and shame.

The repeated impression at the beginning of the account, that Thecla's preoccupation with Paul's word is incompatible with the modesty of a virgin, is an assessment that she lacks shame. Her fiancé, Thamyris, proclaims in distress: 'Thecla, my betrothed, why dost thou sit thus? And what is this passion that holds thee distracted? Turn to thy Thamyris and be ashamed' (3.10; cf. 3.8–9). It is not surprising that in a society where sexual purity represents the essence of a woman's moral character, Paul's role is cast as one of seducer and corrupter of women (3.14–15). The description of his negative influence is heightened by his being called a stranger: he lives outside of the elite group of Iconians. Their concern to guarantee the chastity of their women and to protect their wealth and status, involves essentially endogamous marriage practices (3.13). Like Jesus whom Celsus described as a magician who had a bewitching hold on his followers (on Mary Magdalene in particular), Paul is described as a sorcerer, a *magus* (3.15; cf. 3.19)!

The threat that Thecla poses to the societal values of honour and shame are illustrated by her treatment of Alexander and his reaction. In the text cited above Thecla assumes the offensive stance of the male guardian and protects her own honour. Assuming that Paul was Thecla's guardian, Alexander offers Paul money and gifts in exchange for her. Yet, in a manner that parallels Peter's denial of Christ, Paul denies that Thecla is his or even that he knows her (3.26). It seems that we are to conclude that Paul leaves the virgin to fend for herself. She is so successful in doing this that she ridicules Alexander in the public eye; she shames him.

Alexander's response nevertheless seems harsh: bringing Thecla before the Governor and ultimately sentencing her to the beasts (3.27). In Mediterranean societies, however, it is barely an exaggeration to say that public humiliation can amount to a threat to life itself. By defending herself with strength and courage, Thecla has assumed the traditional role of the male in the public honour context (cf. 3.25, 40). In the challenge-riposte dynamics of interaction in Mediterranean society, Alexander feels bound to answer to the challenge in an equal or more forceful way.[95]

The development of Thecla's Christian role in the *Acts* includes not only a gradual severance of the ties with the household and community, but also an increasing independence from Paul. While the Apostle maintains an important place to the end (3.41), his protection is not always reliable (3.21, 26). Sometimes she must endure humiliations and torture. Her persecution includes being stripped naked in public, the ultimate symbol of a shameless woman (3.22, 33–4, 38). Even here, her purity is not compromised, for a miraculous cloud of fire protects her from being touched by beasts and from being seen naked (3.34). She faces (sexual?) temptation, but does not succumb to it (3.25, 40). By the end of the tale the only reliable protection Thecla receives is from women. They cheer for her and denounce her persecution as unjust (3.27–8, 32–3, 35, 38). It is from the wealthy widow Tryphaena, whose own daughter has died, that Thecla receives shelter (3.27–9). Tryphaena's house eventually becomes the home-base for Thecla's ministry (3.39–40). Tryphaena's intervention is explicitly related to the preservation of Thecla's purity (3.27, 31).

This account of the adventures of Paul and Thecla is 'almost certainly a fabrication'.[96] However, scholars believe that the work mirrors the actual experiences of early Christian women in the second century who rejected marriage and who found themselves in violent confrontations with society. This account might be understood as a narrative of how early Christian women destroyed the traditional Greco-Roman household (a microcosm of the state), and how they constructed an alternate household commu-

---

[95] See Plevnik, 'Honour/Shame', in Pilch and Malina (eds.), *Biblical Social Values*, 96–7,100.
[96] Kraemer, *Her Share*, 154. See her comments in general about the historicity of this work.

nity. With words that seem to set out the boundaries of their new community, the widow Tryphaena embraces Thecla: 'Come inside and I will transfer everything that is mine to you' (3.39). It is significant that Thecla's state is described as that of a transient outsider in a desperate situation; she is a 'desolate stranger' whom Tryphaena takes into her home to replace her own daughter who is dead (3.28). A new household of family members is created, where the bonds are not of blood, but of Christian commitment. Despite the dangerous consequences of its public manifestations, the community of women resolutely adheres to its vision of community life modelled on the family.

There is further evidence to suggest that communities of unmarried early Christian women existed in the second century. I Timothy 5.16, for example, may be translated literally as a reference to believing women who 'have widows'. Although this verse has frequently been understood as a reference to believing women who have relatives who are widows, an expanding appreciation of the complex lives of celibate women in the church is leading scholars to view the text as having a broader scope; it probably refers to relatively well-to-do women who have taken in poor widows, not necessarily only their relatives.[97] Yet, the scope of the instruction for believing women who have widows to assist them in 1 Timothy 5.16 is limited by the recommendation that all younger widows should remarry, thereby reducing the risk of public scrutiny (5.14). In other church groups, however, such restrictions seem to have been absent. A community of unmarried women that may have included younger and older women, women who were widows, and women who had never been married, may be in view when Ignatius of Antioch greets the 'virgins called widows' at the beginning of the second century CE in such a way as to imply a distinction from the households of the brethren with their wives and children (Ign. *Smyrn.* 13.1).

Read in relation to 1 Timothy 5.3–16, the *Acts of Paul and Thecla*

---

[97] There is some manuscript variation with respect to 1 Timothy 5.16. Instead of simply believing woman (πιστή), some authorities have believing man or woman (πιστὸς ἢ πιστή), or believing man (πιστός). The latter two variations have been viewed as an attempt to improve the text; see Verner, *Household of God*, n. 40, 139; Dewey, '1 Timothy', 357.

offers valuable insight into what happened in the early church when the private became public. These texts help us to see the dynamics of societal response to a way of life adopted by early Christian women. Since Paul's day, this lifestyle had been the subject of public scrutiny and at the heart of church concerns about social respectability. Later, it became the focus of public hostility and church crisis. The author of the Pastorals responds to societal criticism by exhorting that the private world of the early church visibly conform to public standards. On the other hand, the community that would see Thecla as a heroine stands resolute in its effort to encourage all women to deal with the world as though they had no dealings with it, and to embody the form of the world that is passing away (1 Cor. 7.30–1). Public hostility is confronted, and the private meetings of celibate women continue despite great dangers. Although both communities draw upon Pauline tradition, it is the community reflected in the *Acts* which epitomizes Celsus' fear about the public becoming private in early Christianity. In this community, the stable hierarchical household (a reflection of the order of society) has been abandoned in favour of an alternate vision of the household that was dreamt up in 'women's places', but intended for the salvation of all of humanity (3.43; cf. 3.17).

Conclusion

The material on early Christian women in the Pauline circle that we have considered in this section offers several indications that the nature of the public opinion expressed by outsiders (examined in Part 1) was of real concern to early church communities. For a group intent on winning the world, public opinion simply could not be ignored. Even in the earliest stages of the Pauline movement, exhortations intended to direct the lives of celibate women were shaped by a concern for social respectability. Yet, the teaching in 1 Corinthians 7 is fraught with ambiguity, for the lives of early church women who remained unmarried also carried symbolic significance as an expression of distinct communal identity. The celibacy of the women holy in body and spirit functioned as an important means of setting the church apart from the world.

Conclusion

Although little attention has been given here to the difficult question of the motives of women who chose to join the church and remain unmarried (an issue that will be discussed in Part 3), I have endeavoured to present the consequences of their choices, both for their lives in the church and for their place in the wider context of Greco-Roman society. Because women remained unmarried, the convictions of outsiders that new religious groups corrupted the women of the Empire were strengthened. Remaining unmarried was readily interpreted as a challenge to the order of the household. It is ironic that celibacy, inspired by a desire to be holy and pure, often raised questions about a woman's fidelity and basic morality. Consequently, the preference for celibacy which appears to be especially strong among Christian women is, as early as 1 Corinthians 7, the subject of careful monitoring in a church intent on winning the world. Definitions of situations when a wish to remain unmarried should be abandoned (1 Cor. 7) develop into full-blown constraints (1 Tim. 5.3–16). Hostility between church and world has increased at the beginning of the second century, and the activities of celibate women are now perceived in church circles as being directly responsible for this mounting tension. In fact, church teaching concerning the inappropriate religious inclinations of Christian women echoes general public opinion about the effect of illegitimate religion on Greco-Roman women. Structures are put in place which ensure that as many Christian women as possible remain at home, exemplifying the most exacting ideal of the Greco-Roman wife.

When the Pastoral Epistles are read in relation to the *Acts of Paul and Thecla*, it becomes clear that the strong movement towards social respectability represents only one possible response to hostile public opinion in Pauline circles. In the *Acts*, Thecla boldly confronts public opinion. The result is that the reader is offered a picture of the violent consequences of asceticism. Thecla dramatically acts out rejection of the world, a perspective which must be accepted by those women who enter the church and remain unmarried. There is no doubt that the response to the world reflected in the *Acts* is more strongly sectarian than that disclosed by the Pastoral Epistles. But the unmistakable desire to draw a line separating the community from the evil world in the *Acts* is nevertheless still coupled with a hope to win the world. Thecla is an evangelical teacher who not only is successful in converting an extended household, but gains a reputation as a teacher who enlightened many with the word of God (3.43). Moreover, despite the hostility which the world directs at Thecla, even the non-believing officials are portrayed as ambivalent in her presence. As Thecla was brought in naked to be burned we are told that 'the governor wept and marvelled at the power that was in her' (3.22). This is perhaps an indication that the favourable opinion of outsiders is still important to the community.

Because honour and shame were such central values in ancient Mediterranean society and were so closely related to sexuality and gender distinctions, the conceptual structures were in place for celibate women to embody the shame of the community and its concern for (church) reputation. Male members of the community saw their own honour expressed through the chastity of widows and virgins. The woman whose chastity was rendered beyond question to such an extent that she neither married nor remarried came to symbolize the boundaries that separated the whole community from the outside world. But because of the way in which the values of honour and shame functioned in Greco-Roman society, it was inevitable that the behaviour of women would be scrutinized by critics of early Christianity. Likewise, when the community was criticized by outsiders, church authors were bound to respond to challenges to their honour by directing the behaviour of church women. The precarious attempt to establish public esteem in the Pastoral Epistles took the form of limiting the acceptance of a celibate way of life for women and strict restrictions governing their lives. In contrast, in the *Acts of Paul and Thecla* challenges to community honour were met with determination to present the life of a celebrated virgin whose purity remained unstained even in the face of the most frightening societal menace.

If we trace the trajectory in Pauline Christianity stretching from 1 Corinthians 7 to the *Acts of Paul and Thecla*, it becomes clear that although the significance of the life of the celibate woman is tied to the cultural values of honour and shame, in some communities, the usual means of maintaining these values has been transformed. Specifically, when Paul and the author of the *Acts* legitimize the choice of women of all ages to remain unmarried, they are allowing women to be removed from the auspices of husband and/or father and are making these women responsible for defending their own honour and for representing the honour of the community. Because the association of women with the private, domestic sphere and men with the public sphere is one of the important ways that honour and shame are played out in Greco-Roman society, it is not surprising that a threat to usual household arrangements creates such a strong reaction. Moreover, it is not surprising that early Christian literature frequently associates women with the boundaries of the church community and reveals an interest as to where their lives stand on the intersection between public and private. In Corinth unmarried women holy in body and spirit have taken on special significance for the ascetic party in defining the nature of their allegiance to the group; Paul's exhortations not only recognize their importance for the church in a world that is passing away, but also reveal an awareness of the significance of their behaviour for relations with the outside world. In the Pastoral Epistles married women and older widows who have a history of exemplifying the virtues of an ideal wife become central to projecting a church image that will quiet slander. In the *Acts of Paul and Thecla* the virgin acts as a symbol of a community that is persecuted by the outside world, but who confronts that world with courage and is never corrupted.

Celibate women in early Christianity announce to the world the shape of church boundaries. There is no doubt that in some communities their lives are severely restricted and that their sexuality may serve as a commodity in male struggles for honour and prestige.[98] But the way that they symbolize corporate identity calls us to reflect upon their power. The virgin and widow in early Christianity are powerful in their ability loudly to confront society and to transform community boundaries. Their visibility sometimes leads church authorities carefully to guard their actions, but they nevertheless remain vulnerable to violent confrontations with a hostile society. The risks experienced by the next group of

---

[98] See the feminist critique of the ideology of virginity in Castelli, 'Virginity and its Meaning', 86.

women we will encounter are perhaps even greater, and the advances they make on Greco-Roman society are not nearly so loud. In the lives of the women married to unbelievers we find further evidence for the power of early Christian women in Greco-Roman society. They may aptly be called the quiet evangelists.

PART THREE

Marriage, women, and early church responses to public opinion

In recent years many scholars have suggested that women's attraction to early Christianity was related to the freedoms offered in celibacy. Dennis R. MacDonald, for example, estimates that groups of widows, which in some early Christian circles may have included virgins who had never been married (cf. Ign. *Smyrn.* 13.1), were a counter-cultural force within their patriarchal society: 'Perhaps we should interpret this virginity as a rebellion – conscious or unconscious – against male domination. Perhaps it symbolized not only moral purity, but also independence, dedication to a calling, and criticism of conjugal society.'[1] The criticism of society that MacDonald and others associate with celibate early church life is of particular importance for this book because it implies confrontation between early Christians and public opinion about the proper behaviour of women. When scholars address the situation of married women in the church, they often come to very different conclusions about the role these women played in church relations with the world. Elisabeth Schüssler Fiorenza contrasts the liberation from social constraints offered to celibate women by early Christianity, with the fate of the married early Christian women. Unmarried women acquire an independence which produces conflict with society; but married women remain, in conformity to society, confined within the patriarchal family:

---

[1] MacDonald, *The Legend and the Apostle*, 40. For a similar line of thought see also Burrus, *Chastity as Autonomy*, 108.

Marriage, women, and early church responses

Paul's advice to widows who were not necessarily 'old' – since girls usually married between twelve and fifteen years of age – thus offered a possibility for 'ordinary' women to become independent. At the same time, it produced conflicts for the Christian community in its interaction with society. Paul's theological argument, however, that those who married are 'divided' and not equally dedicated to the affairs of the Lord as the nonmarried, implicitly limited married women to the confines of the patriarchal family. It disqualified married people theologically as less engaged missionaries and less dedicated Christians. It posited a rift between the married woman, concerned about her husband and family, and the unmarried virgin who was pure and sacred and therefore would receive the pneumatic privileges of virginity. One can only wonder how Paul could have made such a theological point when he had Prisca as his friend and knew other missionary couples who were living examples that his theology was wrong.[2]

Because married early church women exhibited virtues that were commonly encouraged for wives in Greco-Roman society, they have often been associated with patriarchy, accommodation to the standards of the world, and apology. However, because I seek to explain how women figured both in public opinion about the church and in early church responses to public opinion, it is important to examine carefully any argument which polarizes the lives of married and non-married women in terms of their significance for church relations with Greco-Roman society.

Without denying the recent important work accomplished on studying celibate early Christian women over the past number of years, Fiorenza's critique of Paul has caused me to rethink common assumptions about the involvement of married women in the early church, and the attraction of early Christianity for women in general. Perhaps there is less of a dichotomy than is often thought between what early Christianity offered married women and what it offered unmarried women. For modern western women, the lives of ascetic early Christian women may seem immediately attractive. Early Christian women who rejected marriage are identified as brave women who resolutely opposed the cultural ethos of Greco-Roman society.[3] One thinks of ascetic

---

[2] Fiorenza, *In Memory of Her*, 225–6.

[3] Note that E. Clark identifies martyrdom and asceticism as frameworks 'within which Christian women's rejection of the political order could be manifested as fully and gloriously as men's. . . ' See 'Early Christian Women', 26.

women such as the legendary Thecla. Her determination to remain celibate is portrayed as enabling her to break through the cultural expectations imposed on her as wife, mother, and mistress of slaves, and even to surpass the usual constraints placed on women in terms of early Christian ministry. For those of us engaged in a reconstruction of the lives of early Christian women, the story of Thecla is enormously significant. But the recent work of researchers (discussed in the Introduction to this book) which incorporates anthropological approaches to study biblical women, reminds us of the importance of considering the experiences and priorities of women which may be very different from those of modern western women.[4]

In the Introduction to the collection of essays edited by Amy-Jill Levine, 'Women Like This': New Perspectives on Jewish Women in the Greco-Roman World, Levine offers an interesting example of recent critical evaluation of the relationship between modern preoccupations and historical reconstructions of early Christian women. She notes that the 'richly varied lives and images of Jewish women in the Hellenistic and Roman periods' has been neglected in some feminist reconstructions of early Christianity, and warns that 'the Jewish systems in both Palestine and the Diaspora may not have been as repressive as has been claimed'. Of particular importance for this study is Levine's assertion concerning an underlying idea in some theories about why Jewish women chose to follow Jesus: 'some writers suggest that for Jesus to liberate women to their full potential, he had to liberate them *from* something; this "something" is then described as the repressive, patriarchal, Jewish system'.[5]

The assumption uncovered by Levine as highly problematic for an accurate understanding of Jewish women – early church women had to be liberated from something – is related to a desire to find an emancipating element in early Christianity. Furthermore, this assumption is rooted in a desire to shed light on motives for conversion. However, the problem is that an accurate

---

[4] Part 1, pp. 13–15. See especially Meyers, *Discovering Eve*, 33. See also Lefkowitz, 'Wives and Husbands', esp. 31–2.

[5] Amy-Jill Levine, *'Women Like This': New Perspectives on Jewish Women in the Greco-Roman World* (Atlanta: Scholars, 1991) xvi–xvii. A full bibliography is provided on p. xvii n.2.

understanding of the motives of early Christian women is extremely difficult, if not impossible, to ascertain. For example, the investigation of marriages between believers and unbelievers in this section raises a haunting historical question: why would a woman join an illicit religious group, given potentially dangerous results such as living in the house of a hostile spouse? Perhaps the hope of discovering something that early Christianity liberated women from – a desire which may inadvertently lead to the painting of unrealistically bleak pictures of Jewish and, indeed, pagan women – may be inspired partially by the attempt to identify demonstrable benefits which accompanied conversion. However, the goal of acquiring personal or individual benefits through one's course of actions may be far more important to the modern personality than it was to women who entered the early church. Even early Christian widows who have been described as a counter-cultural force in a patriarchal society, I will argue, engaged in a manner of living which was still fundamentally connected to the lives of women outside the church. As I will show, if too much weight is placed on the social liberation of the individual as the motive for the celibate participation of women in the church, the intimate connection between the lives of married and unmarried women in early Christianity becomes obscured. To recall the concerns discussed by Levine in relation to Jewish women, the problem in this case becomes one of indirect contribution to an 'anti-married woman' bias.

There is no doubt that in comparison to the significantly innovative lifestyles of the celibate women discussed in Part 2, married women led lives that were dictated by centuries of tradition. Despite significant changes in the legal status of women, Mary Lefkowitz has argued that as we move from classical Athens to the Roman Empire, notions of the proper role of wives do not seem to have undergone any radical change. Traditional virtues such as chastity, care for husband and children, and exemplary management of the household, continue to frame the portrait of the ideal wife over a great range of time and geography. The type of marriage envisioned in Plutarch's *Advice on Marriage*, which permits the education of the wife (to the extent that she is to have her husband as a philosophical mentor) nevertheless offers a good example of the persistence of traditional attitudes.[6] As for early Christianity, married women in the church at the turn of the second century have been characterized as 'discreet and modest wives' who stood as 'exemplary apologists for the new faith'.[7] According to E. Clark, 'patristic evidence suggests that traditional Greco-Roman marriage ideals received minimal revision by early Christian writers'.[8] She has argued that early Christianity offered only two innovations to the marital ethics of late ancient pagan society: a single standard of sexual morality, and the condemnation of divorce and remarriage.[9]

As early church authors begin explicitly to discuss appropriate marriage ethics, their deep roots in Greco-Roman culture are evident. While Paul's thought may move towards a significant transformation of marriage relations (1 Cor. 7; Gal. 3.28), the household codes of the later Deutero-Pauline literature contain a vision of the ideal Greco-Roman household made up of benevolent householders, obedient slaves, disciplined children, and circumspect wives – an image only thinly veneered with Christian spirituality (Col. 3.18–4.1; Eph. 5.21–6.9; cf. 1 Pet. 2.13–3.17). When Clement of Rome wrote to the Corinthian church in the generation that followed the death of Paul, he seemed far more determined than the Apostle had been to communicate the importance of the believing wife's subjection to her husband. Having studied 1 Cor. 7, it is striking to hear Clement speak of the church as having a reputation as a community which instructs wives 'to remain in the rule of obedience and to manage their households with seemliness, in all circumspection' (*1 Clem.* 1.3; cf. *1 Clem.* 21.6–7).[10] Priorities have changed. Composed at the beginning of the second century CE, Ignatius of Antioch's letter to Polycarp is cautious concerning those who remain celibate 'to the honour of the flesh of the Lord'. Ignatius aims to ensure that marriage between Christians becomes a spiritual vocation by making it subject to the authority of the bishop; the instructions are intended to guarantee that marriage will be 'according to the

---

[6] Lefkowitz, 'Wives and Husbands', 46; see pp.41–6; on Plutarch see also Brown, *The Body*, 13–14.   [7] Clark, 'Early Christian Women', 22.   [8] Ibid.   [9] Ibid., 20–2.

[10] Trans. K. Lake, *The Apostolic Fathers*, 2 vols. (LCL 1912–13). All references to *1 Clem.* in this chapter are to this translation. See MacDonald, 'Women Holy', 180–1.

Lord' and not 'according to lust' (ἐπιθυμία; Ign. *Pol.* 5.1–2; cf. Ign. *Pol.* 4.3).[11]

Similarities between Ignatius, *Letter to Polycarp* 4.1–5.2 and the conventional structures of the household in late Antiquity are evident. However, my investigation of the Ignatian correspondence and other contemporary texts has convinced me that it is simplistic to view the emergence of the ideal of the Christian couple as only a 'return to patriarchy' which had solely negative consequences for early Christian women. A dichotomy between married and unmarried women may distort the historical evidence. In this chapter, I will demonstrate that it is misleading to applaud the early church as a haven for celibate women while denouncing it as a place of further subjugation for married women.

In Part 2, I demonstrated that restrictions on the lives of celibate women were sometimes the result of the church's encounter with increasingly hostile public opinion. Marriage could be recommended as an antidote to slander. But we will see that even married early Christian women, who led the quietest and most circumspect lives, could be subject to critical evaluations. Even a small trespass on their part probably would be viewed as an indication of their immoral nature and of the immoral nature of their church. In this section I will illustrate that the lives of married and unmarried women in the church had much in common, and that their situation in the face of hostile opponents was much the same. Moreover, with respect to the first group of married women we will be discussing (those married to non-believers), it is evident that their membership in church groups required tremendous initiative. The lives of church women married to non-believers were severely restricted; but because they maintained intimate contact with the non-believing world, their participation in church rites required perhaps the greatest resolve and, at times, unshakeable bravery.

The diverse group of texts discussed in this section of the book

---

[11] This text is the subject of a detailed study in my article, 'The Ideal of the Christian Couple', 105–25. For the translation of Ignatius employed here see n. 10 above. With respect to the authenticity of the Ignatian correspondence and textual problems I am following the 'modern consensus' as defined by Schoedel following Lightfoot and Zahn. See W. R. Schoedel, *Ignatius of Antioch: A Commentary on the Letters of Ignatius of Antioch* (Philadelphia: Fortress, 1985) 3–7.

have been selected because they offer evidence that teaching directed at married early Christian women was affected by early Christianity's encounter with public opinion. With the possible exception of 1 Corinthians 7.12–16, all the passages on marriage between believers and non-believers reflect the church's encounter with a hostile public reaction. Nevertheless, 1 Corinthians 7.12–16 illustrates that in the earliest period of church history, believers certainly experienced hostility within the home, at the hands of non-believing spouses. They were instructed to view their marriages with the hope that non-believers might be won for Christ.

1 Corinthians 7.12–16 – the evangelizing potential of household relations

As church communities emerged in the cities of the Roman Empire, difficulties arose because some individuals were joining these groups without their spouses. Already in Paul's correspondence with the Corinthians, the way this issue is addressed implies both that community members were uncertain about whether mixed marriages should continue, and that such marriages were subject to strife (1 Cor. 7.12–16).

Perhaps in response to those Corinthians who saw divorce as an escape from the immoral influence of an unbelieving spouse[12] and/or as release from marital tensions, Paul argues in favour of the continuation of mixed marriages by appealing to the status of the children. He expects that his audience will be convinced of the sanctifying nature of these marriages because the offspring are not unclean, but holy. Paul's argument needs to be examined carefully. First, it is important to recognize that by welcoming the wives of unbelieving husbands as members of the community, Paul is sanctioning what might be understood as a type of marital infidelity. As I illustrated in Part 1, a Greco-Roman wife's faithfulness to her husband included faithfulness to his gods: a dutiful wife would ensure that children also shared in the religion of the household.[13]

---

[12] On the ascetic currents in Corinth see MacDonald, 'Women Holy', 161–81.

[13] See especially Plutarch's remarks about the need for a wife to share not only her husband's friends, but also his gods in Plut. *Moralia* 140D, trans. F. C. Babbit (LCL 1927–69). See also Portefaix, *Sisters Rejoice*,146–7; Wire, *Corinthian Women Prophets*, 85.

Second, it is important to ask why the issue of children plays such an important role in Paul's argumentation, especially when, as a whole, 1 Corinthians 7 hardly seems concerned with propagation. Commentators have pointed to the Jewish background of Paul's thought in this passage, noting a typically Jewish concern with the status of the children of marriages between Jews and non-Jews.[14] But if we aim to understand why Paul would expect to convince a largely Gentile community to preserve mixed marriages by appealing to the status of the children, we must also think in very concrete terms about the role of children in the community.

Paul presumes that the holiness of the children will be obvious to the Corinthians; surely such visibility would not be possible unless the children of such unions were mainly believers. Thus, in pointing to the example of the children, it is as if Paul were saying: Look at the success we have already had within your households![15] But we should be cautious about understanding entry into the community in terms of modern notions of conversion. Given the importance of household relationships in the building-up of church communities, it is likely that the children of believers accompanied them into the church. It may be that such allegiance is best understood in terms of the symbiotic relations of kinship. From early Christian times onwards there is significant evidence of the powerful influence of Christian teaching that is absorbed at a mother's side.[16] In the descriptions of Christians offered by both

---

[14] On the Jewish background of Paul's thought on mixed marriage see Newton, *Concept of Purity*, 105–6, 145 n. 31.

[15] Certainly we cannot conclude on the basis of this text that all children of mixed marriages were believers. Indeed there is a sense in which Conzelmann is correct when he says: 'It looks as if holiness is crassly regarded as a thing; it is transferable, without faith (and even baptism) being necessary.' See Conzelmann, *Commentary on the First Epistle to the Corinthians*, 121; see pp. 121–3 for summary of various ways the reference to children has been understood. No matter how one understands the implications of Paul's thought here, if we focus on why the example of children serves Paul in an attempt to make his point about the 'saving' possibilities of mixed marriages, we inevitably confront the potential influence of believing children in the household. See also the response to Conzelmann, focusing on the Jewish elements of Paul's thought, by Newton, *Concept of Purity*, 105–6.

[16] See Jean Delumeau, *La religion de ma mère: les femmes et la transmission de la foi* (Paris: Cerf, 1992). On women's responsibility for the religious education of children in Greco-Roman society and the implications of this for church life see Portefaix, *Sisters Rejoice*, 33–6, 193–4.

Lucian and Celsus, the involvement of women accompanied by children is highlighted. Yet, it is not inconceivable that, once they had been integrated into the holy community, children played an important part in the winning of the remaining non-believing members of households. At any rate, Paul uses the point about the holiness of the children in his central argument about the continuation of mixed marriages. Such marriages must be preserved because of their inherent potential for winning new members. Paul's treatment of the problem culminates in the question applied equally to believing men and women: how do you know whether you will save your husband/wife (1 Cor. 7.16)?[17] In 1 Corinthians 7.16 Paul does not go so far as to say that a nonbeliever is actually a member of the community, but the example of the holy believing children confirms the general holiness of the marriage and holds out the promise of a future acceptance of the gospel by the spouse.

In 1 Corinthians 7.12–16 the hope that mixed marriages will yield new community members overrides any scruples about believers becoming 'mismated with unbelievers' (2 Cor. 6.14; cf. 1 Cor. 6.15–20).[18] But Paul does not believe that these marriages must be preserved under all circumstances. In the case where the non-believing partner is unwilling to remain married, a brother or sister is not 'enslaved' (δουλόω; 1 Cor. 7.15). Antoinette Clark Wire aptly has described the intent of Paul's concession as 'the freeing of the abandoned'.[19] Church members are to do all they can to preserve the unions, but sometimes the unions dissolve in a way that is apparently beyond the control of the believing member. Paul's teaching leads to the obvious conclusion that some non-believers are not consenting to remain married, and hence are

---

[17] On the missionary intent of this text see Yarbrough, *Not Like the Gentiles*, 111–12. The text has sometimes been taken to reflect resignation in light of the non-believer's desire to separate: 'Do not resist your partner's wishes, since after all you have no way of knowing whether you can effect his salvation.' Yarbrough has argued convincingly against this alternate interpretation (p.112).

[18] On 2 Corinthians 6.14–7.1 and 1 Corinthians 6.15–20 see Newton, *Concept of Purity*, 102–14.

[19] The *NRSV* translates δεδούλωται (a derivative of the verb δουλόω) as 'bound'. I prefer Wire's more revealing translation of the graphic verb Paul employs as 'enslaved'. See *Corinthian Women Prophets*, 85–6.

treating the believing spouse with hostility. Although Paul is not explicit about suffering in this text, a veiled reference to it is probably contained in Paul's proclamation: God has called you to peace (1 Cor. 15.7).[20] What seems to be beyond question is that there are serious problems in the households of believers married to unbelievers; some community members have taken the initiative in removing themselves from the situation, while others essentially have been abandoned by unbelievers who no longer consent to live with them. In an effort to extend the scope of salvation as broadly as possible, the Apostle insists that believers do all they can to remain in what must have been very difficult situations. Seen from the perspective of the unbelievers, Paul offers us one of the earliest examples of the church acting as an irritant to Greco-Roman society. The effect of his exhortation is to legitimize the existence of 'the house divided against itself'. When one reads 1 Corinthians 7.12–16 in light of Celsus' comments that when Christians 'get hold of children in private and some stupid women with them, they let out some astounding statements as, for example, that they must not pay any attention to their father and school-teachers',[21] the implication of Paul's teaching (which would shape subsequent church advice on the matter) stands out sharply; in recommending the continuation of mixed marriages, he sanctioned a pattern of Christian behaviour that threatened the very heart of the household in the ancient world.

This disruption would be particularly likely if it was mainly the *women* of Corinth who were involved in mixed marriages. There are good reasons for thinking this to be the case. In keeping with his tendency to speak about the mutual obligations of men and women in 1 Corinthians 7, Paul makes parallel references to men and women who were married to unbelievers. I have argued previously, however, that behind this deliberate attempt at equivalence

---

[20] It is impossible to be certain how this proclamation should be interpreted. Should it be read together with the first part of the verse, as offering further support for the notion that where there is lack of consent on the part of the non-believer, the believer should be considered freed from the marriage? Should it be read in conjunction with v.16 as a further reason not to separate from the non-believing spouse? Although the first case seems to me most likely, in either case the phrase points to difficulties in the marriage which are either insurmountable, or may be overcome only through God's call to peace.

[21] *C. Cels.* 3.55. See discussion of Celsus in Part 1 of this volume.

throughout 1 Corinthians 7 lies a special concern for divorced women, widows, and virgins.[22] There is another factor in support of the contention that mixed marriage mostly involved believing women. Given the social arrangements of Greco-Roman society, Christian men would be less likely to be married to non-believing women than the reverse. The accounts of entry into the church of male believers and their households are indications that wives usually shared their husbands' allegiances from the outset (e.g. Acts 16.32–3; 18.8; 1 Cor. 1.16).[23] Yet, by far the most convincing argument in favour of reading 1 Corinthians 7.12–16 as directed mainly to women is the testimony of later evidence which refers almost exclusively to believing women involved in such arrangements.[24]

Understood from the perspective of church women, 1 Corinthians 7.12–16 acts both as an indicator of the complexities and restrictions that characterized the lives of early Christian women, and as a testimony to their initiative. Despite Paul's concession that a believing woman is not 'bound' to remain married when the non-believer refuses consent (i.e. she essentially has been abandoned), one wonders if Paul's exhortations sometimes had the effect of locking women within a difficult domestic setting. Beginning in the late first century CE Christian authors comment on the cruel treatment of Christian women by their pagan husbands. Clement of Rome, for example, connects the suffering of believing women who were divorced by pagan husbands with the indignities suffered

---

[22] This is the main point I argued in 'Women Holy'. See also Part 2, pp. 133–44. Wire sees evidence in 1 Corinthians 7.12–16 of a special focus on women, when Paul uses a masculine article to refer the spouse: 'If the unbeliever leaves, let him leave (7.15).' See *Corinthian Women Prophets*, 85–6. However, the rhetorical balance in the discussion of male and female in 1 Corinthians 7.12–16 is so strong that it seems better to look for arguments in support of a focus on women which are external to this particular text.

[23] Prominent women, in contrast, are depicted as independently joining the movement (e.g. Acts 17.4, 12, 34). The tale of the conversion of Lydia does, however, offer us an example of a woman who joined the church with her household (Acts 16.13–15, 40). Lydia, a native of Thyatira now living in Philippi, was a seller of purple goods. She is described as being a 'worshipper of God' (perhaps a pagan women with an allegiance to Judaism). The great initiative and independence that Lydia demonstrates, coupled with the fact that no husband is mentioned, have led scholars to estimate that she may have been a relatively well-to-do widow. See, for example, Thurston, *The Widows*, 34.

[24] This evidence will be examined below, but see also my article, 'Early Christian Women', 221–34; Fox, *Pagans and Christians*, 310–11.

by women before martyrdom.[25] It seems reasonable to assume that even as early as Paul's day some women found life with an unsympathetic spouse intolerable, and they themselves took the initiative in separation. Perhaps this is what Paul is acknowledging in his puzzling admission, inserted in the midst of his prohibition of divorce, that some women are separating from their husbands in the community and should subsequently remain single or be reconciled to their husbands (1 Cor. 7.11). In an intriguing text (further analysed below) the second-century apologist Justin Martyr records the fact that a church woman initiated a divorce from her pagan husband, despite earlier attempts to be faithful to Paul's position on the matter. But we must be careful about assuming that women immediately would have wanted to extricate themselves from mixed marriage. There were very serious legal reasons why a woman might want to remain married. A believing mother's special opportunity to evangelize her children might be lost, if her husband refused to live with her: 'After divorce, the father retained *potestas* [control], and with it the right to keep the children with him.'[26] Moreover, while the issue of the motivation of the women who joined the church is perhaps the most difficult to evaluate historically, there is no good reason to doubt that they would have shared Paul's hope that they could act as evangelists in their own homes. The very least we can say about the women in Paul's day who entered the church without their spouses is that they acted with tremendous resolve. Further, as tensions between church and world increased with the passing decades, the believing female partners of mixed marriages must have been nothing less than courageous.

Reflecting only early stages of church institutionalization, 1 Corinthians 7.12–16 does not display the kind of caution that is characteristic of later exhortations. As we move on to discuss 1 Peter 3.1–6 (probably composed near the end of the first century CE), we will find an implicit acknowledgment of the precarious sit-

---

[25] *1 Clem.* 6.2–3 (LCL *Apostolic Fathers*). For a similar sentiment see also Tertullian *Apology* 3 (*ANF* III.20); *Recognitions of Clement*, 2.29.

[26] Gardner, *Women in Roman Law and Society*, 146. She notes that from the time of Antoninus Pius, appeals could be made to a magistrate so that a child might continue to live with his mother, but the father's *potestas* remained otherwise undiminished.

uation of women who were married to non-believers: husbands who do not obey the word may be won without a word by the behaviour of their wives (1 Pet. 3.1). While both 1 Corinthians 7.12–16 and 1 Peter 3.1–6 share an interest in mission, in Paul's exhortation there is no indication that community members are being taught to keep their church affiliations a secret. 1 Corinthians 7.12–16 might be characterized as a particularly bold acknowledgment of the evangelizing potential of household relationships. In fact, this is how the text was read in subsequent generations. In the fifth century, the erudite but scandal-haunted Jerome wrote a letter to Laeta, advising her on how to rear a virgin Christian daughter. He cites Paul's treatment of mixed marriage. He begins his quotation at 1 Corinthians 7.13 with the case of the woman with the unbelieving husband (he omits the previous reference to a man with an unbelieving wife), suggesting that this was the situation with which he was most familiar. In order to illustrate the wisdom of Paul's counsel he notes that Laeta, although herself married to a Christian spouse, was the offspring of a Christian mother and of a pagan father: her mother's piety had influenced Laeta, despite her father's unbelief. Like Paul, Jerome was convinced that the example of believing children held out the promise of the future acceptance of the Gospel by family members. With respect to her grandfather (a man of the highest distinction but who still walked in darkness) Laeta's daughter is cast in the role of unrelenting child-evangelist: 'When she sees her grandfather, she must leap upon his breast, put her arms round his neck, and, whether he likes it or not, sing Alleluia in his ears.'[27]

1 Peter 3.1–6 – recovering the lives of the quiet evangelists

Of all early Christian women, probably none faced the dangerous consequences of visibility more than those who were married to non-believers. Often encouraged by early Christian exhortation to remain married despite any personal inclinations to the contrary, these women inevitably led a 'double' life. Lucius Apuleius'

---

[27] *Letter 107*, Jerome to Laeta; excerpt from Kraemer, ed., *Maenads*, 130; see pp.127–30.

description of the marriage between the pitiful baker and the woman who worshipped a god called 'only' alerts us to the fact that society's reaction to mixed marriages could be categorically negative. This, no doubt, goes a long way towards explaining the nature of the advice that women married to unbelievers received in church circles: appeals to remain steadfast were coupled with warnings about the importance of quiet and submissive wifely behaviour. Ironically, women also were encouraged to engage in discreet evangelizing efforts within the contexts of their own homes. Even early Christian authors sometimes appear somewhat uncomfortable about sanctioning behaviour that, while necessary to their group's growth, disrupted the commonly accepted ideal of harmony within the home. The result was that some married early Christian women found themselves in the awkward and even hazardous daily situation of eating with, sleeping with, and caring for the children of non-believers. Their goal of maintaining single-hearted loyalty to Christ and to the members of their communities must have been tested by the great prudence their way of life demanded and by the complex manoeuvres necessary if, as was recommended by the author of 1 Peter, their participation in church rites was to remain a secret.[28]

In his important book, *A Home for the Homeless*, J. H. Elliott has described the central focus of 1 Peter as: 'the interaction of Christians and society, the social contrasts and conflicts which have created a crisis for the Christian movement in Asia Minor. 1 Peter is addressed to resident aliens and visiting strangers who, since their conversion to Christianity, still find themselves estranged from any place of belonging.'[29] Elliott's study illustrates that norms and ideals associated with the household are strongly evident in 1 Peter, and that the topic of household is prominent in hostile public reaction to church communities. 1 Peter 2.18–3.7 reveals that Christian marriages and the behaviour of Christian slaves were under suspicion.[30] In speaking generally about the setting of the addressees of 1 Peter, Elliott has pointed to social tensions

---

[28] On the complexity of Christian life in Mediterranean society in general see P. Brown, 'Late Antiquity', in P. Veyne (ed.), *A History of Private Life, Vol 1: From Pagan Rome to Byzantium* (Cambridge, Mass., and London: Belknap Press of Harvard University, 1987) 259. [29] Elliott, *A Home,* 48. [30] Ibid., 80.

caused by population movement and the meeting of diverse cultures in the urban and rural regions of four provinces of Asia Minor: Pontus-Bythinia, Galatia, Cappadocia, and Asia.[31] He provisionally dates the letter between 73 and 92 CE. Although this was a period before any direct confrontation with Rome, Elliott nevertheless feels justified in speaking of a crisis which is threatening community life:

It was a time when the expansion of the Christian movement in Asia Minor and its growing visibility as a distinct socio-religious entity was being encountered and challenged with suspicion, fear and animosity. Spread throughout all the provinces north of the Taurus, the sect had attracted rural as well as urban elements of the population, former Jews as well as a predominant number of pagans. Living on the margin of political and social life, these *paroikoi* 'resident aliens' no doubt had seen in this new salvation movement new opportunity for social acceptance and improvement of their economic lot. Coming from the already suspect ranks of strangers, resident aliens and lower classes, however, these 'Christ-lackeys' gained only further disdain for the exotic religion they embraced. Sporadic local outbreaks of slander and abuse had led to the suffering of these Christians here as elsewhere throughout the Mediterranean world.[32]

For Elliott, however, the crisis does not only lie in the suffering of Christians per se, but in the threat that suffering poses to their very social distinctiveness.

The crisis situation outlined by Elliott may at least partially explain why the statement in 1 Peter 3.1–6 concerning wives whose husbands are non-believers is decidedly more cautious than Paul's exhortation in 1 Corinthians 7.12–16 concerning mixed marriages.[33] As we will see, the enthusiasm for evangelism is still present but it is restrained, and one gets a far greater sense of the vulnerability of the believing partner. In fact, a perception of injustice is echoed throughout 1 Peter. While the hope is expressed that the good behaviour of Christians will have a positive effect on outsiders (maybe even lead them to glorify God), it also appears that the ignorance of certain foolish individuals has led to the feeling that Christians are being mistakenly accused of wrongdoing, and

---

[31] Ibid., 59–73.   [32] Ibid., 83–4.
[33] The full text of 1 Pet. 3.1–6 is cited in the Introduction, p. 44.

perhaps even of civil disobedience (cf. 1 Pet. 2.12, 13–17; 3.16).[34] That Christians would seek to behave in such a way as to meet even the most stringent expectations of societal propriety should not come as a surprise, given the powerful influence of impression, rumour, and stereotype we have seen in the earliest records of pagan criticism of Christianity. Living on the crossroads between the church and the world, women who were married to unbelievers were especially susceptible to scrutiny. 1 Peter 3.1–6 gives us every reason to believe that these women were being treated with hostility by mates who may also have played a part in the slander of the community.[35]

1 Peter 3.6 strongly suggests that these women had been suffering. They are to let nothing terrify them. It is as if the author[36] were saying that even if they are harshly treated despite their most valiant attempt at quiet behaviour, they should not be afraid. Believers are to fear God (1 Pet. 2.17; cf. 1.17), but not fear those who oppose their faith (1 Pet. 3.14). Those who suffer according to God's will are to deliver themselves to the care of the faithful creator (1 Pet. 4.19). David L. Balch has noted that some philosophers in the Greco-Roman world taught that the wife must fear the husband.[37] As part of an effort to instil a sense of hope, the author seems to go against a cultural norm. A woman married to a nonbeliever is not to fear her husband;[38] the main focus of her trepidation should be God. The focus of her attention ultimately is

---

[34] Note that Elliott also draws attention to these texts in *A Home* (p. 80), but his interpretation differs somewhat from mine.

[35] The expression, 'those disobedient to the word' in 1 Peter 3.1, implies active opposition to Christianity rather than passive disbelief (cf. Acts 14.2; 19.9; Rom. 15.31). See Balch, *Let Wives*, 99.

[36] For the sake of convenience, 'author' is used in the singular throughout this discussion. However, because of 1 Peter 5.12–13 some scholars have thought it preferable to speak of authors. Elliott, for example, speaks of the letter as originating from a Petrine group in Rome. See *A Home*, 272; 270–80.

[37] Balch, *Let Wives*, 105. He notes Xeneophon, *Concerning Household Management*, 7.25 and ps.–Aristotle, *Concerning Household Management*, III.144.2. Balch offers an excellent detailed discussion of all of 1 Peter 3.1–6 on pp. 95–105.

[38] 1 Peter 3.2 refers to the reverent (ἐν φόβῳ – literally 'in fear') behaviour of Christian wives which might win their husbands. Although it is possible that the reference is to 'due reverence to the husbands', 1 Peter 1.17, 2.17 and 3.6 strongly suggest that what is in view is reverence to God. E. Best, for example, understands it in this way; see *1 Peter* (Grand Rapids: Wm B. Eerdmans, 1977) 125.

outside of the household. It is important to recognize, however, that for those women who were married to unbelievers, the advice to be quiet and submissive offered no guaranteed protection against the suspicion of wrongdoing, nor against a hostile spouse. That the exhortation to wives in 1 Pet. 3.1–6 culminates in the instruction that women should not be afraid means that the focus of the text as a whole is primarily on how they should relate to non-Christian husbands.[39] In instructing the Christian wives of unbelievers to live modestly, quietly, and in submission to their husbands, the author of 1 Peter clearly is acknowledging the authority structures which define relationships in the household. Such close proximity to the unbelieving world means that it is prudent for wives to go about their business quietly. In fact on one level, women who are in view seem to be extremely confined, as secluded from the menacing powers outside as is possible given the precariousness of their situation. While it may seem that there is little more to be said about instructions which clearly reinforce hierarchy in male/female relations, when we recall the distinction between authority and power discussed in the Introduction to this book we may detect new levels of meaning.

The author directly reinforces the authority of the unbelieving husbands with the plea that women accept the authority of their husbands. Obviously, early Christian teaching matches cultural norms in this case.[40] The traditional ideal of a quiet wife is expressed in the hope that husbands will be won 'without a word' (1 Pet. 3.1) and in the idea that a wife's best adornment is a gentle and quiet spirit (1 Pet. 3.4). In speaking of the marital relationship, Plutarch says that 'like the flute-player, she [the woman] makes a more impressive sound through a tongue not her own'.[41] In 1 Peter 3.5–6 biblical women who were submissive to their husbands,

---

[39] The preceding exhortation to slaves (2.28–5) also focuses on suffering, suggesting that what the author has primarily in mind here is the interaction of Christians with non-Christian members of the household (in this case, masters). Ibid., 96. Note however that the structure of 1 Peter 3.1 implies that the author may also have been speaking generally to wives. See Edward G. Selwyn, *The First Epistle of St Peter* (London: MacMillan & Co, 1958) 183.

[40] Plutarch's *Moralia 142E* , trans. Babbitt (LCL) offers an especially good parallel where the verb also appearing in 1 Peter 3.1, 5 occurs: ὑποτάσσω. Balch gives other examples; *Let Wives*, 97–9, 143–9.

[41] Plutarch, *Moralia*, 142D; trans. Babbitt (LCL).

including Sarah who called Abraham 'Lord' (Gen. 18.12), are held out as examples for Christian women to emulate (1 Pet. 3.5–6).[42] Given the hazardous circumstances of Christian women living in the households of unbelievers, the practical effect of these exhortations is unmistakable: prudence is recommended in relation to a society that expects a wife to share her husband's customs and religion.

A particularly interesting instruction, given the concern in 1 Peter about the conflict between Christians (insiders) and society (outsiders), and which is related to the plea for Christian wives to be submissive to their non-Christian mates, is found in 1 Peter 3.3–4. Wives are not to become caught up in the external adornment of jewels and clothing, but rather their adornment is to be 'the inner self with the lasting beauty of a gentle and quiet spirit, which is very precious in God's sight' (1 Pet. 3.3).[43] Like the community that is battered by aggressive forces from outside and looks inward for support, the believing woman is to look to her inner self for sustenance in the hostile world of her own home. One might say that the modest unadorned woman becomes a model for, and a microcosm of, the community of those who are truly God's people: those finding in their inner selves what is more precious than the tainted gold of the world outside. 1 Pet. 1.7 in fact calls genuine faith that which is more precious than gold which, though perishable, is tested by fire.[44]

There is a sense where the exhortation found in 1 Peter 3.1–6 (which encourages the wife married to the unbelieving husband to respect his authority) offers the woman protection from the hostile world outside. Elements in the text which reinforce traditional authority structures are interwoven with other elements which foster security, home-centredness and isolation. However, in keeping with 1 Peter as a whole, 1 Peter 3.1–6 also displays a certain openness to the world outside, specifically, an interest in evangelism. J. H. Elliott notes that, on the one hand, 1 Peter presents the relationship between believers and the outside world as one of alienation and hostility. On the other hand, '[the text]

---

[42] On the use of Genesis 18.2 in this text see Best, *1 Peter*, 126–7.   [43] Trans. *NRSV*.
[44] Balch draws attention to the relationship between 1 Peter 3.3 and 1 Peter 1.7. See also his discussion on the ideal of modest dress for women in *Let Wives*, 101–2.

speaks in positive, optimistic terms concerning the eventual conversion of these outsiders (2.12; 3.1–2), supports a neutral, if not favourable, view of civil government (2.13–17), and utilizes the secularly popular model of the household to discuss the roles and relationships of distinctive Christian behaviour (2.18–3.7; 5.1–5).'[45] Even with respect to the tense arrangement of mixed marriages, 1 Peter speaks in optimistic terms about the eventual conversion of unbelievers. Husbands may be won without their wives speaking a word, but by their reverent and chaste behaviour (ἀναστροφή, 1 Pet. 3.1–2; cf. 3.6; 2.14). The importance attributed to the woman's behaviour in 1 Peter 3.1–6 is in keeping with the emphasis on doing good throughout this work and, according to Balch, should be read in relation to 'the omnipresent suspicion in Roman society that foreign cults were sexually immoral' (cf. 1 Pet. 2.11; 2.16). [46] Thus the focus on the chaste conduct of the wife married to the unbeliever probably has an apologetic function. In addition, quietness and gentle behaviour (1 Pet. 3.4) as an appropriate response to slander, and one that might actually convince the opposing partner, is known in ancient literature.[47] Yet it remains remarkable that the author articulates such confidence in the possibility that a husband might be won in the hazardous social setting of the unbelieving household. Even if it were the case that moral example was a more powerful evangelizing tool in the ancient world than in our modern context, at some point ideal behaviour would need to give way to teaching. It is impossible to determine to what extent such marriages did lead to 'conversions'. From the evidence I have collected from the first four centuries of church history, I am inclined to conclude that an overtly hostile reaction from the husband was more common than a change of heart; but we do know of women who were successful in the conversion of other members of the

---

[45] Elliott, *A Home*, 108. In order to explore this tension in 1 Peter, Elliott makes use of the model of the conversionist sect developed by sociologist Bryan Wilson and discussed in Part 2 of this volume.

[46] Balch, *Let Wives*, 101. See also his discussion of the importance of conduct in Jewish and early Christian settings, 100–1.

[47] A particularly interesting example noted by Balch comes from Musonius, *Must One Obey One's Parents under all Circumstances?* (*Orations* XVI). Gentleness and control of the tongue are recommended as the best approach to take when a father refuses to allow his son to study philosophy; see pp.99–100; see also pp. 100–3 for further examples.

household, especially children.[48] Whatever the 'success rate' may have been, it is evident that the author of 1 Peter is even more determined than Paul was that such marriages be preserved, even in the face of heightened suffering. There is nothing resembling the 'Pauline Privilege' in 1 Peter 3.1–6. The author hopes to bolster the resolve of the quiet evangelists by comparing them to holy biblical women and calling them the children of Sarah.[49]

If we consider the role of the woman evangelist that emerges from 1 Peter 3.1–6, what seemed at first glance to be simply a Christian appropriation of dominant patterns of hierarchy now looks much more complicated. The exhortation directed to the wife married to the unbeliever confines her to her home, yet, para-doxically, also pushes her outside of the home. 1 Peter 3.1–6 expresses what Dubisch has called a 'cultural acknowledgment of female power'. This acknowledgment takes place despite the fact that it is clearly illegitimate power according to the norms of the non-believing world. The acknowledgment of the power of the wives of unbelievers does not receive the strong legitimation that would be the result of calling women to evangelize their husbands boldly, disobey them overtly, or leave them categorically. In other words, the power of these women is not reinforced with clearly articulated authority structures. However, while the author of 1 Peter's acknowledgment of female power may be said to be indi-rect, even cautious, there is no doubt that such a recognition takes place. The power is recognized as effective: wives may win their husbands. The women are acknowledged as leading a venerable Christian life: they are compared to the holy women of old and called the 'daughters of Sarah'.

As we move from the implications of the author's response to focus specifically on the actual situation of the quiet evangelists, it is useful to recall that the domestic sphere of the believing woman enabled her to touch many lives, not only that of her husband.

---

[48] See, for example, *Letter 107*, Jerome to Laeta cited above. The most famous example of a woman being successful in winning her husband is the case of Augustine's mother Monica; see *Confessions*, 9.19–22.

[49] Balch notes that Sarah was sometimes regarded as the mother of women proselytes. Philo allegorically interpreted her role as helping Abraham in his progress towards phi-losophy. See *Let Wives*, 105.

Slaves and children come immediately to mind, but the life of the extended household in the Greco-Roman world may also have offered opportunity for exchange with clients and business associates of various kinds.[50] Church records provide examples of the faith spreading from women to their children, such as 2 Timothy which describes Timothy's faith as a faith that dwelt first in his grandmother Lois and in his mother Eunice (2 Tim. 1.5). By remaining married to an unbeliever and by leading the life of an ideal mother and wife, a woman increasingly may succeed in exercising power as she emulates more closely the ideal. The denial of a woman's authority in relation to her husband in the household, and the reinforcement of the 'traditional' female life that occurs in 1 Peter 3.1–6, by no means eliminates female power. In addition, while this power clearly is exercised in the domestic sphere, it extends its influence deeply into the public sphere: it contributes to the spread of a new religious movement that will defy political authorities in its determination to worship the one God and will come to threaten the very order of the society as a whole.

Recent anthropological thought criticizes the assumption that norms which identify women with the household limit the role of women exclusively to the private sphere. In this light, it is useful to see the woman married to the unbeliever as being a mediator between realms.[51] On the one hand, she ventures into the public sphere, moving and manoeuvring to secure Christian membership; yet she also returns to her private home, intent on transforming the house. However, as we noted previously, we must be careful when describing the early church as a public entity, because the locus of so much of its activities was the private domain. It is indeed perhaps only because of the ambiguous relationship between public and private, manifested in early Christianity, that women married to unbelievers were able to join the movement at all; for movement outside of one's house in the early church was essentially movement occurring between a network of houses.

---

50 See discussion in Meeks, *Urban Christians*, 30.
51 See Dubisch, 'Culture Enters', 207–8; 210–11.

In a world that was convinced that women were especially susceptible to bizarre religious impulses and which by the second century clearly was denouncing early Christianity for corrupting women, it remains remarkable that women would have the courage to enter church communities without their husbands. If one is convinced by Elliott's social profile of 1 Peter's addressees as 'resident aliens and strangers' (*paroikoi*) living on the margins of social and political life, the actions of these women seem even more striking. Yet in such a community, women would have found much rich symbolism to give meaning to their experiences of being strangers in their own homes.

The evidence concerning the circumstances of the wives married to non-believers revealed by this analysis of 1 Peter 3.1–6 nevertheless calls for further investigation and caution with respect to the line of argument where the choice of joining an early church community is linked directly with improved social conditions.[52] As I noted above, scholars often have looked for social liberation offered by the Christian movement when dealing with the thorny issue of the motives of women who joined the movement.[53] However, the difficulty in identifying significant social advantage offered to women who joined Christian communities without their spouses, coupled with the likely increase in domestic hostility, reminds us of how little we understand about why these women became members on their own initiative. The author of 1 Peter offers us an interpretation of their Christian lives by pointing to their roles as evangelists, and they may certainly have shared the author's enthusiasm for a possible transformation of their households. Yet, much about the precise circumstances of their conversions will remain in the shadows. As we will see, one intriguing account offered by the second-century apologist, Justin, does enable us to recover a remarkable amount of information about the experiences and activities of one woman who had a pagan husband; this text may shed further light on the circumstances addressed in 1 Peter.

---

[52] See for example Elliott, *A Home*, 83–4.

[53] On motivation see Kraemer, *Her Share*, 139–40. She notes: 'To enquire about motivation is far more problematic than to enquire about consequences. Intertwined with our own perspectives, the very concept of motivation is thorny' (p. 139).

Justin's woman married to an unchaste husband: religious sensibilities and life with a pagan husband

Written from Rome around 155–7 CE and addressed to Emperor Antoninus Pius, his sons, as well as to the Senate and the whole people of the Romans, Justin's *Apology* illustrates how marital scandal can be at the heart of the persecution of Christians.[54] In order to illustrate the unjust treatment of the Christians, Justin Martyr records an account of a Roman woman who joined the church without her spouse. In contrast to the advice given to wives by the author of 1 Peter, this woman set out to evangelize her husband boldly, 'explaining the Christian teachings and warning him of the eternal punishment by fire reserved for those who live without chastity or right reason'.[55] This resulted in the kind of marital strife and public scrutiny that the author of 1 Peter seemed intent on preventing. Advised by friends to persevere in the hope that her husband might change his ways in the future, the wife suppressed her initial inclination to divorce him (despite the fact that he had completely lost her affections). But, eventually, a report of her husband's increasingly immoral behaviour during a trip to Alexandria caused her to seek divorce.

It is interesting to compare this woman's actions with the previously discussed exhortations in 1 Corinthians 7.12–16 and 1 Peter 3.1–6. On the one hand, we see continuity between these texts. For the sake of the possibility of the husband's future 'transformation' and despite marital tension, the wife initially resolves to remain married. On the other hand, there is a clear departure from Paul and 1 Peter on the matter. The marriage eventually breaks down, and Justin leaves no doubt that it is the woman who initiates the divorce. These events reveal two important facts. First, although women were counselled in church circles to remain married to

---

[54] There has been considerable debate concerning the relationship between the works known as 'First Apology' and 'Second Apology'. Robert M. Grant argues that it is probable, though uncertain, that there was originally one petition. See discussion in *Greek Apologists of the Second Century*, 54–5.

[55] Justin, *Second Apology*, 2. Trans. Thomas Falls, *Saint Justin Martyr* (Fathers of the Church 6; Washington: Catholic University, 1948). All subsequent references in this book are to this translation. For the Greek text and a French translation see André Wartelle, *Saint Justin, Apologies* (Paris: Études Augustiniennes, 1987).

unbelievers, they did not always do so (and Justin nowhere implies that the woman should have acted otherwise). Second, the woman's wavering decision implies that the course of action she should adopt was by no means completely clear. This was particularly the case when the pagan husband persisted in overtly immoral activities. The *Shepherd of Hermas,* of Roman provenance and from roughly the same period as Justin's *Apology*, deals with the question of whether a husband who finds that his wife is engaging in adultery should continue to live with her. While not specifically addressing the question of mixed marriage, it does lead us to wonder whether responses to the issue of the continuation of marriages to non-believing spouses could be tempered by the behaviour of the non-believing partner. In the *Shepherd of Hermas,* husbands who know of their wives' immorality are said to be partakers in her sin and they are instructed to 'put her away'. They are not to remarry, but they may accept the woman's repentance.[56]

A comparison of 1 Peter 3.1–6 and Justin's account of the woman with the unchaste husband suggests that Christian women who were married to non-believers could find themselves in a variety of social circumstances. It should be noted that we are dealing with settings that are at least fifty years apart, and are likely discussing different social strata. While 1 Peter may have been composed in Rome (1 Pet. 5.13), its addressees were the rural and urban populations of Asia Minor that included dispossessed strangers.[57] Justin's gaze is on the centre of the Empire, and he turns his phrases to address an elite audience. Moreover, the woman at the centre of the controversy in Justin's *Apology* is clearly at least relatively well-to-do. There are several status indicators[58] in the text. In the first place, her husband's impious adventures in

---

[56] *Herm. Man.* 4.1.5–9 (LCL *Apostolic Fathers*). See also discussion of the *Apocryphal Acts* below which exhibit a radical departure from Paul's advice on mixed marriage.

[57] See 1 Peter 5.13. Babylon sometimes appears as a name for Rome in early Christian literature. In the warning against luxurious adornment in 1 Peter 3.3, the author was probably drawing on a well-known topos concerning feminine virtue in order to call women to focus on their inner characters and, therefore, the text by no means necessarily implies that any women in the community were well-to-do.

[58] Social status in Greco-Roman society is a very complex issue involving more than wealth. On criteria for determining social status in early Christian literature see Theissen, *Social Setting*, 73–96.

Alexandria indicate a capacity for travel. More importantly, however, the woman's own pre-Christian life is described as one characterized by the leisure required to engage in reckless evil actions with 'servants and employees', a time when she 'took pleasure in drunkenness and every wicked action'. The text, in fact, implies that the woman might well have been in a position to control a substantial amount of money even after divorce: legal entanglements involved complications having to do with the recovery of her dowry. In the end, Justin offers us a portrait of a Roman matron who acts with the kind of independence in divorce matters which, according to the ancient historian Gillian Clark, was rare for women in the Roman Empire.[59] If we read Justin's account in relation to other early Christian texts, including 1 Peter, we are warned once again against assuming that all early Christian women lived within the same social parameters.

Unlike 1 Corinthians 7.12–16 and 1 Peter 3.1–6, Justin's account of the scandal caused by mixed marriage offers us an explanation of why a woman would find a continuing marriage with a promiscuous pagan husband so abhorrent. At the outset Justin describes the woman's attitude as the result of her Christian allegiance. Like her husband she had once been unchaste, but now was self-controlled. Her initial inclination to divorce her husband was because 'she considered it sinful to live any longer with a husband who sought in every way those means of sensual pleasure contrary to the law of nature and in violation of every right'. But the scandalous behaviour in Alexandria precipitated the divorce proceedings for she did not wish 'to participate in his sinful and impious acts by continuing to live with him by sharing his table and his bed'.

The language Justin employs in his description of the woman's acceptance of a chaste life 'depicts the normal course of conversion as he describes it'.[60] Moreover, in stressing the woman's moral resolve he reveals not only the priorities of much of second-century Christianity, but also speaks in a manner that would win the respect of an elite whose moral ideals included respect for

[59] Gillian Clark, 'Roman Women',193–212, esp. 205; see also S. Pomeroy, *Goddesses*, 150–63.   [60] Grant, *Greek Apologists*, 69.

sexual restraint.[61] It seems likely that at the heart of Justin's account lie authentic historical events, and that his interpretation of the woman's motivation explains why many women married to non-believers would have found such proximity to the pagan world abhorrent. The religious sensibilities expressed in this work call to mind the activities of Thecla discussed in Part 2, and of women in general in the legends of the *Apocryphal Acts of the Apostles*. As in Justin's description of the woman with the unchaste husband, these *Acts* reveal the strong influence of Christian asceticism on the dissolution of unions with pagans[62] and they attribute a great deal of initiative to church women. The *Acts of Peter*, for example, tell the story of Xanthippe who was inspired by Peter to separate from her husband. Albinus, horrified that his wife 'would not even sleep in the same bed with him, was raging like a wild beast and wished to do away with Peter'.[63] Although referring to the dissolution of an engagement rather than a marriage, we have seen that the *Acts of Paul and Thecla* similarly convey vividly the challenge that asceticism could hurl at Greco-Roman society. For the women in these legends, separation from the pagan world means conflict with the cultural ideal of wife, mother, and mistress of the household; the ultimate result is violence. As we will see, violence is also the outcome of the marital scandal described by Justin.

Before we consider the connection between marital scandal and persecution in Justin's text, we should pause to focus on an aspect of the religious sensibilities which the Apologist attributes to the woman with the pagan husband. The key phrase is: 'continuing to live with him by sharing his table and his bed'. The fact that the consequences of remaining joined to a non-believing mate are expressed both in terms of food and sexuality calls to mind a similar interest in the relationship between marriage and separation from the pagan world, in the Greco-Roman Jewish romance

---

[61] See Brown, *The Body*, 34.

[62] According to Grant, in Justin's account, 'the woman's attitude was strongly influenced by ascetic rigor'; *Greek Apologists*, 70. Justin does not claim that the woman's goal is to devote herself to perpetual celibacy like the women of the *Apocryphal Acts*, but if we apply the teaching from the *Shepherd of Hermas* cited above, celibacy might have been the result. Although it is by no means certain, Grant has linked the woman with Valentinian circles; see R. M. Grant, 'A Woman of Rome: Justin, *Apol.* 2,2', *CH* 54 (1985) 461–72.

[63] *Acts of Peter* 34, trans. E. Hennecke, *NT Apoc*: 2, 298–9.

Joseph and Aseneth. This work was written between the first century BCE and the second century CE, probably in Hellenistic Egypt.[64] The words of Joseph to the as yet unconverted Aseneth express the sentiments of a believer married to an unchaste spouse. Like Justin's woman, Joseph is anxious to avoid associations which yoke him intimately with the pagan world:

It is not fitting for a man who worships God, who will bless with his mouth the living God and eat blessed bread of life and drink a blessed cup of immortality and anoint himself with blessed ointment of incorruptibility to kiss a strange woman who will bless with her mouth dead and dumb idols and eat from their table of strangulation and drink from their libation cup of insidiousness and anoint herself with ointment of destruction.[65]

The connection between abhorrence of food sacrificed to idols[66] and repulsion at the thought of physical intimacy with a spouse who partakes of such food would not surprise an anthropologist. Commenting on life in rural Greece, Jill Dubisch observes: 'Concern with what comes and goes in the body, with things that move from inside to out and those that go from outside to in, parallels the concern with what goes inside and outside of the house and reflects the larger preoccupation with the boundaries of the family and their protection. Through bodily orifices pollution can occur.'[67] In the case of the woman Justin describes, the concern is for her own body. By sharing her husband's bed or even his food, his sinful and impious acts will enter her. Such activities have a profound symbolic significance: in essence, they make her body an impious body, her house a pagan house, and they leave her family

---

64 See Kraemer, *Maenads*, 408.

65 *Joseph and Aseneth*, 8.5, trans. C. Burchard, in J. H. Charlesworth (ed.), *Old Testament Pseudepigrapha*, vol. 2 (Garden City, N.Y.: Doubleday, 1983–5). Manuscript variations have led to substantial disagreements about the shape of the earliest version of this work. See comprehensive discussion in Kraemer, *Her Share*, 110–13. These debates do not, however, call into question the brief citation here.

66 The problem with food sacrificed to idols in early Christianity was that when meat was purchased in the market, ritual actions in a pagan cultic setting may have accompanied the slaughter of the meat. For a full discussion of the issues see Wendell Lee Willis, *Idol Meat in Corinth: The Pauline Argument in 1 Corinthians 8 and 10* (Chico, Calif.: Scholars, 1985); see also Theissen, *Social Setting*, 121–43.

67 Dubisch, 'Culture Enters', 201–3. See also the work on body symbolism by Mary Douglas in *Purity and Danger* and *Natural Symbols* .

outside the boundaries surrounding those who have been made chaste through the teachings of Christ.

It is interesting to note that a variety of New Testament texts connect the pollution of sexual immorality with eating food sacrificed to idols (e.g. 1 Cor. 10.8; Rev. 2.14, 20).[68] While mixed marriage was often accepted by the church as non-polluting, the attitudes of the rigourist Corinthians that Paul may have been admonishing in 1 Corinthians 7.12–16, the heroines of the *Apocryphal Acts*, and Justin's woman married to an unchaste husband suggest that some early Christians were not convinced by the line of argument offered by Paul and the author of 1 Peter. With respect to idolatrous food, Paul's moderately lenient advice gave way to the conviction that complete avoidance was the best course of action.[69] Concern about both of these issues was related to a preoccupation with the boundaries of the social group. For the woman Justin described, the risks of participating in the wicked world were dramatically manifested in eating with and sleeping with her husband. What was at stake was not only marital unity, but the nature of her entire association with a tainted pagan society.

The Christian woman's response to this confrontation with immorality was to give her husband a bill of divorce (the sole requirement for divorce) and to leave him.[70] However, the account does not end here. The bill of divorce sets in motion an array of legal conflicts which often culminates in Christians losing their lives. It is difficult to identify the precise nature of the conflicts in which the main characters are embroiled (Justin mentions them in passing in order to move the story to its climax, which is the martyrdom of innocent Christians). It seems that because the woman

---

[68] See C. K. Barrett, 'Things Sacrificed to Idols', *NTS* 11 (1964–5) 138–41. An interesting text to consider here is 2 Corinthians 6.14–7.1. Although frequently regarded as an interpolation, this passage would lead one to question whether remaining married to a non-believer was appropriate. For relevant bibliography see Meeks, *Urban Christians*, 227 n.113.

[69] Barrett, 'Things Sacrificed', 138–41. See also Theissen, *Social Setting*, 132–4. Theissen notes that by the second century a liberal attitude to meat sacrificed to idols came to be associated with gnostic groups. Justin in *Dialogue with Trypho*, 35.6 (*ANF* I.212) associates the eating of meat sacrificed to idols with Marcionites, Valentinians, Basilidians, and Saturnilians.   [70] See Grant, *Greek Apologists*, 72.

left her husband against his will, he decided to accuse her of being a Christian. She, in turn, petitioned the emperor for a delay; first, to be able to set her household affairs in order and secondly, to defend herself against the accusation. According to Robert Grant, the woman's petition to the Emperor indicates that dowry matters were involved; presumably the husband wished to retain at least a portion of the dowry.[71] The desire to prove that the woman had done something disgraceful may well have been inspired by financial incentives.[72] At any rate, the woman's petition for delay was successful. Apparently prevented from proceeding any further for the moment, the husband turned his attention to the woman's Christian teacher, Ptolemaeus.[73]

Justin offers a detailed discussion of Ptolemaeus' trial before the judge Urbicus, praetorian prefect of Rome. In keeping with the fact that he is a 'true Christian', Ptolemaeus admits his identity. That Ptolemaeus' is sentenced to execution leads a Christian onlooker, Lucius, to protest strongly to Urbicus:

What is the reason for this sentence? Why have you punished this man who is not an adulterer, a fornicator, or murderer, or thief, or robber, nor in a word convicted of any crime at all, but only confesses that he bears the name of Christian. Your judgment, Urbicus, does not become the Emperor Pius, nor the Philosopher [Marcus Aurelius], son of Caesar, nor the sacred Senate.[74]

But this loud protestation only leads to the executions of Lucius and of another protester.

As Lucius' words make clear, Justin's account, culminating in the

---

[71] Ibid., 72. Grant offers a thorough discussion of the legal entanglements.

[72] He may have accused her of immoral behaviour; Justin states that her life before association with Christianity was promiscuous. On divorce and the dowry see Clarke, *Secular and Christian Leadership*, 80–5.

[73] This attack which turns towards the woman's teacher calls to mind the *Apocryphal Acts*, where the conversion of women leads to the death of the Apostles. Grant argues: 'Since Justin says nothing of her martyrdom or even imprisonment, it seems . . . likely that while she had been impressed by "the teachings of Christ" she was not seeking baptism or even adherence to a Christian group or school.' I am not convinced by Grant's argument, for it fails to account for why so much attention is given to the woman in an effort to illustrate the unfair treatment of Christians. See 'A Woman of Rome', 468.

[74] This section of *Second Apology*, 2 has been examined by Elaine Pagels in 'Christian Apologists and "The Fall of the Angels": An Attack on Roman Imperial Power?', *HTR* 78 (1985) 301–25.

arbitrary execution of Christians, functions as an indictment of the whole system of imperial power.[75] As he is about to be led away we are told that Lucius 'expressed his thanks, since he knew that he would soon be freed from such evil rulers and would go to the Father and King of Heaven'. What is especially interesting for the present study is how quickly the story moves from its setting in the home of a married couple to the public domains of law and government. Justin offers us a detailed, early Christian description of how the conversion of a woman who was married to a non-believer might trigger violence against Christians. What is remarkable is that this violence extends well beyond the particular household in question (Justin leaves us guessing with respect to the woman's ultimate fate) to snuff out the lives of the Christian teacher and two particularly bold protesters.

Studying the situation of believers married to non-believers has made me cautious about assuming that married early church women were completely confined by the structures of the Greco-Roman household while celibate early church women were unrestricted by these structures. In a manner that calls to mind Thecla's initiative, the woman who divorced her pagan husband in Justin's account bravely confronted the hostility of Greco-Roman society. Moreover, it is important to recognize that even women who were married to non-believers, and who followed the kind of teaching reflected in 1 Peter 3.1–6, were remarkable in their determination to remain church members under such circumstances. They were powerful in their potential to transform households. Admittedly, if we compare the teaching on mixed marriage in 1 Corinthians 7.12–16 to that in 1 Peter 3.1–6, we can see a move towards traditional roles for wives, a similar development to that visible when the teaching on celibate women in 1 Corinthians 7 is compared to instructions concerning widows in 1 Timothy 5.3–16. In both 1 Peter and 1 Timothy traditional marriage is recommended as a response to slander. In 1 Peter the brave woman who joins the church and hopes to win her husband and family becomes the quiet evangelist in her own home. In 1 Timothy the young widow becomes the dutiful wife.

<hr/>

[75] See Pagels, 'Christian Apologists', 301.

What, then, are we to make of this composite picture? Thus far the collection of materials on unmarried and married early church women, selected in light of the church's encounter with public opinion, has revealed a combination of responses to the world, ranging from accommodation to worldly standards to overt challenges to the social order. While early Christian writers attribute greater importance to marriage as the church encounters increasingly hostile public opinion by the end of the first century CE, this development is not uniform. Church reaction to the place of women in public reaction to early Christianity was complex and diverse. The next material to be analysed is particularly significant for illustrating this point. In the correspondence of Ignatius of Antioch we discover the promotion of the ideal of the Christian couple and the creation of endogamy rules as defensive strategies against the immoral outside world. However, Ignatius combines strong measures to promote Christian marriages with an acceptance of asceticism for women. Investigation of the roles of individual women mentioned in these works, coupled with an analysis of texts where family relations are in view, reveals surprising possibilities for women's involvement in church life at the beginning of the second century. References to married women, widows, and virgins point to a certain fluidity with respect to the roles adopted by women. In addition, evidence in Ignatius' letters will lead us to explore the significance of married life for *all* early church women during a time of increasing tension between the church and the world. Even those early Christian women who at first glance seem virtually invisible due to the traditional nature of their lives will be seen as playing a vital role in church response to public opinion. The church woman who is a partner in Christian marriage becomes the best representation of the believer who is consistently faithful to Christ and resolutely unmoved by the seductions of pagan society.

Married life and the social reality of women in the communities of Ignatius of Antioch

When it comes to the involvement of women in the early church, Ignatius' writings are striking in many ways. Written at about the

213

same time as the Pastoral Epistles, Ignatius' letters display a similar interest in the hierarchical organization of the church and in the winning of outsiders (Ign. *Eph.* 10.1–3; Ign. *Trall.* 8.1–2; cf. Ign. *Smyrn.* 4.1; 7.1–2).[76] However, this collection of writings does not reflect the connection, evident in the Pastoral Epistles, between concern for social respectability, focus on church offices, and restriction of the activities of celibate women. Rooted in a social setting where hostile public reaction has turned into active persecution (Ignatius is on his way to Rome to face martyrdom), it is surprising to hear him warmly greet widows and virgins without any indication of efforts to limit their activities (Ign. *Smyrn.* 13.1). We would expect his insistence on the acceptance of the threefold ministry of bishop, presbyters and deacons – which seems to have been articulated with the intention of including only male officials – to have silenced any commendation of prominent female members. But this does not happen. In considering the women who are specifically named in the Ignatian correspondence we are reminded that we are closer to the organizational and leadership patterns of Paul's day than it might first appear. As with Paul's letters, among the references to individuals, an important place is occupied by women.[77]

The women named in Ignatius, Letter to the Smyrnaeans 13.2 and Ignatius, Letter to Polycarp 8.2–3 in light of references to church couples

The household of Tavia is greeted in Ign. *Smyrn.* 13.2. Ignatius refers to the personal spirituality of Tavia; he prays 'that she be confirmed in faith and love, both of the flesh and spirit'. The fact that Tavia is singled out apparently as the leader of her household suggests that she may be a widow. 'Virgins called widows' and 'families of the brethren with their wives and children' are distinct social groups making up the church according to Ignatius, *Letter to the Smyrnaeans* 13.1. Tavia may even be the leader of a household of celibate women (perhaps comprising young unmarried women, widows and children; cf. 1 Tim. 5.16) and as such would draw

---

[76] On the attitude to the world displayed by the writings of Ignatius of Antioch see MacDonald, 'The Ideal of the Christian Couple', 105–25.

[77] This has been noted by Fiorenza; see *In Memory of Her*, 247–8.

strength from the encouragement offered by Ignatius. Ignatius apparently feels that celibacy requires caution (cf. Ign. *Pol.* 4.1, 5.2) in the Greco-Roman world.[78]

A second woman is greeted in such a way as to lead us to believe that she is in charge of a household, but she is labelled with deference to the identity of her husband (Ign. *Pol.* 8.2). If the wife of Epitropus were part of a missionary couple such as Prisca and Aquila or Andronicus and Junia (cf. Rom. 16.3, 7; 1 Cor. 16.19; Acts 18.1–3) we would expect the husband to be greeted as well. She could be the widow of a well-known Christian, but it is also possible that she is the wife of a pagan paterfamilias, perhaps a relatively well-to-do pagan official, as may be suggested by the alternate translation of 'ἐπίτροπος', as 'procurator'.[79] That she, as the wife of an unbeliever, could play an active role in the church seems remarkable since one would expect that such a woman would need to keep the lowest profile possible. Indeed, as we have seen, the church itself sometimes recommended to such women only quiet, discreet behaviour (cf. 1 Pet. 3.1–2). However, some second-century Christian women who were married to pagans did not go about their business in silence, as is demonstrated by Justin Martyr's description of the matron of Rome. Scholars have been perhaps too quick to assume that women who are mentioned as independently offering services to the church were unmarried.

From what we know of a third woman mentioned in the Ignatian correspondence, close association with the pagan world does not always seem to have hampered service to the church. Alce, a person dear to Ignatius (Ign. *Pol.* 8.3; Ign. *Smyrn.* 13.2) is likely the same Alce mentioned in *Mart. Pol.* 17.2: 'Niketas, the father of Herod, the brother of Alce'.[80] The mention of Herod is suggestive

---

[78] On Ignatius' cautious attitude towards celibacy see Schoedel, *Ignatius*, 272–3. Schoedel prefers the possible translation of Ign. *Smyrn.* 13.2 as 'whom I boast ('εὔχομαι') is established in faith and love both fleshly and spiritual' believing it to be 'more likely that Ignatius mentions those whom he fondly remembers as firm in the faith' (p. 253 n. 29). However, the translation by K. Lake adopted here seems to fit best with Ignatius' cautious attitude towards celibacy expressed in his letter to the Bishop of Smyrna. Ignatius prays for the well-being of Tavia and her household rather than asserting it confidently.

[79] 'Procurator' covered a wide range of administrators and the exact status of this official is thus impossible to determine. See Schoedel, *Ignatius*, 280 n.14.

[80] On the rare name Alce referring to a woman see ibid., 253. For the translation of the *Martyrdom of Polycarp* employed here see n. 10 above.

of a family of relatively high social status, for Herod was an *eirenarch*: he held an office which was filled by members of the upper classes.[81] It is also to be noted that Herod was the official responsible for the arrest of the aged Polycarp (cf. *Mart. Pol.* 6.2; in 8.2 he is assisted by his father in his work) and that Alce had relatives who were enemies of the church. Of prominent standing in society at large, of prominent standing in the early church among Christians in Smyrna and Philomelium (to whom the *Martyrdom of Polycarp* is addressed), of a family which included prominent non-believing members, this woman lived dangerously, but apparently successfully, close to the boundaries separating the church from the world.

If we limit our study of married early Christian women to passages in Ignatius where women are specifically named, we quickly run out of evidence. Moreover, as I made clear in the previous discussion, it is impossible to be certain that any of these women were married.[82] Even when we find individual married women mentioned, such as is the case with women who were members of the missionary couples we know from Paul's correspondence (Prisca and Aquila, Andronicus and Junia, and possibly also Philologus and Julia, as well as Nereus and his sister), the evidence is by no means easy to assess.[83] In interpreting the significance of the presence of missionary couples in the Pauline circle, 1 Corinthians 9.5 comes to mind. With this text Paul maintains the right of an apostle to be accompanied by a wife as a sister (ἀδελφὴν γυναῖκα).[84] Elisabeth Schüssler Fiorenza argues that it is best to understand 'sister' in the sense of missionary co-worker. The importance of the wife as missionary co-worker gains further support from the fact that when Paul speaks of such wives as Prisca or Junia, 'their

---

[81] See Schoedel, *Ignatius*, 253; *Early Christian Writings*, A. Louth (ed.) (Penguin Classics, 1987) 133 n. 9. On Alce see also Fiorenza, *In Memory of Her*, 248.

[82] See remarks of Patricia Wilson-Kastner who evaluates the role of the married woman in the early church in relation to the question of female authorship in Wilson-Kastner (ed.), *A Lost Tradition: Woman Writers in the Early Church* (Lanham, N.Y.; London: University Press of America, 1981) vii–xxiv. On the difficulty of dealing with evidence for the lives of early Christian women who were married see also Graham Gould, 'Women in the Writings of the Fathers: Language, Belief and Reality', in W. J. Sheils and D. Wood (eds.), *Studies in Church History 27: Women in the Church* (Oxford: Basil Blackwell/ Ecclesiastical History Society, 1990) 1–13, esp. 11.

[83] For a full discussion of these couples see Fiorenza, *In Memory of Her*, 172–3; 180.

[84] See discussion in Part 1, pp. 103–4.

traditional status and role as wives does not come to the fore, but rather their commitment to partnership in the work of the gospel. Moreover, we have no indication whatever that the work of these women missionaries laboring in tandem with their partners was restricted solely to women, as patristic exegetes suggest.'[85] Here Fiorenza has in mind Clement of Alexandria, *Stromateis* 3.6.53.3: '[They] took their wives around as Christian sisters rather than spouses, to be their fellow-ministers in relation to housewives, through whom the Lord's teaching penetrated into the women's quarters without scandal.'[86] While there is no evidence that the work of female co-missionaries was restricted *solely* to women in Paul's churches, I wonder if the second-century Church Father portrays reality more accurately than Fiorenza suggests. There is a direct correspondence between the fear of scandal articulated by Clement of Alexandria, and the impression of the critics (discussed in Part 1) that early Christian groups penetrated women's quarters and corrupted women. Even in its infancy, the Pauline movement had to operate within the social structures of the Greco-Roman city. Despite the visibility of some women in the public domain, the cultural ideal of the woman at home remained dominant.

The home, a domain traditionally associated with women, was the place where the *ekklesia* gathered. This setting offered opportunity for the involvement of women, and it also suggests an important missionary strategy. Paul, devoted to establishing a community set apart from the world while leaving every possible door open to win the unbeliever (cf. 1 Cor. 8; 10; 14.22–5), certainly is aware of the evangelizing potential of household relationships. This potential is suggested indirectly by his mention of household conversions (1 Cor. 1.14–16; 16.15–18; cf. Acts 16.32–3; 18.8) and explicitly by his treatment of mixed marriage (1 Cor. 7.12–16), discussed previously. We may ask some practical questions. Given that in addressing the believing partners of mixed marriage Paul probably refers primarily to women, how were these women evangelized in the first place? It is evident that their marriages sometimes were

---

[85] Fiorenza, *In Memory of Her*, 173.
[86] *Clem. A.l. Strom.* 3.6.53.3., trans. J. Ferguson, *Stromateis Books 1–3*, Fathers of the Church vol. 85 (Washington: Catholic University, 1991) 289. See Fiorenza, *In Memory of Her*, 201 n. 43.

subject to considerable tensions (1 Cor. 7.15). How would the community maintain contact with a woman who was under the watchful eye of a disapproving household? Prisca was commended for risking her neck (Rom. 16.3). Did her work involve evangelizing women, and was this a typical practice?

The remarks of Clement of Alexandria cited above indicate the importance of the role of women in the evangelizing of other women. The comments point to more than a division of labour (with an implicit lessening of the woman's ministry because it is 'private'); here there is a positive acknowledgment of the dangerous work of penetrating pagan households done by early Christian women. In later times, early Christians unashamedly gave deaconesses the special responsibility of infiltrating pagan households to minister to their women.[87] While we must be careful about reading the social realities of later times back into earlier periods, our previous observations concerning the dominance of the cultural values of honour and shame in the New Testament suggest that there is good reason for seeing Clement's remarks as shedding light on the entire period being discussed in this book. In a world where women embody the shame of their community by means of their chastity, the married woman whose sexuality is safely contained by the structures of her household might well be seen as the most trusted companion of other women and, consequently, the missionary most likely to succeed! The wives of the apostles mentioned in 1 Corinthians 9.5 may not have been involved in purely spiritual marriages as Clement believes, but their partnership with missionary husbands must have involved a good deal of expediency when it came to travel and the winning of believers in the ancient world.[88] At any rate, when reading early Christian evidence that links women's ministry with entrance into pagan households and the evangelization of women, it is important to realize that the indoor world of the house was not an inferior world for the early Christians, it was a world that was penetrated with great gusto.

[87] See *Constitutions of the Holy Apostles* 3.15; excerpt from Kraemer ed., *Maenads*, 239. Cf. also R. H. Connolly, ed., *The Didascalia Apostolorum*, chap.16, pp.146–8.

[88] Perhaps Paul is acknowledging this expediency when he states in 1 Corinthians 9.5 that being accompanied by a wife is one of the rights which he has given up. Certainly in 1 Corinthians 9.3–7 being accompanied by a wife is directly related to missionary work.

Returning more specifically to the beginning of the second century, although missionary couples are absent from the Ignatian correspondence and these works reveal an interest in defining a male church leadership, we must be careful not to assume too quickly that the wives of male office-holders were of little consequence in the life of the church. When we read texts that illustrate the undeniable connection between household ethics and the articulation of the qualities of church officials, the picture which emerges of the church official's wife is one of an obedient, faceless woman who manages her household with great circumspection (e.g. 1 Tim. 3; Pol. *Phil.* 4–6). But two second-century texts that list sins of church leaders offer an interesting insight into the relationship between spouses. The sin of Valens (once a presbyter among the Philippians) is a source of great disappointment for Polycarp, the bishop of Smyrna. That Valens' wife is implicated in his wrongdoing (probably avarice) is implied by Polycarp's reaction: 'I am deeply sorry for him and for his wife and "may the Lord grant them true repentance"' (Pol. *Phil.* 11.4).[89] Have the joint heirs here become co-conspirators? Similarly, the wife of the visionary Hermas plays a key role in his sinful past. Hermas is embedded in the sin of his household, the wickedness of his children and the impropriety of his wife who 'does not refrain her tongue, with which she sins' (*Herm. Vis.* 2. 2.3; *Vis.* 1.3.1).[90] We cannot be more precise about the nature of her transgression but it does seem to have involved a considerable measure of her own initiative. That Hermas should be punished for the sins of his household strikes him at one point as being unjust, but during a vision, the angel of punishment explains: '"They cannot", said he, "be punished in any other way, than if you, the head of the house, be afflicted. For when

---

[89] For the translation of *Polycarp to the Philippians* employed here see n. 10 above. The case of Valens and his wife calls to mind the story of Ananias and Sapphira who are equally culpable in their sins of greed and deceit and who both fall down dead at the feet of the apostles (Acts 5.1–11).

[90] For the translation of the *Shepherd of Hermas* employed here, see n. 10 above. There is extensive debate with respect to dating and authorship of this document. I am assuming here that this document comes from about the same period as Ignatius' writings. See arguments in favour of an early date and of a single author in H. O. Maier, *The Social Setting of the Ministry as Reflected in the Writings of Hermas, Clement and Ignatius*, Dissertations SR 1 (Waterloo, On.: Wilfrid Laurier, 1991) 55–8. On women sinning with their tongues see 1 Timothy 5.13.

you are afflicted, they also will necessarily be afflicted, but while you prosper, they cannot suffer any affliction' (*Herm. Sim.* 7). Robin Lane Fox refers to this pronouncement as sounding a 'hideous note of collective punishment'.[91] This certainly offends modern sensibilities which value the autonomy of individuals in the family, but it also illustrates that relations between husbands and wives and between household members could have a very different significance in early Christianity than in our own society. To take the argument one step further: relations between husbands who were church leaders and their wives may well have had a very different significance for early church leadership and organization than is the case with such marriages in modern Christian contexts.

Ignatius, *Letter to Polycarp* 4.1–5.2 reveals the importance of household relationships as a means of envisioning the constituency of the church. The text suggests that ministerial roles developed along the structures of the Greco-Roman household. Husbands and wives, slaves, and widows (who likely hold a church office at this stage, cf. Ign. *Smyrn.* 13.1) are singled out in exhortation. Moreover, the instructions are followed immediately by a call in Ignatius, *Letter to Polycarp* 6.1 to be subject to the bishop, presbyters and deacons.[92] Although our main focus is on married couples, it is wise to consider them in relation to other groups, since to be part of a household was to be part of a network of relationships far broader than our nuclear family; connections between members were more 'symbiotic' than is usually the case in our contemporary setting.[93]

The slave women of Ignatius, Letter to Polycarp 4.3 and early church teaching on permanence in marriage

It is by no means easy to come up with a tidy definition of what constituted 'marriage' in the Roman Empire. According to Roman law, legal capacity for marriage existed between two free citizens.

---

[91] Fox, *Pagans and Christians*, 387.

[92] H. O. Maier has argued that the house-church provides the setting for community division and meetings in the time of Ignatius. He has suggested that the house-church patron had a central role to play in the leadership of Ignatius' communities. See *Social Setting of the Ministry*, 147–56. [93] See Dubisch, 'Culture Enters', 208.

But this simple statement receives great qualification in relation to various categories and classes of persons. Even where there was no legal capacity for marriage, such as was the case in marriage between slaves, marriage terminology could be used.[94] While the stability of slave families in the Roman Empire is difficult to determine, church officials who allowed such families to continue could have been giving practical expression to the advice 'to treat slaves justly' one encounters in Deutero-Pauline household codes (Col. 4.1; cf. Eph. 6.9) or to Ignatius' counsel to avoid being 'haughty to slaves, either men or women'.[95] It would be difficult for the Christian master so extolled to separate a slave couple from each other or from their children when the believing master had also been lectured on the virtue of fidelity and permanence in marriage (Ign. *Pol.* 4.3–5.1).

The fact that Ignatius is so precise concerning slaves, mentioning both men and women, is striking in comparison with the more general references to slaves in the Deutero-Pauline literature.[96] His exhortation reads like an intentional effort to include women. Pliny's account of the torturing of two female slaves who were also deacons is an indication of the visibility of female slaves in the churches of Ignatius' day.[97] Since the exhortation is made to Polycarp as bishop of Smyrna (indirectly to the community as a whole) and not specifically to believing masters, the group of slaves under consideration most likely included slaves who were part of unbelieving households (cf. 1 Tim. 6.1–2). While the expediency of allowing slaves to maintain marriages and have children is by no means unknown in Greco-Roman literature, the Christian slave of the pagan master would be unable to appeal to the image of union

---

94 See Gardner, *Women in Roman Law and Society*, 31–2; see also pp. 31–44.

95 On family relations among slaves ibid., 213–18. Dale B. Martin is somewhat more confident about the stability of slave marriages and immediate family relations than Gardner. See his evaluation of inscription evidence in *Slavery as Salvation: The Metaphor of Slavery in Pauline Christianity* (New Haven and London: Yale, 1990) 2–7.

96 A parallel is found in a first-century BCE inscription from a private religious association in Philadelphia: 'those entering this house, men [and women], bond and free'. But this seems to be more of a general parallelism – a means of including all people – rather than an attempt to ensure that both male and female slaves are in view as in Ignatius. See Frederick C. Grant, *Hellenistic Religions* (New York: Liberal Arts, 1953) 29; this text is discussed by Schoedel in *Ignatius*, 270 n. 9, 272 n. 1.

97 See discussion in Part 1, pp. 53–5.

between man and woman as a reflection of the relationship between Christ and the Church, in an effort to convince a master especially determined to break up a family.[98] Female slaves of unbelieving households would certainly be vulnerable and in need of careful consideration. Written near the end of the first century CE, *1 Clement* offers some interesting material on the suffering of women. *1 Clem.* 6.1–4 refers to the indignities suffered by women during martyrdom. Condemned women were apparently made to participate in theatrical representations before their deaths: 'Through jealousy women were persecuted as Danaids and Dircae, suffering terrible and unholy dignities . . .' (*1 Clem.* 6.2). This jealousy also estranged wives from husbands (*1 Clem.* 6.3). While the text might refer to unbelieving husbands condemning their wives, it also could refer to the separation of women from their spouses under a variety of circumstances, such as a master's rage at the infidelity and insubordination displayed by the women of his household. Clement of Rome also speaks of members of the church delivering themselves into bondage that they might ransom others; his discussion suggests that he has mainly women in mind (*1 Clem.* 55.2–6). Some provided food for others with the price they received for themselves. Women performed many deeds of 'manly' valour – women who followed the examples of Judith and Ester and delivered themselves into danger are noted. What these veiled references suggest is that there were a variety of situations where female slaves would need careful consideration, even rescue (cf. *Herm. Man.* 8.10; *Sim.* 1.8), despite the fact that Ignatius himself gives only the rather tame instruction to not be 'haughty' to slaves. At the beginning of the third century in North Africa, the slave woman Felicitas is said to have given birth prematurely and in great pain while imprisoned. She gave birth to a girl who was raised by one of the 'sisters'.[99]

It is interesting to consider the interrelationship between teachings on marriage, permanence in family life, and the involvement of slaves in early Christianity. While manumitted male slaves were

[98] See Martin, *Slavery*, 26–8. See, for example Varro, writing in the first century BCE, *On Agriculture*, 1.17.5, cited p. 27.
[99] See *Martyrdom of Saints Perpetua and Felicitas*, 15 in Kraemer (ed.), *Maenads*, 104.

sometimes in a position to buy their wives themselves,[100] there is evidence to suggest that women had a better chance of manumission, perhaps partially because their work as slaves was considered less lucrative by their owners.[101] Unless she had been manumitted for the purposes of marrying an owner, a freedwoman would be anxious to secure her future. If she was already 'married' to a slave who had not yet been manumitted, should she seek a new partner? Gardner tells of Petronia Justa's effort to establish herself as free-born, since she was a freedwoman who likely had been manumitted only informally: 'As an informally manumitted *Latina*, Petronia might face considerable difficulty making any match with a Roman citizen, to whom she could offer neither legal marriage, legitimate children, nor an inheritance for the children. She brought her case to try to establish her free birth, possibly because there was a Roman in the offing whom she wanted to marry.'[102] If Petronia were a Christian woman who had previously had a slave partner who remained in captivity, Paul's advice to her may well have been to remain in the state in which she was called, rather than seek out new opportunities that manumission might bring (1 Cor. 7.20–4). If she found herself separated from a Christian partner on account of having been manumitted or sold with little consideration for her own wishes, should she remain single in the hope of a possible reconciliation with her husband (cf. 1 Cor. 7.11)?

Ignatius' teaching moves even more strongly in the direction of slaves remaining slaves than does Paul's instruction. He refers to the danger of slaves 'being puffed up' and he is concerned with the church not becoming overly taxed by slaves who hope that the community will buy their freedom or perhaps will buy a family member who remains in captivity. But the aspect of the slave teaching which points to its connection with the marriage teaching in Ignatius, *Letter to Polycarp* 5.1–2 is the notion that slaves who seek to

---

[100] Gardner, *Women in Roman Law and Society*, 225. Some funerary inscriptions describe women as both freedwoman and wife. According to Gardner, this is probably an indication that the wife had been properly manumitted and the children were citizens.

[101] Ibid., 225–6. It must be remembered that manumission and the permanence of slave marriages were to a large extent out of the control of slaves. See discussion of this complicated issue pp. 222–6. See also Corley, *Private Women, Public Meals*, 48–52.

[102] Gardner, *Women in Roman Law and Society*, 224–5.

be set free are slaves of lust. The same danger frames the exhortations in both 4.3 and 5.2 ('ἐπιθυμία') . Endorsing the possibility of a sexual significance in Ign. 4.3, Schoedel has argued that Ignatius is afraid of the removal of the restraints of slavery because freedpersons frequently had little choice but to take up prostitution to survive.[103] Moreover, there is evidence to suggest that slave women made use of prostitution in order to earn their purchase price. In the ancient world, assumptions concerning the sexual promiscuity of slave women seem to have emerged from the sexual availability of these women and their need to sell sex for a livelihood. The fact that slave women were always available to their masters as sexual commodities, were present at public banquets as servers and entertainers when respectable matrons were noticeably absent, and sometimes acted as prostitutes to earn income, meant that their lives were likely to be interpreted as shameless and as a violation of the gender distinctions of private: woman/ public: man. A reputation for impropriety and immorality could apparently follow slave women into their existence as freedwomen, even if they had never participated, or had long ceased participating, in 'immoral' trades.[104] Given this cultural background, the mention of lust would seem to be a particularly effective, though thoroughly conventional, means of categorizing the inappropriate aspirations of female slaves.

In addition to sexual immorality, the risks of slaves desiring to be set free might also have included the danger of illicit 'marriages', marriages which were not 'in the Lord', but according to lust, marriages which did not have the sanction of the bishop (Ign. *Pol.* 5.2). A woman might have had little option other than to seek out a new partner, even a pagan partner, simply in order to survive. Gillian Clark has described the limited possibilities before the freed slave-woman as follows:

she might be a prostitute, a *mima*, or, if she were lucky, a housewife, doing much the same work as an *ancilla* did but in her own home. If she had caught the fancy of someone of high social status, she would be his *con-*

---

[103] Schoedel, *Ignatius*, 271. He reads the reference to 'evil arts' in 5.1 in the same light. On the involvement of slave women in prostitution and as a source of income for manumission see Corley, *Private Women, Public Meals*, 50–1.

[104] See Corley, *Private Women, Public Meals*, 48–52.

cubina not his wife: it was not respectable to marry a *libertina*, though it had been known to happen even before Augustus allowed it for non-senators.[105]

From the point of view of slaves who were women, church support might need to extend well beyond manumission (cf. 1 Tim. 5.16).

The widows of Ignatius, Letter to the Smyrnaeans 13.1 and Ignatius, Letter to Polycarp 4.1 – celibate life and traditional women's work

As we consider the difficult circumstances encountered by slave women, a second group of needy women discussed by Ignatius comes to our attention, the widows. Despite the somewhat cautious attitude Ignatius displays towards celibacy in Ignatius, *Letter to Polycarp* 5.2, he calls for widows not to be neglected and for Polycarp to be their protector (Ign. *Pol.* 4.1; cf. Pol. *Phil.* 6.1; *Herm. Sim.* 9.27.2–3). The letter to the Smyrnaeans includes a greeting to 'the virgins called widows' (τὰς παρθένους τὰς λεγομένας χήρας; Ign. *Smyrn.* 13.1). This intriguing phrase probably points to the admission of virgins to the group or 'order' of widows (cf. 1 Tim. 5.3–16) which we know existed at this time.[106] Thus, 'virgins called widows' might be a broad category comprising various types of unmarried women who probably had no means of support apart from the church. But unlike the author of the Pastoral Epistles, Ignatius demonstrates no interest in limiting 'enrolment' in this

---

105 Clark, 'Roman Women', 198. Economic reasons such as inability to produce a dowry, and restrictions on marriage between certain categories of people meant that some women became concubines rather than wives. Evidence suggests that concubinage occurred less frequently among the freeborn, with a tendency for men to be of a higher status than women and with a noticeable number of freeborn men. See Gardner, *Women in Roman Law and Society*, 56–8. Lilian Portefaix has discussed the difficulty faced by women who found themselves outside of the legal marriage relationship. See Portefaix, *Sisters Rejoice*, 26–32. For example, Portefaix has drawn our attention to Lucian's description of a poor widow, unskilled in her husband's craft as a 'smith' and left with no recourse other than to propose her daughter as a prostitute. See especially, pp. 26–7; cites Lucian, *Dialogues of the Courtesans*, 6.

106 See discussion in Schoedel, *Ignatius*, 252. As indicated in n. 11, I am following the modern consensus with respect to the authenticity of the Ignatian text. The longer version of the letter to the Philadelphians (ch.4) does, however, contain further instructions concerning widows which are usually understood as the work of a later editor. This material is very much in keeping with the concern for the proper behaviour of widows one sees in the Pastoral Epistles. See discussion in Thurston, *The Widows*, 60–3.

group to older women (cf. 1 Tim. 5.9–16). In addition, there seems no reason to doubt that some of these women in need of the bishop's protection would have had children young enough to require care (cf. 1 Tim. 5.10; 5.4). These women may have lived together in the house of a more well-to-do believing woman; this is implied by 1 Timothy 5.16 and is suggested by the greeting of 'virgins called widows' in Ignatius, *Letter to the Smyrnaeans* 13.1 which distinguishes this group from believing families made up of house-holders, wives and children. We may assume that the daily lives of at least some of these women would be taken up by the same activities that made up the days of married women. Gillian Clark summarizes the drudgery involved in housework in the ancient world:

there was spinning and weaving and sewing and mending, cooking and cleaning, and water carrying and baby-minding. Doubtless one reason for child mortality was the impossibility of keeping a swaddled baby clean on the fourth floor of a tenement with the water-supply at the end of the street. Soranus . . . said babies should be bathed and massaged once a day; the undersheets aired and changed and one should watch for insect bites and ulceration. It sounds optimistic.[107]

The involvement of children in the lives of some unmarried women also may be reflected in the practice of pairing the care of orphans with the care of widows. Nowhere is this more clearly evident than in the Epistle of James, where such behaviour is described as the essence of religiosity: 'Religion that is pure and undefiled before God and the Father is this: to visit orphans and widows in their affliction, and to keep oneself unstained from the world' (Jas. 1.27; cf. *1 Clem.* 8.4; *Herm. Man.* 8.10; *Barn.* 20.2.). While this may represent a stylized manner of speaking about those who are in need,[108] it is significant that Ignatius refers to the neglect of orphans and widows as the vice of his docetic opponents; here he undoubtedly has specific behaviour in mind (Ign. *Smyrn.* 6.2).[109] A fascinating statement where widows and orphans are exhorted as though they form a group (perhaps members of the same household?) is found in the *Shepherd of Hermas*: 'Grapte

---

[107] Clark, 'Roman Women', 198.
[108] Community protection of orphans and widows had long been recognized as an ethical obligation within Judaism see e.g. Jeremiah 7.6; Deuteronomy 24.19–22.
[109] See discussion in Maier, *Social Setting of Ministry*, 154–5.

shall exhort the widows and orphans' (*Herm. Vis.* 2.4.3). In Part 1 we saw that the involvement of women accompanied by children plays an important role in descriptions of early Christianity by pagans. Lucian tells of aged widows and orphan children visiting the imprisoned Peregrinus. Celsus sees the church as contributing to insubordinate behaviour among women and children. The church is depicted as eager to attain converts among children and to corrupt young minds.[110]

In her recent study of widows in early Christianity, Bonnie Bowman Thurston has gone so far as to claim this order of widows represented 'the most prominent group of women in the first three centuries of the church'.[111] Modern interest in this group inadvertently has caused the role of married Christian women to fade to a new level of pallor; it perhaps has also contributed to an exaggerated dichotomy between the lives of married women and their non-married sisters. Our discussion in Part 2 of the widows exhorted in the Pastoral Epistles (1 Tim. 5.3–16) demonstrated that the travel of widows from house to house was probably rooted in adherence to a strongly ascetic Pauline teaching, and that this practice may indicate that widows adopted teaching roles. The author of the Pastorals hoped to put an end to this kind of behaviour among young widows by encouraging them to take on the household duties of wives, implying that there were activities undertaken by widows which were not commonly undertaken by wives. However, the allusions to the ministerial roles of the widows in the Pastoral Epistles and in other works from the first half of the second century also point to some common experiences of wives and widows in the early church. It is clear that widows were especially devoted to the task of intercessory prayer (1 Tim. 5.5; Pol. *Phil.* 4.3). But in setting examples of modesty, restraint, and sensibility they acted out the ideals of womanly behaviour that were also required of wives (cf. 1 Tim. 5.6; Pol. *Phil.* 4.3; 1 Tim. 2.9; Tit. 2.3–5).[112] 1 Timothy 5.10 indicates that the criteria for the selection of widows for admission to the order included a past characterized by such home-based activities as hospitality, bringing up

---

[110] See Part 1, pp. 75–6; 110–13.   [111] Thurston, *The Widows*, 7–8.
[112] On widows expressing feminine ideals, ibid., 68.

children, and the relief of suffering; it is reasonable to conclude that widows would continue in such acts of service after enrollment. The instructions in Titus 2.4–5 calling for older women to teach younger women to be model wives, mothers, and household managers point to a duty that may sometimes have been shared by both widows and older married women.

We need to consider one more aspect of the portrait of widows that emerges from early Christian scholarship, one which may be related to an exaggeration of the difference between the lives of widows and wives. Because of the desire to assert that widows were not merely passive recipients of community charity, but were actively involved in ministerial roles, there has been a tendency to downplay the ethical ideal of the church as protector of widows.[113] Disputes over the care of widows indicate that this issue was not merely an abstract ideal; it had serious consequences in day-to-day community life (cf. Acts 6.1; 1 Tim. 5.16). It is safe to assume that some widows who turned to the church were indeed very poor. As is made clear in the case of a second-century widow who, as a last resort, proposed her daughter as prostitute, widowhood could lead to destitution.[114] A remarkable text in *1 Clement* also is worth considering. In keeping with his tendency to hold up biblical women as models for believers (cf. *1 Clem.* 55.3–6), Clement of Rome may offer us insight into church constituency. Lot's disloyal, 'double-minded' wife is contrasted with Rahab the harlot who is saved for her 'faith and hospitality'. Moreover, according to Clement, Rahab offers an example not only of faith, but also of prophecy (*1 Clem.* 11–12; cf. Heb. 11.31; Jas. 2.25). It is not difficult to imagine what needy women who had been forced to adopt a life of prostitution and who had turned to the church for support would have heard in this text. Freedwomen who carried with them a rep-

---

[113] The active and not merely passive role of widows is an important line of argument, for example, in Thurston's exploration of the 'widow as altar' symbol (Pol. *Phil.* 4.3); see *The Widows*, 106–13.

[114] See n. 105 above. Note that widows and virgins are mentioned by John Chrysostom as being among the poor supported by the Antiochian church in the fourth century. When speaking about this group of needy women he notes that 'the list of them hath already reached unto the number of three thousand' (John Chrysostom, *Homily on Matthew* 66,3; cited in Portefaix, *Sisters Rejoice*, 182 n. 37). John Chrysostom is explicit about a phenomenon which probably existed much earlier.

utation of promiscuity, and who sometimes had very little hope of engaging in a marriage that would earn them the status of a matron, may also have found their existences validated.[115] While the woman who has the honoured status of wife may lack faith (cf. *1 Clem.* 1.3; *1 Clem.* 21.6–7), the woman with even the most dishonourable of pasts might serve as a model of piety. Unmarried women who found refuge in church circles might be called upon to exhibit the virtues of the ideal wife, but acceptance in the group for those who had faith was not prohibited on the basis of immoral past associations. Despite respectable appearances and virtuous backgrounds, married church women needed to cultivate an attitude of single-hearted loyalty to husbands and to Christ in order to remain unstained from the immoral world (Eph. 5.21–33; Ign. *Pol.* 5.1–2).

Early Christianity demonstrated a surprising openness to women who did not emulate the ideal *materfamilias* and, in sanctioning the possibility of women remaining unmarried, it allowed for extraordinary independent behaviour in the social realm. Yet, we must be cautious about polarizing the issue. We should not read the involvement of the unmarried woman exclusively in terms of abrogation of traditional female roles, and the involvement of the married woman as limited to passive cooperation with her husband's conversion. Studying material from Ignatius' correspondence and several other texts from the same era has enabled us to consider the relationship between unmarried women and married women in early Christianity; we have been made aware of complexity that cannot be reduced to dichotomous patterns of life. In addition, placing early Christian exhortation against a background of increasing tension between the church and the world has helped us identify a certain fluidity with respect to the lives of married and unmarried women in early Christianity. A variety of life-circumstances are intertwined: the slave woman whose destiny lies beyond her control, the widow dependent on the church for support, the wife quietly heeding advice to be tolerant of the pagan partner, and the wife in the model Christian household caring for

---

[115] Corley, *Private Women, Public Meals*, 52. The question of marriage possibilities for freedwomen is complicated; see discussion p. 50. See also Rousselle, *Porneia*, 97–9.

children. In the next section we will move from the daily realities of women's existence to consider how the life of the married woman could take on symbolic proportions as an expression of the essence of Christian identity.

From Ephesians 5.21–33 to Ignatius, *Letter to Polycarp* 5.1–2 – the evolution of authority structures governing the lives of married women

In the context of examining Paul's teaching on marriage and celibacy in Part 2, we noted that in the earliest stages of church development, marriage practices were used as an important means of establishing the distinction between believers and outsiders. The sexual behaviour of outsiders was a point of reference for setting the ethical standards for church members. Drawing upon the sociological model of the conversionist sect, we noted that marriage practices can act as a vehicle of social protest: they are a distinctive behaviour that communicates both to believers and to non-believers how standards of conduct in the church exceed those on the outside. Moreover, endogamy rules – designed to encourage marriage between group members – serve to insulate the group from the outside world. 1 Corinthians 7 reveals an understanding of marriage between believers where divorce is prohibited; this restriction acts as a means of containing the immorality that threatens to penetrate the group from the outside world.

Probably written for a Pauline community (or group of communities) in the generation after the Apostle, Ephesians displays elements of the marriage teaching we have seen in Paul's letters.[116] It is likely that when community members listened to the detailed exposition given to the topic of marriage between believers, a discussion set in the midst of exhortations concerning household relationships (Eph. 5.21–6.9), they would have heard a strong encouragement to marry only 'in the Lord' (cf. 1 Cor. 7.39). As in Paul's letters (1 Cor. 6.15–20; 1 Thess. 4.4–5), there is the idea in Ephesians 5.21–33 that union with a pure female body has sym-

---

[116] The historical situation of Ephesians and the nature of the document are disputed by scholars. See discussion in MacDonald, *Pauline Churches*, 86–7.

bolic importance in expressing the nature of the separation from a past way of life. As a reflection of the holy and unblemished church, the pure bride stands in contrast to the evil world outside (Eph. 5.25–7; cf. Eph. 5.1ff; 4.17ff). In contrast to 1 Corinthians 7, however, there is no hint in Ephesians 5.21–33 that celibacy is preferred for those who can stave off temptation. Nowhere in Paul's letters does the significance of marriage receive the same detailed attention as it does in this Deutero-Pauline work, dating probably from the last third of the first century. Here, the Christian couple is given a central place in church life. Their relationship is infused with religious significance: their marriage is an expression of the mysterious relationship between Christ and the Church (Eph. 5.32).

Ephesians 5.24–5 exhorts wives to be subject to their husbands as the Church is subject to Christ, and husbands to love their wives as Christ loved the Church and gave himself up for her. The husband, Christ/ wife, Church comparison in Ephesians 5.21–33 reminds us of Hosea's use of the metaphor of marriage to describe the relationship between God and Israel. The comparison of the relationship between humanity and divinity to concrete relations between husbands and wives also calls to mind the frequent use of the topos of household management in ancient Jewish and pagan literature. The household codes which appear in Pauline-influenced works of the first and second centuries CE often participate in the morals and philosophical thought of the Roman empire. There is an interest in the interaction between the pairs of relationships in the household: wives/husbands, children/parents, and slaves/masters (Col. 3.18–4.1; Eph. 5.21–6.9; 1 Pet. 2.13–3.7; 1 Tim. 2.8–15, 3.4, 6.1–2; Tit. 2.1–10, 3.1; Ign. *Pol.* 4.1–5.2; Pol. *Phil.* 4.2–6.1). In Greco-Roman literature a frequent connection is drawn between the household and society at large, with submission and order in the household reflecting submission and order in the state. The comparison in Ephesians of marriage to the relationship between Christ and the Church is in keeping with the tendency to depict household relationships as a reflection of a wider social reality in the early church. Furthermore, the development of rules governing behaviour in Christian households in the generations that followed the initial organization of early Christian groups (when the church became increasingly visible and subject to hostility) has been understood in light of the growing need for apology. Many scholars cite the appearance of the topos of household management in Jewish apologetic literature, which aimed to illustrate the stability of the Jewish household, to make a case for a similar apologetic function in early church household codes.[117]

Although less obviously framed with an interest to lessen tense relationships with the non-believing world than the household material in 1 Peter (cf. 1 Pet. 2.15; 3.15–16), the household code of Ephesians, with its focus on the marital relationship, probably served some apologetic functions.[118] Given what we have learned about the critique that early Christians experienced and the desire in Pauline circles to respond to public opinion, we should understand Ephesians 5.21–33 as an early stage of a development which becomes pronounced in the second-century apologetic *Epistle to Diognetus*: it is an attempt to explain that Christians marry as other people do, and even exceed their neighbours with respect to moral rectitude (cf. *Diogn.* 5.6–10). It is important to remember that the ideal of the Christian couple in early Christianity was established in light of rumours of scandalous sexual impropriety. The text attributed to Marcus Cornelius Fronto, studied in Part 1 as offering a particularly good illustration of the influence of impression and stereotype on public perception of early Christianity, is useful to recall here. What was portrayed as reprehensible about early Christianity was that it operated through secret tactics and that it engaged in the kind of clandestine and immoral activities that required the seclusion of the private home. Although the household should have sheltered women and children from such destructive forces, it was depicted as the very arena of their corruption.[119]

---

[117] See especially Philo, *Apology*, 7.3–5; Josephus, *Against Apion*, II.199. The most important work on the apologetic function of the New Testament household codes is Balch, *Let Wives*. See also discussions in MacDonald, *Pauline Churches*, 106–11; E. Elizabeth Johnson, 'Ephesians', in Newsom and Ringe (eds.), *The Women's Bible Commentary*, 340–1.

[118] Cf. Ephesians 5.15 and Colossians 4.5 where relations with outsiders are clearly in view (the author of Ephesians relied heavily on the letter to the Colossians). Johnson believes that Ephesians 5.21–6.9 reveals an interest in the church's public image; see 'Ephesians', 341. See also Craig S. Keener, *Paul, Women and Wives: Marriage and Women's Ministry in the Letters of Paul* (Peabody Mass.: Hendrickson, 1992) 139–56; 258–79.

[119] See Part 1 pp. 60–1.

Placed against this background, we see Ephesians 5.21–33 as representing the further institutionalization of an inclination, already detectable in Paul's letters, to see Christian marriage as protection against a world that misunderstood church practices and could corrupt and destroy the pure church. Under such circumstances, the unblemished bride became the perfect image to convey to the public. She was an ideal representation of community shame, that is, concern for public reputation. Rule-like statements which guaranteed the purity and submissiveness of the Christian wife became a defensive strategy in a world that was watching her particularly closely for signs of immorality and subversion.

Given the influence of Pauline Christianity on Ignatius of Antioch and the fact that he found a model for his own martyrdom in Paul (Ign. *Eph.* 12.2), it is not surprising to see in Ignatius, *Letter to Polycarp* 5.1–2 a contrast between marriage with bishop's consent, related to the Lord, and marriages according to lust (ἐπιθυμία).[120] In keeping with the Pauline understanding, Ignatius articulates a vision of Christian marriage which is thought to stand in sharp contrast to the ethical patterns of non-believers. As in Ephesians we discover an appeal to household code traditions (which is combined with an interest in church offices; cf. Ign. *Pol.* 6.1–2; 1 Tim. 3.1–13) and the ideal Christian marriage is viewed as a reflection of the love of Christ for the Church: wives are to love the Lord and be satisfied with their husbands in flesh and spirit and husbands are to love their wives as the Lord loved the Church.[121] In both Ephesians and Ignatius' letter to Polycarp we see the symbol of the church-bride serving as a metaphor for the whole community and acting as a guide to relations between the married couple. The reference to 'flesh and spirit' in Ignatius, *Letter to Polycarp* 5.1 means that there is no question of the symbol of the woman church being used in relation to 'ascetic, spiritual'

---

[120] On the Paulinism of Ignatius see Schoedel, *Ignatius*, 9–10; R. M. Grant, *The Apostolic Fathers*, vol. 4: *Ignatius of Antioch* (London: Thomas Nelson & Sons, 1966) 24. On the significance of references to lust in Ignatius, *Letter to Polycarp* 4.1–5.2 see MacDonald, 'The Ideal of the Christian Couple', 109–10.

[121] It is impossible to be certain that Ignatius knows the text of Ephesians 5; he may simply share with its author a traditional theme. However, it is evident that both authors are articulating a vision of the ideal Christian couple and are very interested in the theme of unity. On Ephesians and Ignatius see Schoedel, *Ignatius*, 9.

marriages.[122] The importance of a wife's chastity within marriage is forcefully conveyed.[123] Like the wife who is ever content with her one true husband, the church-bride is faithfully united with Christ.

There are many similarities between the marriage teaching in Ephesians 5.21–33 and Ignatius, *Letter to Polycarp* 5.1–2. However, Ignatius exceeds the measures adopted by the Deutero-Pauline author to encourage Christian marriage in one important sense. For Ignatius, a couple desiring to marry must be united with the consent of the bishop. This new development in early Christianity represents more than the extension of the bishop's authority over the personal lives of believers.[124] If we recall the discussion in Part 2 of how marriage practices are an important means setting sects apart from the world, the requirement that men and women be married with the consent of the bishop is best understood as a bolstering of the rules of group endogamy. Ideal marriages between Christians, who undoubtedly will raise Christian children (cf. Pol. *Phil.* 4.2), serve both as an important means of protecting the community from polluting influences and of announcing its identity to the outside world. If we speculate as to what this extension of the bishop's authority might have meant at the practical level, a few scenarios come to mind. The precarious situation created by marriage between believers and non-believers suggests that it is unlikely that the bishop would have given his permission for a new marriage to take place with an unbeliever. Further, the bishop

---

[122] See discussion of the polarity, 'flesh and spirit' in Schoedel, *Ignatius*, 23. In contrast to the usage in the Ignatian correspondence, such language appears in *2 Clement* to support asceticism (cf. *2 Clem.* 14.1–15.1; 6.9; 7.1–6; 8.6; 9.3; 12.2–5). It is also important to note that in early Christianity the church-bride symbol could be employed in a more 'counter-cultural' sense to speak of virgins who were brides of Christ. See discussion in Fox, *Pagans and Christians*, 370–4.

[123] See MacDonald, 'The Ideal of the Christian Couple', 123–4. A particularly interesting parallel to the marriage teaching in Ignatius, *Letter to Polycarp* 5.1–2 is offered by a private religious association from Philadelphia in the first century BCE where fidelity within marriage is clearly the responsibility of both husband and wife, and ethics have serious religious consequences; see Grant, *Hellenistic Religions*, 29. See also Schoedel, *Ignatius*, 272; note 96 above. For a second parallel from the first century CE see Musonius Rufus, *Fragment*, 12, cited in Malherbe, *Moral Exhortation*, 152–4.

[124] The bishop's authority also extends over the lives of celibate members of the community; cf. Ignatius, *Letter to Polycarp* 5.2. For patristic evidence on the authority of the Church in marriage and weddings see L. Godefroy, *Dictionnaire de Théologie Catholique* 9 (Paris: Librairie Letouzey et Ané, 1927) 2104–5.

likely would aim to instil in the couple virtues that exceeded the standards of the non-believing world, in the hope that the couple would be conveyors of true Christian identity.[125] In order to ensure that marriage was truly 'according to the Lord' (Ign. *Pol.* 5.2) it would be vital to ensure that neither member of the prospective union had been lured by false teaching, for sometimes this vice was particularly difficult to detect (Ign. *Pol.* 3.1; Ign. *Smyrn.* 4–8).

There are several aspects of the life of the early church at the beginning of the second century CE that relate to the tightening of authority structures governing Christian marriage in Ignatius, *Letter to Polycarp* 5.1–2. Early church literature from this period displays considerable ambiguity and ambivalence with respect to whom one may marry. In addition to the case of marriages between believers and non-believers we have examined in detail, early church members struggled with such issues as whether the prohibition against divorce applied to the case of an adulterous wife (*Herm. Man.* 4.1.4–11; cf. Matt. 19.9; 5.32) and whether the remarriage of widows was acceptable (*Herm. Man.* 4.4.1–2; cf. 1 Cor. 7.39–40). In studying how marriage practices define sectarian identity, I noted in Part 2 that broad and ambiguous marriage rules increase the risks of compromise with the world. Such compromise may lead to the ultimate threat to the life of the group: apostasy.

A source which offers further evidence of the shape of early Christianity in Asia Minor at the beginning of the second century, Pliny's (governor of Pontus-Bythinia, 111–13 CE) letter to the emperor Trajan, speaks of those who ceased to be Christians.[126] In the study of Pliny's correspondence in Part 1, we examined his description of the arrest and torture of two female slave deacons. Two points were especially important. The public visibility of these

---

[125] On the relationship between early Christian marriage teaching and pagan ideals see Brown, 'Late Antiquity', 246–51, 259–66. W. R. Schoedel believes that Christian marriage is one of the many areas where Ignatius expresses a relatively positive attitude towards pagan society; see 'Theological Norms and Social Perspectives in Ignatius of Antioch', in E. P. Sanders (ed.), *Jewish and Christian Self-Definition* vol.1: *The Shaping of Christianity in the Second and Third Centuries* (Philadelphia: Fortress, 1980) 50.

[126] See Pliny, *Epistles*, 10.96 discussed in Part 1 pp. 51–9. It is generally thought that Ignatius was arrested during the reign of Trajan, 100–18 CE; see Schoedel, *Ignatius*, 5. On mixed marriage leading to apostasy see especially Philo, *Special Laws*, 3.29 (cited in Yarbrough, *Not Like the Gentiles*, 15–16.)

women was probably a function of their role as women with power to influence pagan households. Further, the hostile reaction of government officials was likely the result of rumours of gatherings involving female promiscuity. It is against such a background that Ignatius' effort at social control by means of the bishop's authority should be understood. In marriage and matters of sexuality generally, the bishop should offer safety and guidance. The bishop should be the special protector of widows (Ign. *Pol.* 4.1). He should test the motives of those who remain continent to honour of the Lord's flesh, by requiring of them the ultimate sign of discretion: silence. He should guide the married couple to become a microcosm of the community, faithful to Christ against which the snares of the 'prince of this world' (Ign. *Magn.* 1.2) will never prevail (Ign. *Pol.* 5.1–2).[127]

In both Ephesians 5.21–33 and Ignatius, *Letter to Polycarp* 5.1–2 the ideal of the Christian couple is communicated by an appeal to the husband, Christ/ wife, Church symbolism and by authority structures that range from household rules to the enforcement of episcopal control. However, the effectiveness of the ideal in shaping the lives of believers is also related to the fact that it encompasses ethics which permeated Greco-Roman society. The church could present its own vision of the ordered sexuality evident in the work of Ignatius' contemporary, Plutarch's *Advice on Marriage*, or in the sarcophagi of Italy and Asia Minor in the second and third centuries.[128] According to historian Peter Brown, the unity of the Christian couple could be seen to mirror the love between Christ and the Church in much the same way as 'the concord of a married couple was made to bear the heavy weight of expressing the ideal harmony of a whole society'.[129] The effort

---

[127] See MacDonald, 'The Ideal of the Christian Couple', 119. It is impossible to be certain about what Ignatius is calling for when he limits knowledge of one's continence to the bishop in Ignatius, *Letter to Polycarp* 5.1. He is perhaps being somewhat cautious with respect to a way of life which sometimes led to the hostile treatment of Christians by outsiders; see MacDonald, 'The Ideal of the Christian Couple', 114.

[128] This is how Brown reads Ignatius; see *The Body*, 58–9. On Plutarch and the sarcophagi see pp. 13–17.

[129] Ibid., 57. Brown here is speaking about the use of marriage imagery in Ephesians, but his comments also apply to the use of imagery in Ignatius. See *The Body*, 57. On the relationship between control of sexuality and Christian identity see S. Laeuchli, *Power and Sexuality: The Emergence of Canon Law at the Synod of Elvira* (Philadelphia: Temple University, 1972) 90–3, 109–12.

to speak in language the outside world could understand and to encourage marital behaviour that could not lead to the slander of the community has rightly been judged as having had important consequences for early Christian women. Believing women who in Paul's day often seem to have been spared the inevitable difficulties of a 'procreating existence' in Greco-Roman society by maintaining their virginity or by remaining unmarried after widowhood or separation (1 Cor. 7), now assume a life that is remarkably similar to that of the matrons who live in the world that was left behind.[130] Struck by the importance of the commonplace household arrangements in Ignatius' vision of church and Christian life, Brown observes: 'The mystical end of an undivided church was to be achieved by singularly prosaic family arrangements.'[131] E. Elizabeth Johnson has recently concluded that Ephesians 5.21–33 represents a contradiction of Paul's understanding of relations between men and women. She reads the adoption of the household code as a response to perilous relations with outsiders and concludes that this development had unfortunate consequences for women: 'By subordinating the interests of the women in the congregation to the interests of the church's public image, the author apparently operates more from fear than from faith.'[132]

There is no doubt that the ideal of the Christian couple which emerges from Ephesians and Ignatius' letter to Polycarp represents the institutionalization of Pauline marriage teaching in a specific, but not inevitable, direction. Discussed in Part 2, the *Acts of Paul and Thecla* demonstrate that hierarchical marriage teaching was not the necessary outcome of Paul's understanding of the relationship between men and women. Yet, there are also significant lines of continuity between Paul's marriage teaching as a means of drawing the faithful apart from the world, and the hierarchical teachings contained in Ephesians 5.21–33 and Ignatius, *Letter to*

---

[130] Brown notes that the 'exquisite ideal of marital concord deliberately stared past the grief, pain, and illness associated with childbirth'. See *The Body*, 24. He draws attention to treatises on virginity: Ps. Athanasius, *Vita Sanctae Syncleticae*, 42 (which speaks of the physical suffering of the married woman) and Eusebius of Emesa, *Sermon* 6.5; see pp. 24–5. See also the discussion of the *Acts of Thomas*, pp. 99–100.   [131] Ibid., 59.

[132] Johnson, 'Ephesians', 341.

Polycarp 5.1–2. Moreover, before we interpret the 'prosaic' developments we see in Ignatius as a simple compromise in order to speak the language the pagan world could understand, or as being retrogressive in relation to earlier, more 'revolutionary' teaching, we need to understand as best we can the full impact of this teaching for the lives of women.

Roman ideals of fidelity, the concord of the married couple, and the permanence of marriage, which correspond to concepts in Ephesians 5.21–33 and Ignatius, *Letter to Polycarp* 5.1–2, must be tempered by evidence of a reality at odds with these ideals. The marriage laws of Augustus functioned to guarantee the chastity of women within marriage and supported a 'double-standard' on fidelity within marriage.[133] When we compare the strict stance of the early church against divorce to the relative ease with which divorce was procured in Greco-Roman society, the pagan world appears to be much closer to our own understanding of what is humane or liberal. Yet, while it is true that Christian teaching might lock women into oppressive relationships, we must consider whether women had any real opportunity to initiate divorce, and the consequences of a woman being divorced in the Roman Empire. Ancient historians have expressed doubt about the extent to which the power of divorce lay in the hands of women, despite the evidence of a few elite women who were notorious for 'independently' divorcing their husbands:

A *filiafamilias* could not choose her husband unless she could get round her father; could not divorce him without her father's economic support; and could not prevent herself from being divorced at the instigation of her husband, her father, or his father. She was, indeed, almost her husband's equal in this: he too was subject, at least in theory, to his father's financial control, required his consent to marry (but could refuse his own) and perhaps to divorce, and could be made to divorce: but sons had, in practice, more scope. A woman *sui iuris*, like a man could make independent decisions, allowing for family and financial constraints. But she had one major disadvantage. If she decided to divorce she would lose her children, for they belonged to the father's family. Women cannot adopt, says the

---

[133] On the details of the Augustan legislation of 18 BCE and 9 CE (*lex Julia et Papia*) in general see Gardner, *Women in Roman Law and Society*, 77–88; on adultery pp.127–31. See also Brown, *The Body*, 23–5; discussion in Part 2, pp. 167–8.

jurist Gaius . . . for not even the children of their own bodies are in their *potestas*.[134]

As for the reasons to divorce a woman, one emerges as particularly tragic: infertility seems almost without exception to have been understood as the fault of the woman.[135] The single standard of sexual fidelity required in Christian marriage, coupled with the prohibition against divorce, may seem at first glance to be a fairly minor (perhaps even repressive) alteration to Greco-Roman marriage ethics. But this 'minimalist' revision may have had an importance for women that we can barely appreciate.[136]

The husband, Christ/ wife, Church comparison intertwined with household ethics, and the extension of the bishop's authority over marriage, functioned to ensure that the ideal of the Christian couple reached fruition in everyday life. It is important to realize that the exhortations in Ephesians 5.21–33 and Ignatius, *Letter to Polycarp* 5.1–2 held out the promise of a permanent home to those who might otherwise be abandoned. It is also likely that the ideal of the permanently united Christian couple could benefit women who found themselves abandoned and destitute on account of conflict with non-believing husbands or due to the casualties of life that might require them to adopt desperate, but immoral, measures. A woman who had been divorced by a non-believing husband would not be completely abandoned. A destitute widow would not need to promote her daughter as a prostitute. The woman who was childless would not find herself put aside. In Ignatius' letters the means to protect those who have been rendered solitary by life's circumstances stands as the corollary of stringent measures to protect the unity of the couple (Ign. *Smyrn.*

---

[134] Clark, 'Roman Women', 204–5; see also Pomeroy, *Goddesses*, 158, see pp. 150–63; Gardner, *Women in Roman Law and Society*, 260. Freedwomen who were married to their patrons were apparently not allowed to divorce them without their consent. See pp. 82–3; 86–7.

[135] See Gardner, *Women in Roman Law and Society*, 81–2, 224; see also Portefaix, *Sisters Rejoice*, 29–30. The shame of infertility is mentioned as one of the causes for the suffering of married women in Ps. -Athanasius see. n. 130 above.

[136] See conclusions of Clark above, n. 8. Here it is interesting to consider the involvement of women in the cult of Isis which emphasized the goddess as the protector of marriage, a model spouse, and defender of chastity. See discussion in Meeks, *Urban Christians*, 25. See also G. Paterson Corrington, 'The Milk of Salvation: Redemption by the Mother in Late Antiquity and Early Christianity', *HTR* 82:4 (1989) 393–420; see pp. 402–3.

13.1–2; Ign. *Pol.* 4.1). While being somewhat cautious in tone, Ignatius' teaching left open the possibility of remaining alone 'to the honour of the flesh of the Lord' (Ign. *Pol.* 5.2).

The discovery of possible positive aspects in the marriage teachings of Ephesians and Ignatius' letter to Polycarp does not negate the traditional, even socially conservative tone of these texts. Such a tone also is found in the concurrent teaching on slavery (Eph. 5.21–6.9; Ign. *Pol.* 4.1–5.2). The husband, Christ/ wife, Church comparison reveals the presence of common experiences and expectations with respect to male and female roles in the Mediterranean world. But if we recall the theoretical discussion of the distinction between power and authority in the Introduction, we are reminded that women may find routes to power 'through their acquiescence to the cultural value system'. [137] The traditional Christian wife who symbolizes the pure church is subject to authority structures which dictate her submission in the home and the church community, and this denial of authority has been used to sanction terrible acts of oppression of women which continue in our own time. But in an early church setting, it is nevertheless important to recognize that the traditional Christian wife was powerful in her role as mediator between the church and the world.

The church-bride and married women as mediators between the church and the world

The use of the woman-church symbol is related to the tendency to see woman as a resource that must be protected and kept pure – as a means to produce legitimate heirs, and as a means to proclaim male honour. As has been noted previously in this study, the Mediterranean woman represents her household's shame; she embodies its concern for reputation and hence by means of her chastity announces the moral rectitude of her home to the outside world. The impact of the church-bride symbol in early Christianity may be more fully appreciated when we draw on the findings of anthropological studies of modern Mediterranean

---

[137] Dubisch (ed.), *Gender and Power* , 17–18.

societies where woman appears as an important symbol of the identity of the group. It is possible here to offer only a few examples from the work of anthropologists which suggest further lines of inquiry. In her work on Greek village life, Juliet du Boulay has noted the tendency for women to be referred to quite literally as 'the house'. This is an especially intriguing phenomenon given the importance of the household setting in early Christianity. The seriousness of the sin of Hermas' wife (*Herm. Vis.* 2. 2.3) immediately comes to mind as one reads du Boulay's observations about the symbolic association of a wife's fidelity with other character traits. Suspicious absences from the home, neglect of household duties, and even such vices as excessive gossiping and general troublemaking which may be completely unrelated to sexuality, will nevertheless be seen as related to a woman's moral nature and have devastating consequences for the family:

In this way a woman's absence from the house is contrary to her role, not fundamentally because such absence is taken by the community to indicate adultery – although it may be so represented – nor again because her absence is seen to cause practical chaos in the house, but essentially because such absence is recognized to be in itself a sort of spiritual infidelity, an action damaging to the unity of the house which, without the woman, falls apart. Economically and symbolically, unity and harmony are constructs from which, because of the nature of the temporal world, humanity is continually falling away. The continual reconstruction of this harmony in the house can take place through the agency of the woman, and because of this she must continuously be present: 'Without the housewife', the villagers say, 'the house cannot function.'[138]

Woman as a symbol of corporate identity in Greek life also is of interest to anthropologist Jill Dubisch who warns, however, against supposing that symbolism coincides neatly with gender roles. To read the husband, Christ/ wife, Church comparison simply as a statement of the symbolic association of men with divinity and women with humanity (and ultimately only as a testimony to the devaluation of women)[139] perhaps is to engage in the kind of over-

---

[138] See du Boulay, *Portrait of a Greek Mountain Village*, 133; see pp.131–3.

[139] This is not deny that the marriage metaphor can be put to dangerous use. See Renita J. Weems, 'Gomer: Victim of Violence or Victim of Metaphor?' *Semeia* 47 (1989) 87–104, esp. 99–101.

simplification Dubisch has noted among anthropologists who analyse gender simply in terms of symbolic oppositions such as nature/culture, pollution/purity, public/private, sacred/profane. Rather than women being equated simply with only one side of these oppositions, her investigations of rural Greece have led her to conclude that 'women are concerned with maintaining boundaries, mediating between realms, and transforming substances suitable for one realm into those proper for another'.[140] Woman is more than simply a 'static' symbol of family stability; through her housework she transforms matter into a culturally accepted substance and maintains it in this state. For example, through her cooking, food becomes suitable to eat. A woman keeps dirt from penetrating the house. She prevents family matters from becoming gossip. Moreover, concern about what comes in and goes out from the house parallels concern for maintenance of the woman's body. These attitudes reflect a larger preoccupation with the identity of the family:

> The natural impulses of sexuality must be transformed through marriage and controlled through a woman's *dropi*, or sense of 'shame', so that they are channeled into a culturally circumscribed and acceptable act that ensures family continuity. Illicit sexual penetration is a violation of the family; it is like gossip, 'matter out of place', dirt, and like all dirt, polluting. Through a woman's sexual orifice, dishonour can occur. Through her mouth, gossip and the revelation of family secrets can run uncontrolled. A woman's body thus becomes the symbol of family integrity and purity and, more generally, of society as a whole . . .[141]

Far from being an insignificant aspect of early church history, the use of the female body as a symbol for the church is an important feature in the early Christian identity: it points to the drawing of boundaries between the sacred community and the world so full of lust (Eph. 5.26–7; Ign. *Pol.* 5.2, cf. 1 Thess. 4.4–5). How this symbolism was acted out in the lives of women requires further study, but it is not difficult to find examples of women mediators between the church and the world, both among wives who remained married to unbelievers and women who quietly made their way into the households of unbelievers to minister to the women

---

[140] Dubisch, 'Culture Enters', 208; see pp. 207–8.   [141] Ibid., 210–11.

therein.[142] Even the Christian wife of a Christian householder who spent much of her time caring for children and managing her household (1 Tim. 5.14) should not be viewed simply as a static participant in hierarchical marriage arrangements designed to quiet the hostile reaction of the outside world. Life in ancient Mediterranean society required her continually to reconstruct the harmony of her house. Life in the church, which may well have met in her house, required her continually to reconstruct the harmony of the Church, the bride of Christ.

Conclusion

In this section we have seen that the household, traditionally the locus of women's activities, functions as a kind of crossroads between the private and the public in early Christianity. As is made clear by the appropriation of household language to express church identity in both its local and universal manifestations, the private home could be used as a symbol for the public entity of early Christianity. Moreover, in much the same way that women in Mediterranean societies are referred to literally as the house, the early Christian bride came to be called the 'church'. An awareness of the symbolic association between woman, church, and house is vital for understanding how women figured in early church responses to public opinion in Greco-Roman society.

The household acted as the locale for many early Christian activities, and it was an important model for church structure and ideology. The actions of women, which might have been seen as subversive in the public domain, lost some of their offensiveness in this domestic setting. In the early church, the membership of women who were married to non-believers was facilitated by the fact that movement outside of one's own house for Christian purposes was essentially movement between a network of houses. But the fluid relationship between the private home and the public domain in early Christianity was not without problems for women involved in such marriages. Even if their roles were enacted within

---

[142] Brown has collected evidence to suggest that under conditions of martyrdom women could penetrate prisons more easily than men who sought to avoid the public spaces of the pagan city; see *The Body*, 154.

a context of a network of houses and their activities were generally of the kind that would not draw public attention, women could not count on being completely sequestered from public gaze. Our reading of second-century pagan critics of early Christianity has drawn attention to the tendency to view early Christianity as violating the cultural ideal of the woman 'at home'. Women who rejected their husband's gods in favour of a god called 'only' were especially susceptible to a barrage of stereotypical critiques, ranging from gullible fool, to adulteress, to whore.

The seeds of assault on Greco-Roman society already were sown with 1 Corinthians 7.12–16. Read from the perspective of early church women, Paul's instruction that the believer should remain married to the non-believer unless the non-believer wishes to terminate the relationship, sanctions a type of insubordination in society. The text reveals that as early as Paul's day, mixed marriages were leading members to experience hostility from outsiders. The hope expressed in Paul's exhortation that such marriages could win over non-believers, however, explains why Paul was willing to accept the continued involvement of church members in tense domestic settings. It was not only the spouse that could be transformed and made holy in such marriages, but also the children. Written in the earliest stages of the institutionalization of church communities, when the church's challenge to Greco-Roman society was only beginning, 1 Corinthians 7.12–16 stands out as a bold acknowledgment of the evangelizing potential of household relationships.

Composed at the end of the first century CE in response to a crisis in community life involving increased tension between believers and outsiders, 1 Peter 3.1–6 is decidedly more cautious than 1 Corinthians 7.12–16. With its exclusive focus on women involved in mixed marriage, this text introduces us not only to the problems they experienced, but also to the influence they wielded, despite being subordinate members of the household who were in the early church against the wishes of the head of the household. By exhorting women to evangelize their husbands 'without a word', the author offers us a glimpse of the treacherous manoeuvres that must have been required if participation in church rites was to remain quiet. The call to evangelize even in the face of a hostility that could terrify women, gives us a sense of the instability of the 'double' life these women were bound to lead; they obviously could not be so secretive about their Christian affiliation as to preclude conversions.

Social-scientific reflection on the distinction between power and authority has facilitated our analysis of the 'balancing act' evident in this text. In emphasizing the subordinate behaviour of women married to unbelievers, the author of 1 Peter is reinforcing the kind of authority structures that were commonly in place in Greco-Roman society. But by stressing the role of these women as quiet evangelists, the author expresses a cultural acknowledgment of female power, even though it is clearly illegitimate power according to those who are in positions of authority in society. This recognition of female power is indirect and cautious, but it has the unmistakable effect of pushing women beyond their confinement in the household to act as mediators in the quest to win over the Greco-Roman world.

1 Peter 3.1–6 offers a window into the lives of some very quiet and hidden early Christian women: those who remained married to non-believers. They lived their lives at the edge of the non-believing world, in the hope that they would transform that world. However, Justin's account of the woman who was married to the unchaste husband indicates that by the second century Christian women were known for independently divorcing their pagan husbands. But it is important to note that the woman from Rome that Justin described was of high social status, and that the resources available to her to guarantee her survival after separation were probably much greater than those available to many early Christian women faced with the same problem. If women married to non-believers were among the resident aliens living in Asia Minor who were the focus of concern in 1 Peter, it is likely that these women had fewer possibilities open to them. As is generally the case with the study of early Christian women, it is important to recall that early church women married to unbelievers lived under a variety of social conditions.

Yet even in the light of social privilege, it remains remarkable that the woman described by Justin would seek so boldly to extricate herself from marriage to a pagan, during a time of pronounced hostility between early Christianity and the pagan world. From what Justin tells us about the woman's fear of the polluting influences of union with her promiscuous mate, it is evident that problems in marriages between believers and non-believers should not be understood as being independent from ascetic currents in early Christianity. Like women who rejected marriage altogether in favour of devotion to God, women who joined the church without their spouses could be accused of launching an assault on the cultural ideals expressing woman's primary responsibility to the household. In the case of the woman whom Justin described, a specific marital conflict set in motion a wave of persecution and violence that extended far beyond her home.

What is perhaps most striking about the passages concerning women in the early church married to non-believers is that the actions of these women are described as having results that transcend their individual circumstances. The woman who remains married to the non-believer becomes an evangelist in her home: she is a powerful mediator between the church and the world. The language used to exhort her often is cautious, but it also discloses an awareness of the importance of her role. Nevertheless, while the actions of the woman who is married to the non-believer may advance the quest to win over the Greco-Roman world, they may also heighten the threat to the lives of community members. To a hostile outsider, this woman becomes a vivid illustration of the threat to society that comes with the privatization of religion. In the end it may be said that the actions of the woman involved in such a marriage are symbolic of the struggle for Christian identity.

Pagan critics tended to focus on the behaviour of women in new religious groups. Some women in early Christian circles either rejected marriage altogether or rejected the prerogatives of the head of the household in determining the religion of the household. There was a cultural climate that linked household reputation with the chastity of women. With these factors involved, it is fitting that the symbol of the female body played an important part in expressions of corporate identity in early Christianity. We have studied how the symbol of the church-bride functions in maintaining the boundaries between the church and the world. By examining Ephesians 5.21–33 and Ignatius, *Letter to Polycarp* 5.1–2 we have aimed to understand how this symbolism is related to the lives of women who were married to fellow believers.

The ideal of the married couple in these texts, which appears to enshrine the 'traditional' wife so permanently in early Christian history, is usually seen as a sign of the developing patriarchal identity and structure of the church. Such teaching moves from household codes governing relations between Christian members within a household and house-church, towards a more formal system of church offices based on the structures of the household. It is often thought that this development eroded avenues open to women. But a broad view of historical trends needs to take full account of the lives of community members during this era. Writings that come from the late first century and the early second century, for all their prosaic ethics, are fascinating for the light they shed on early Christian relations with the non-believing world. It is at this time that early Christianity became unmistakably visible and women played an important role in this visibility. If we consider the material in this section in relation to the discussion in Part 1, it becomes clear that women took on a symbolic significance in both public opinion about the early church and in early church response to public opinion. There is truth in the statement that the married woman became 'an apologist' for the new faith, but in a more profound sense than as an ideal wife on display with the hope of convincing outsiders that Christians married and had children like normal people. The married woman came to symbolize the believer who was ever-faithful to Christ, resolutely unmoved by the seductions of a tainted pagan society, but nevertheless committed to the household that formed such an important foundation of that society.

If we move from how married women were depicted to how they themselves experienced their lives, we must of course admit that we do not know if 'the wives of the brethren' would have preferred to be counted among the 'virgins called widows' (Ign. *Smyrn.* 13.1) any more than we can be certain about the motives of married women who entered the church. It appears, however, that there was a profound connection between married and unmarried women, both in terms of their situation in Greco-Roman society in general, and with respect to the lives they led in the church. The conventional lives of married women which included the physical challenges of bearing children and housework no doubt contributed to their invisibility in the public sphere. Yet, thinking about early Christian married women has, perhaps above all, led me to be cautious about interpreting conventional behaviour as inconsequential behaviour. The interplay between the ideal of the church bride and ethical exhortations which call wives to be subject to their husbands masks aspects of the lives of early Christian married women which become evident when one recalls that the conventional behaviour takes place in an illegitimate group countering hostile public opinion. The fact that church meetings were located in households meant women's household management was directly related to the harmony and protection of the group. Their involvement in traditional wifely duties meant that they were in a position to protect and evangelize destitute orphans and widows, and discreetly visit women who were married to non-believers.

The study of the texts on married women in this chapter confirms the impression derived from the non-believers' description of early Christianity that the reality of women's lives in the early church was shaped by the complex interchange between concrete historical events and the symbols which encoded how women should behave in both church and society. The patriarchal legacy of early Christian texts that call for traditional behaviour including circumspection and submission should never be underestimated. But when one learns to read such texts in relation to expressions of public opinion about female involvement in the church, a woman emerges who offers a powerful challenge to a world that would label her as hysterical.

General conclusion

My main goal in writing this book has been to illustrate that the history of early Christian women includes the public reaction to their lives. I have shown that an understanding of how women figured in public opinion about the church furthers our knowledge of early Christian women in several important ways. Most obviously, the collection of references to church women by second-century critics highlights the presence of women in public impressions of Christianity. Previous treatments of pagan reaction to early Christianity have stressed that an outsider's perspective should be valued as an alternative source of information about church groups to that available from Christian sources. I have argued a similar case with respect to what can be known about Christian women from non-Christian sources. The pagan critics convey information about such important matters as the evangelical efforts of women, the nature of their leadership roles, and the general shape of their daily lives as celibate and married women.

Beyond offering us interesting information about women's lives which complements and, at times, even challenges conclusions about the history of Christian women based on Christian texts, the comments of the second-century pagan critics analysed in Part 1 contribute to our comprehension of the interaction between church groups and Greco-Roman society. The mounting tension between the church and the world that begins to be discernible in New Testament works of the late first century CE is directly related to the activities of early church women and to perceptions about Christianity as a home-based, women's religion. An awareness of public opinion revealed by the comments of non-Christian authors alerts us to indications of the desire to respond to public opinion in church texts. Such indications are especially clearly visible in ethical exhortations directing the lives of married and unmarried women; they are present in works that both pre-date and are contemporary with the comments of the second-century pagan critics of early Christianity.

The non-Christian descriptions of early Christianity in the second century CE reveal stereotypical opinions concerning the effect of Eastern religions, including Judaism, on Greco-Roman women. Women were understood as especially susceptible to the influence of illegitimate religious groups: their affiliations with such groups were believed to cause them to behave in bizarre and immoral ways. The public perception associating female membership in early Christianity with the deranged behaviour of women is epitomized by Celsus' label of Mary Magdalene as a hysterical woman. This woman is the victim of the low-grade magic of a charlatan, Jesus; but Celsus' acknowledgment of her important role in the creation of the central Christian belief in the resurrection amounts to an indirect acknowledgment of her influence.

In surveying the references to Christian women by the pagan critics of the second century, we have found many examples of the power of early Christian women. But at the same time we have discovered a disproportionate relationship between what women were actually doing and what they were said to be doing. Even if women behaved in a manner that was quite conventional within early Christianity, their very membership in the group meant that they were subject to being characterized in the most negative ways as witches, whores, and enemies of the State. In dealing with the issue of women and public opinion we have constantly been made to reflect on the relationship between image and reality.

I believe that the main contribution of this book lies in the results of a specific focus on the place of women in public reaction to early Christianity. Scholars not primarily interested in how women figured in public opinion about early Christianity, have nevertheless been operating for several years with assumptions about how the interaction between the church and the world affected the lives of church women. One such assumption highlighted in this book is that the growing conservatism of church ethics in some groups in the last decades of the first century and in the second century CE is related to the church's concern with public image. An increasing encouragement of the ideal of the Christian couple, a narrowing of options for women to remain unmarried, and a lessening of possibilities for women to exercise leadership roles, have commonly been identified as results of an increasing concern with social respectability. I have not denied the general accuracy of these trends, but I have aimed to measure the developments in relation to what the first critics were actually saying about early Christian women.

Church efforts to respond to the criticism of outsiders were inspired by much more than a broad interest in illustrating that church members were model householders and citizens. Church responses to public opinion which can be detected in ethical exhortations governing the lives of women should be understood in light of the remarkable importance of the visibility of early Christian women. Women emerge in public opinion as supporters and proponents of church teaching. They are at the centre of the perception that the essence of Christianity's offence lies in the privatizing of religion: the taking of matters tied to the public institutions of city and state and making them affairs of the home. The increasing conservatism of church ethics governing the lives of women in some church groups beginning about the end of the first century CE must be evaluated in relation to the significant presence of women in the exchanges between church groups and the Greco-Roman world.

Often articulated in conjunction with the thesis concerning the progressive social conservatism of church teaching on women, a common line of argument that I have examined in this book might be stated as follows: celibate women were freed to a greater extent than married women from the constraints imposed by the concern with public image in church circles. Thus, the lives of unmarried Christian women were less traditional and there were greater possibilities for them to make significant contributions to the leadership and expansion of Christianity. The comments of the second-century pagan critics of Christianity have caused me to question this dominant understanding of the consequences of marriage or celibacy for early Christian women. For example, references to women (including widows) accompanied by children have led me to believe that scholars have often falsely dichotomized the lives of married and unmarried church women. An examination of the situation of women married to non-believers in light of pagan references to Christianity attracting women and disrupting households, has made me aware of the fact that these women transgressed social boundaries as strongly as those who remained unmarried.

It is misleading to think that a desire for social respectability begins to emerge in ethical exhortations concerning women only with the teaching aimed at Christian wives in the household codes of the Deutero-Pauline works and 1 Peter. In this book I have argued that concern for social respectability shapes 1 Corinthians 7, the earliest detailed attempt to address the circumstances of celibate and married church women. Concern for social respectability has been observed in modern 'conversionist' sects as a necessary outcome of the goal of evangelization. Sociologists have spoken of tension between promotion of social respectability, which tends to lead to accommodation to the standards of the world, and encouragement of separation from non-believers. Understanding how such measures as endogamy rules function to maintain sectarian identity in modern groups can help us see how teaching on marriage and sexuality is fundamental to the development of the inward/outward orientation in early church groups. Knowledge about the patterns demonstrated by modern conversionist sects is extremely useful for evaluating the extent to which early church texts reflect a bold confrontation of societal norms or display a primary interest in group reputation.

Because the Pauline mission took place in a Mediterranean society where the concern for reputation was often expressed through female shame, it was natural for the visibility of women to play a central role in attempts to establish church identity which hovered between engagement of the world and withdrawal from the world. The focus on the holiness in body and spirit of unmarried women in the Pauline movement is in keeping with the primary means through which women demonstrate their shame in Mediterranean societies: chastity. That early church men probably saw their honour defined particularly in relation to the sexual purity of females would also be in keeping with traditional patterns. The celibate early church woman expressed aspects of the ideal chaste woman. Indeed, Galen's reference to ascetic church members reminds us that she could be greatly admired. The celibate early church woman was clearly a controversial figure, but she may also have contributed greatly to early Christianity's appeal.

An understanding of the honour/shame syndrome which has been discussed in depth both by anthropologists of Mediterranean society and social-scientific interpreters of early Christian texts can also shed light upon how church groups threatened dominant cultural values by encouraging women to remain unmarried. The virgins and widows of Corinth, the widows called 'gadabouts' by the author of 1 Timothy (1. Tim 5.13), and the legendary Thecla all participated in behaviour which did not completely abrogate cultural values, but certainly challenged traditional patterns and was probably unusual in the urban context of the Greco-Roman world. Removed from the auspices of male guardians and made responsible for defending their own honour, these women took over roles that were usually reserved for men.

Through her determination to remain unmarried, intriguing mediations between the private, female sphere and male, public sphere, and courageous confrontation of violence, the heroine of the *Acts of Paul and Thecla* emerges as the symbol of the unmarried church woman who loudly confronts society and acts to transform societal boundaries. Thecla is presented in the *Acts* as displaying sexual purity and moral rectitude which are beyond question, but the account also discloses her encounter with public opinion which questions her basic moral nature and ultimately labels her as shameless. This is perhaps displayed most graphically by her encounter with the Syrian, Alexander, who obviously feels this shameless woman is his for the taking. Thecla's rejection of her pre-determined role as wife, sets in motion endless possibilities for her to be accused of the most despicable female vices. An understanding of the symbolic association between woman and house in Mediterranean societies has helped us to appreciate the offensiveness of her actions. Public opinion demanded that she resume her household responsibilities; failure to comply would result in violence.

Many scholars have reflected upon the interesting relationship between the efforts of the author of 1 Timothy to restrict the activities of widows and the asceticism of Thecla. My particular interest in re-examining this relationship has been to shed light upon the circumstances of the author of the Pastorals' acquiescence to public opinion about women. In an effort to quiet slander, 1 Timothy 5 recommends that the young widows (who were probably devoted to an ascetic teaching similar to that revealed by the *Acts of Paul and Thecla*) cease wandering from household to household and take up household responsibilities as wives and mothers. No doubt an encounter with negative public opinion could have dangerous, even violent, consequences for community life and this must always be acknowledged. But it is nevertheless striking to find such blatant correspondence between what critics were saying about early Christianity's effect upon gullible women and what is described by the author of Pastorals as the weakness inherent in Christian women for becoming carried away by false teachers and being incapable of discerning the truth (2 Tim. 3.6–7). In an effort to lessen tension between society and church, church leaders sometimes responded in a manner that had most unfortunate consequences for women: church authors themselves accused women of participating in behaviour that was criticized by outsiders and which had as much to do with stereotypical perceptions about women's involvement in illegitimate religious groups as with their particular actions.

Scholars have argued that the fluid relationship between the public, male sphere and the private, female sphere in early Christianity facilitated the involvement of women and their adoption of unconventional roles. However, an awareness of what the pagan critics of the second century said about early Christian women has led me to explore further consequences of this 'fusing of spheres' for the lives of early Christian women. Locating their activities in women's quarters, early Christians were accused of clandestine activities, of being suspiciously indifferent to traditional authority figures, and of being irresponsible with respect to the affairs of city and state. Who could be more vulnerable to criticism and discovery than early Christian women married to non-believers! They had trespassed on the prerogatives of the *paterfamilias* to determine the religion of the household. In fact, church texts reveal an awareness of the difficulty of their situation. In his *Apology*, Justin Martyr describes how a Christian woman's efforts to divorce her immoral pagan husband set in motion a series of events culminating in the execution of Christians. Early Christian women married to non-believers could challenge dominant cultural values as strongly, and perhaps even more courageously, than the virgins who resolutely refused to marry those to whom they had been promised.

At first glance those women who followed church directives to remain married to unbelievers (1 Cor. 7.12–16; 1 Pet. 3.1–6) appear tragically immobilized by their confinement within pagan households. However, the social-scientific distinction between power and authority which has been used as an analytical tool in this book helps us to gain a broader picture of the shape of these women's lives. 1 Peter 3.1–6 offers an especially good example of the fact that reinforcement of authority structures does not mean the necessary closure of all avenues of power. Women are instructed to obey their husbands in this text, but the expression of hope that these women will win their non-believing mates by their model behaviour is an acknowledgment of the power of these women to act as quiet evangelists. This acknowledgment takes place despite the fact that those outside the church would clearly judge the enterprise of these women as illegitimate and as a violation of the authority of the head of the household. The stakes for the church in encouraging such treacherous behaviour were clearly high. Indeed we have discussed important evidence in this book that the influence of women was central to early Christianity's penetration of the household of Greco-Roman society. Except for their illicit allegiance to early Christianity, women who remained married to non-believers probably led largely traditional lives. But it was through their existence as traditional wives that they found their routes to power: they played a key role in the expansion of a new religious movement.

Throughout this book I have drawn attention to the symbolic association between woman, house, and church in early Christian texts dealing with both celibate and married women. Given the location of early Christian meetings in the private, female sphere of the house during the period we are discussing, the image of the woman church offers the most obvious example of this association. I have traced the development of this image from Ephesians 5 to Ignatius' letter to Polycarp in order to understand how it functions to demarcate Christian identity in ancient society. The use of this image in these texts is closely related to the development of endogamy rules in early Christianity (injunctions to guarantee that new marriages are between believers) and to the tendency to view the Christian woman ever-faithful to her Christian husband as a conveyer of ideal Christian commitment in a non-believing world.

The fact that slave women and widows are mentioned as categories of women in addition to wives in the correspondence of Ignatius of Antioch had led me to reflect upon how the ideal of the permanently united Christian couple could have broad implications for the treatment of women in general in church groups. An acceptance of this ideal might have important implications for protecting the continuity of slave families and might be related to the institutionalization of measures which guaranteed that widows would not be left destitute. Consideration of women's lives in light of the increasing hostility experienced by church groups about the beginning of the second century CE has convinced me that there was considerable overlap between the experiences of the various categories of women in the early church. Pliny's arrest and torture of two women who were slaves and deacons reminds us that we have sometimes been too quick to conclude that relatively well-to-do early church women were the only visible and influential women in early Christianity. As for the tendency to associate the church leadership of celibate women with freedom from household affairs, the widows who were noted by Lucian of Samosata as prominent members of the early Christian group should be considered. These women were not freed from traditional household responsibilities: they were accompanied by children.

The married Christian woman whose traditional life seems so permanently cast into church history by the image of the church bride who obeys the bridegroom, Christ, has been virtually ignored in discussions of the significance of women's contribution to the birth of Christianity. No doubt this is partly due to the fact that her traditional life was usually not considered notable or interesting enough to describe in particular detail. However, the recent theoretical reflection by anthropologists working on women and culture has reminded me that we should not assume that highly conventional behaviour is inconsequential behaviour; it may even carry the possibility of surprising avenues for power. We should not think of the married Christian woman who symbolized the church bride as a static entity. She was a conveyer of the boundaries between the church and the world, and a mediator between realms. She not only represented the church in the passive sense, but continually reconstructed the harmony of the church through her presence. Women's household management may in fact have been as important to the sustained growth of early Christianity as the proclamations of well-known apostles and teachers.

My efforts to comprehend hierarchical marriage arrangements in light of Christianity's encounter with public opinion have convinced me of the need to continue to reflect upon the significance of these arrangements for women's lives within ancient contexts. This goal is very much in keeping with current efforts to incorporate insights from cultural anthropology within the study of Christian origins. Commenting on the methodological challenges involved in applying anthropological studies to biblical narratives Carol Schersten Lahurd has very recently argued that 'biblical exegetes and anthropologists must resist the temptation to reify the appearance of patriarchy and oppression and recognize that such reification can prevent them from seeing both the positive and negative aspects of women's realities'.[1]

My analysis has convinced me that the subject of how early church women figured in public opinion and in church response to public opinion is a complicated one. Because of the close connection between gender and the cultural values through which reputation and concern for reputation were communicated (honour and shame), the visibility of early Christian women in exchanges between the church groups and Greco-Roman society had an importance that I did not anticipate at the outset. In the ancient Mediterranean world the spatial distinctions related to sex (private, woman/ public, man) were a central means of maintaining these

---

[1] LaHurd, 'Rediscovering the Lost Women in Luke 15', 74.

values. If, as in the case of early Christianity, perceptions existed about a group's impropriety and lack of attention to social segregation, the group's women would become objects of scrutiny and would be liable to be labelled as shameless. What all of this means for future study is that scholars investigating non-Christian reaction to the birth of Christianity should no longer ignore the presence of early Christian women. Moreover, discussions about early Christian apology and concern for social respectability must take account of the lives of early Christian women. Studies of the development of Christian identity must consider the importance of female identity for the process of constructing the spaces where people lived and the boundaries that allowed them to make sense of their lives.

I began this book with a strong interest in uncovering aspects of the behaviour of early Christian women which, if not unique in the ancient world, would at least be unusual and unconventional. I indeed found examples of such behaviour especially among celibate church women and women who were married to nonbelievers. But I also found examples of church women acting in traditional ways. During the course of my project, my social-scientific perspective has helped me to realize that conventional behaviour can be highly significant. It is true that when women became members of an illegitimate religious group in the ancient world they tested the limits of conventional existence. The story of Thecla reminds us that early Christian allegiance could sometimes be presented as an almost complete abrogation of past patterns of life for women, and we must continue to think about how such a narrative might be related to the concrete experiences of women. But it is equally as interesting to consider how some church women maintained largely conventional lives caring for homes and nurturing children, despite encountering a barrage of stereotypical critique about their immoral natures and hysterical dispositions.

Bibliography

In the majority of instances, the text and translation of the ancient authors I cite are from the Loeb Classical Library (LCL; Cambridge, Mass.: Harvard University). This is true for most of the Greek and Latin writers, as well as some of the Christian writers. The date of publication and translator varies with each work. Specific references are provided in the notes. Many of the Christian works I cite are from the series *The Ante-Nicene Fathers* (*ANF*), edited by A. Roberts and J. Donaldson (Reprint, Grand Rapids, Michigan: William. B. Eerdmans, 1951). Any other editions of ancient sources are listed below under the editor or translator of the work.

Aubert, Jean-Jacques. 'Threatened Wombs: Aspects of Ancient Uterine Magic'. *GRBS* 30, 1989: 421–49.

Balch, David L. 'Backgrounds of 1 Cor. 7: Sayings of the Lord in Q; Moses as an Ascetic Theios Aner in 2 Cor. 3'. *NTS* 18, 1972: 351–64.

Let Wives Be Submissive: The Domestic Code in 1 Peter, SBLMS 26. Chico, Calif.: Scholars, 1981.

'1 Cor. 7. 32–35 and Stoic Debates about Marriage, Anxiety, and Distractions'. *JBL* 102/3, 1983: 429–39.

Balsdon, J. P. V. D. *Roman Women: Their History and Habits*. London: Bodley Head, 1962.

Barrett, C. K. 'Things Sacrificed to Idols'. *NTS* 11, 1964–6: 138–53.

A Commentary on the First Epistle to the Corinthians. London: Adam and Charles Black, 1968.

Bartchy, S. Scott. *Mallon Chresai: First-Century Slavery and the Interpretation of 1 Corinthians 7. 21*, SBLDS 11. Missoula, Mont.: Scholars, 1973.

Bassler, Jouette M. '1 Corinthians'. In *The Women's Bible Commentary*, Carol A. Newsom and Sharon H. Ringe (eds.), 321–9. Louisville, Kentucky: Westminster/John Knox, 1992.

Bibliography

Batten, Alicia. 'More Queries for Q: Women and Christian Origins'. *BTB* 24, 1994: 44–51.

Bauer, Walter, W. Arndt and F. W. Gingrich. *A Greek-English Lexicon of the New Testament and Other Early Christian Literature*, second edn. Chicago: University, 1958.

Benko, Stephen. 'The Libertine Gnostic Sect of the Phibionites According to Epiphanius'. *VC* 21, 1967: 103–19.
'Pagan Criticism of Christianity during the First Two Centuries AD'. In H. Temporini and W. Haase (eds.), *Aufstieg und Niedergang der römischen Welt*, vol. 23.2, 1055–1118. Berlin and New York: Walter De Gruyter, 1980.
Pagan Rome and the Early Christians. Bloomington: Indiana University, 1984.

Berger, Peter L. and Thomas Luckmann. *The Social Construction of Reality: A Treatise in the Sociology of Knowledge*. Garden City, N.Y.: Doubleday and Company, 1966.

Best, Ernest. *1 Peter*. Grand Rapids: Wm B. Eerdmans, 1971.
'Church'. In Paul J. Achtemeier (ed.), *Harper's Bible Dictionary*, 168–9. San Francisco: Harper & Row, 1985.

Borret, Marcel (ed.). *Origène. Contre Celse. Sources Chrétiennes*. Paris, 1967.

Bourdieu, P. 'The Sentiment of Honour in Kabyle Society'. In J. G. Peristany (ed.), *Honour and Shame: The Values of Mediterranean Society*, 191–241. London: Wiedenfeld and Nicolson, 1965.

Brandes, Stanley. 'Reflections on Honour and Shame in the Mediterranean'. In David Gilmore (ed.), *Honour and Shame and the Unity of the Mediterranean*, A.A.A. Special Publication no. 22, 121–34. Washington, D.C.: American Anthropological Association, 1987.

Brooten, Bernadette J. 'Early Christian Women and Their Cultural Context: Issues of Method in Historical Reconstruction'. In A.Y. Collins (ed.), *Feminist Perspectives on Biblical Scholarship*, 65–91. Chico, Calif.: Scholars, 1985.
Women Leaders in the Ancient Synagogue: Inscriptional Evidence and Background Issues. Chico, Calif.: Scholars, 1982.

Brown, Peter. 'Sorcery, Demons, and the Rise of Christianity from Late Antiquity into the Middle Ages'. In Mary Douglas (ed.), *Witchcraft, Confessions and Accusations*, 17–45. New York: Tavistock, 1970.
'Late Antiquity'. In P. Veyne (ed.), *A History of Private Life, Vol. 1: From Pagan Rome to Byzantium*, 235–311. Cambridge, Mass., and London: Belknap Press of Harvard University, 1987.
The Body and Society: Men, Women and Sexual Renunciation in Early Christianity. London and Boston: Faber and Faber, 1988.

Brown, Raymond. *The Birth of the Messiah: A Commentary on the Infancy Narratives in Matthew and Luke*. Garden City, N.Y.: Doubleday, 1977.

Bibliography

Brunt, P. *Italian Manpower 225 BC – A.D. 14.* Oxford: Clarendon, 1971.

Buckley, Jorunn J. 'The Holy Spirit is a Double Name: Holy Spirit, Mary, and Sophia in the *Gospel of Philip*'. In Karen L. King (ed.), *Images of the Feminine in Gnosticism*, 214–17. Philadelphia: Fortress, 1988.

Burrus, Virginia. *Chastity as Autonomy: Women in the Stories of the Apocryphal Acts* (Studies in Women and Religion 23). Lewiston/ Queenston: Edwin Mellen, 1987.

Cameron, A. and A. Kuhrt (eds.), *Images of Women in Antiquity*. Detroit: Wayne State University, 1985.

Campbell, John K. *Honour, Family, and Patronage*. Oxford: Clarendon, 1967.

Carcopino, Jerome. *Daily Life in Ancient Rome*, trans. E. O. Lorimer. New Haven and London: Yale, 1940.

Carney, T. F. *The Shape of the Past: Models and Antiquity*. Lawrence, Kans.: Coronado Press, 1975.

Cartlidge, David R. '1 Corinthians 7 as a Foundation for a Christian Sex Ethic'. *JR* 55, 1975: 220–34.

Castelli, Elizabeth. 'Virginity and its Meaning for Women's Sexuality in Early Christianity'. *JFSR* 2, 1986: 61–88.

Chadwick, Henry (trans.). *Origen, Contra Celsum*. Cambridge University Press, 1953.

Chadwick, H. and J. Oulton (eds.). *Alexandrian Christianity. Library of Christian Classics*, vol. 2. London: SCM, 1954.

Charlesworth, James (ed.). *Old Testament Pseudepigrapha*, 2 vols. Garden City, N.Y.: Doubleday, 1985.

Clark, Elizabeth A. 'Early Christian Women: Sources and Interpretation'. In Lynda L. Coon (ed.), *That Gentle Strength: Historical Perspectives on Women in Christianity*, 19–35. Charlottesville and London: University Press of Virginia, 1990.

'Sex, Shame, and Rhetoric: En-gendering Early Christian Ethics'. *JAAR* 59, 1991: 221–45.

Clark, Gillian. 'Roman Women'. *Greece and Rome* (ser. 2) 28, 1981: 193–212.

Women in the Ancient World (New Surveys in the Classics 21) Oxford University Press, 1989.

Clarke, Andrew D. *Secular and Christian Leadership in Corinth: A Socio-historical and Exegetical Study of 1 Corinthians 1–6*. Leiden, New York and Köln: Brill, 1993.

Clarke, G. (trans.) *The Octavius of Marcus Minucius Felix*. New York: Newmann, 1974.

Cohen, A. P. *The Symbolic Construction of Community*. London and New York: Tavistock, 1985.

Bibliography

Cohen, David. 'Seclusion, Separation, and the Status of Women in Classical Athens'. *Greece and Rome* (ser. 2) 36, 1989: 3–15.

Connolly, R. H. (ed.). *Didascalia Apostolorum*. Oxford: Clarendon, 1929.

Conzelmann, H. *A Commentary on the First Epistle to the Corinthians*, trans. J. Leitch. Philadelphia: Fortress, 1975.

Corbett, Percy E. *The Roman Law of Marriage*. Oxford: Clarendon, 1930.

Corley, Kathleen E. *Private Women, Public Meals: Social Conflict in the Synoptic Tradition*. Peabody, Mass.: Hendrickson, 1993.

Corrington, Gail P. 'The Milk of Salvation: Redemption by the Mother in Late Antiquity and Early Christianity'. *HTR* 82/4, 1989: 393–420.

Cotter, Wendy. 'Women's Authority Roles in Paul's Churches: Counter-cultural or Conventional?' *NovT* 36, 1994: 350–72.

Crossan, John Dominic. *Four Other Gospels: Shadows on the Contours of the Canon*. Minneapolis: Winston, 1985.

The Historical Jesus: The Life of a Mediterranean Jewish Peasant. San Francisco: Harper, 1992.

Davies, Stevan L. *The Revolt of the Widows: The Social World of the Apocryphal Acts*. Carbondale, Illinois: Southern Illinois University, 1980.

de Labriolle, Pierre Champagne. *La réaction païenne: étude sur la polémique antichrétienne du 1er au VIe siècle*: Paris: L'artisan du livre, 1934.

Delaney, Carol. 'Seeds of Honour, Fields of Shame'. In David Gilmore (ed.), *Honour and Shame and the Unity of the Mediterranean*, A.A.A. Special Publication no. 22, 35–48. Washington, D.C.: American Anthropological Association, 1987.

Delumeau, Jean. *La religion de ma mère: les femmes et la transmission de la foi*. Paris: Cerf, 1992.

Demarolle, Jeanne-Marie. 'Les femmes chrétiennes vues par Porphyre.' *JAC* 13, 1970: 42–7.

Deming, Will. *Paul on Marriage and Celibacy: The Hellenistic Background of 1 Corinthians 7*, SNTSMS 83. Cambridge University Press, 1995.

den Boer, W. 'Gynaeconitis: a Centre of Christian Propaganda'. *VC* 4, 1950: 61–4.

Derrett, J. Duncan M. 'The Disposal of Virgins'. In *Studies in the New Testament*, vol. 1, 184–91. Leiden: E. J. Brill, 1977.

Dewey, Joanna. '1 Timothy'. In *The Women's Bible Commentary*, Carol A. Newsom and Sharon H. Ringe (eds.), 353–8. Louisville, Kentucky: Westminster/John Knox, 1992.

Dibelius, M. and H. Conzelmann. *The Pastoral Epistles*, trans. P. Buttolph and A. Yarboro. Philadelphia: Fortress, 1972.

Douglas, Mary. *Purity and Danger: An Analysis of Purity and Taboo*. London: Routledge & Kegan Paul, 1966.

Natural Symbols. London: Barry and Rockliff, 1970.

Bibliography

(ed.) *Witchcraft, Confessions and Accusations*. New York: Tavistock, 1970.

Dubisch, Jill. *Gender and Power in Rural Greece*. Princeton, N.J.: University Press, 1986.

Du Boulay, Juliet. *Portrait of a Greek Mountain Village*. Oxford: Clarendon, 1974.

Durkheim, Emile. *Les Règles de la méthode sociologique*. Paris: Félix Alcan, 1895.

Eliade, M. *Mephistopheles and the Androgyne*. New York: Sheed and Ward, 1965.

Elliott, John H. *A Home for the Homeless: A Sociological Exegesis of 1 Peter, Its Situation and Strategy*. London: SCM, 1982.

What is Social-Scientific Criticism? Minneapolis: Fortress, 1993.

Esler, Philip Francis. *Community and Gospel in Luke-Acts: The Social and Political Motivations of Lucan Theology*. Cambridge University Press, 1987.

The First Christians in their Social Worlds: Social-Scientific approaches to New Testament Interpretation. London and New York: Routledge, 1994.

Falls, Thomas (trans.). *Justin Martyr. Fathers of the Church 6*. Washington: Catholic University of America, 1948.

Fantam, E. and H. Peet Foley, N. Boymel Kampen, S. B. Pomeroy, H. A. Shapiro. *Women in the Classical World: Image and Text*. New York and Oxford University Press, 1994.

Ferguson, John (trans.). *Clement of Alexandria, Stromateis Books 1–3*, Fathers of the Church, vol. 85. Washington: Catholic University, 1991.

Fox, Robin Lane. *Pagans and Christians*. New York: Alfred A. Knopf, 1986.

Frend, W. H. C. *Martyrdom and Persecution in the Early Church*. New York: University Press, 1967.

Gallagher, Eugene V. *Divine Man or Magician? Celsus and Origen on Jesus* (SBLDS 64). Chico, Calif.: Scholars, 1982.

Gardner, Jane F. *Women in Roman Law and Society*. London and Sydney: Croom Helm, 1986.

Garrett, Susan R. 'Review of Malina, *Christian Origins and Cultural Anthropology*'. *JBL* 107, 1988: 532–4.

Geertz, C. 'Religion as a Cultural System'. In M. Banton (ed.), *Anthropological Approaches to the Study of Religion*, 1–46. London: Tavistock, 1966.

Gilmore, David D. 'Anthropology of the Mediterranean Area'. *Annual Review of Anthropology* 11, 1982: 175–205.

(ed.) *Honour and Shame and the Unity of the Mediterranean* (A.A.A. Special Publication no. 22). Washington, D.C.: American Anthropological Association, 1987.

Gleason, M. W. 'The Semiotics of Gender: Physiognomy and Self-Fashioning in the Second Century CE'. In D. M. Halperin,

Bibliography

J. J. Winkler, F. I. Zeitlin (eds.), *Before Sexuality: The Construction of Erotic Experience in the Ancient World*, 389–415. Princeton: University, 1990.

Gould, Graham. 'Women in the Writings of the Fathers: Language, Belief and Reality'. In W. J. Sheils and D. Wood (eds.), *Studies in Church History 27: Women in the Church*, 1–13. Oxford: Basil Blackwell/ Ecclesiastical History Society, 1990.

Grant, Frederick C. *Hellenistic Religions*. New York: Liberal Arts, 1953.

Grant, Robert M. 'Pliny and the Christians'. *HTR* 41, 1948: 273.

The Apostolic Fathers, vol. 4: *Ignatius of Antioch*. London: Thomas Nelson & Sons, 1966.

'A Woman of Rome: Justin, Apol. 2,2'. *CH* 54, 1985: 461–72.

Greek Apologists of the Second Century. Philadelphia: Westminster, 1988.

Grifiths, J. Gwyn (ed. and trans.). *Apuleius of Madauros: The Isis-Book (Metamorphoses, Book XI)*. Leiden: E. J. Brill, 1975.

Hallett, Judith P. *Fathers and Daughters in Roman Society: Women and the Elite Family*. Princeton, N.J.: University Press, 1984.

Handelman, Don. 'Gossip Encounters: The Transmission of Information in a Bounded Social Setting'. *Man* 8, 1973: 210–17.

Harkins, Paul (trans.). *John Chrysostom, Discourses Against the Judaizing Christians. Fathers of the Early Church 68*. Washington, D.C.: Catholic University of America, 1979.

Heinrichs, Albert. 'Pagan Ritual and the Alleged Crimes of the Early Christians'. In P. Granfield and J. Jungman (eds.), *Kyriakon: Festschrift Johannes Quasten*, 18–35. Münster: Aschendorff, 1970.

Hennecke E., and Schneemelcher, W. (eds.). *New Testament Apocrypha*. 2 vols. English translation edited by Robert McL. Wilson. Philadelphia: Westminster, 1963–5.

Heyob, Sharon Kelly. *The Cult of Isis among Women in the Greco-Roman World*. Leiden: Brill, 1975.

Hock, Ronald F. *The Social Context of Paul's Ministry: Tentmaking and Apostleship*. Philadelphia: Fortress, 1980.

Holmberg, Bengt. *Paul and Power: The Structure of Authority in the Primitive Church as Reflected in the Pauline Epistles*. Philadelphia: Fortress, 1980.

Sociology and the New Testament: An Appraisal. Minneapolis: Fortress, 1990.

Horsley, R. A. 'Spiritual Marriage with Sophia'. *VC* 33, 1979: 30–54.

Hurd, John C. *The Origin of 1 Corinthians*. London: SPCK, 1965.

Isichei, E. 'From Sect to Denomination among English Quakers.' In Bryan Wilson (ed.), *Patterns of Sectarianism*, 182–212. London: Morrison and Gibb, 1967.

Johnson, E. Elizabeth. 'Ephesians'. In *The Women's Bible Commentary*, Carol A. Newsom and Sharon H. Ringe (eds.), 338–42. Louisville, Kentucky: Westminster/John Knox, 1992.

Bibliography

Jones, C. P. *Culture and Society in Lucian*. Cambridge, Mass. and London: Harvard University, 1986.

Jones, Deborah. 'Gossip: Notes on Women's Oral Culture'. *Women's Studies International Quarterly* 3, 1980: 193–8.

Judge, E. A. 'The Social Identity of the First Christians: A Question of Method in Religious History'. *JRH* 11/2, 1980: 201–17.

The Conversion of Rome: Ancient Sources of Modern Social Tensions. North Ryde, Australia: Macquarrie Ancient History Association, 1980.

Kampen, Natalie Boymel. 'Between Public and Private: Women as Historical Subjects in Roman Art'. In Sarah B. Pomeroy (ed.), *Women's History and Ancient History*, 218–48. Chapel Hill and London: University of North Carolina, 1991.

Kearsley, R. A. 'Asiarchs, *Achiereis* and the *Archiereiai* of Asia'. *GRBS* 27, 1986: 183–92.

Keener, Craig A. *Paul, Women and Wives: Marriage and Women's Ministry in the Letters of Paul*. Peabody, Mass.: Hendrickson, 1992.

Kraemer, Ross S. 'The Conversion of Women To Ascetic Forms of Christianity'. *Signs* 6, 1980: 298–307.

'Monastic Jewish Women in Greco-Roman Egypt: Philo Judaeus on the Therapeutrides'. *Signs* 14, 1989: 342–70.

Her Share of the Blessings: Women's Religions Among Pagans, Jews, and Christians in the Greco-Roman World. Oxford and New York: University, 1992.

Kraemer, Ross S. (ed.) *Maenads, Martyrs, Matrons, Monastics: A Sourcebook on Women's Religions in the Greco-Roman World*. Philadelphia: Fortress, 1988.

Laeuchli, Samuel. *Power and Sexuality: The Emergence of Canon Law at the Synod of Elvira*. Philadelphia: Temple University, 1972.

LaHurd, Carol Schersten. 'Rediscovering the Lost Women in Luke 15'. *BTB* 24, 1994: 66–76.

Lampe, Geoffrey W.H. (ed.) *Patristic Greek Lexicon*. Oxford: Clarendon, 1961.

Lefkowitz, Mary R. 'Influential Women'. In Averil Cameron and Amélie Kuhrt (eds.), *Images of Women in Antiquity*, 49–64. London & Canberra: Croom Helm, 1983.

'Wives and Husbands'. *Greece and Rome* (ser. 2) 30, 1983: 30–47.

Levine, Amy-Jill (ed.), *'Women Like This': New Perspectives on Jewish Women in the Greco-Roman World*. Atlanta: Scholars, 1991.

Liddell, Henry George and Robert Scott. *A Greek English Lexicon*, ninth edition. Oxford: Clarendon Press, 1940.

Louth, A. (ed.). *Early Christian Writings*. London: Penguin Classics, 1987.

Love, Stuart L. 'Women's Roles in the Certain Second Testament Passages: A Macrosociological View'. *BTB* 17, 1987: 50–9.

Bibliography

'The Household: A Major Social Component for Gender Analysis in the Gospel of Matthew: A Macrosociological View'. *BTB* 23, 1993: 21–31.

'The Place of Women in Public Settings in Matthew's Gospel: A Sociological Inquiry'. *BTB* 24, 1994: 52–65.

MacDonald, Dennis R. *The Legend and the Apostle: The Battle for Paul in Story and Canon.* Philadelphia: Westminster, 1983.

There is No Male and Female: the Fate of a Dominical Saying in Paul and Gnosticism, HDR 20. Philadelphia: Fortress, 1987.

MacDonald, Margaret Y. *The Pauline Churches: A Socio-historical Study of Institutionalization in the Pauline and Deutero-Pauline Writings,* SNTSMS 60. Cambridge University Press, 1988.

'Early Christian Women Married to Unbelievers'. *SR* 19/2, 1990: 221–34.

'Women Holy in Body and Spirit: The Social Setting of 1 Corinthians 7'. *NTS* 36, 1990: 161–81.

'The Ideal of the Christian Couple: Ign. *Pol.* 5.1–2 looking back to Paul'. *NTS* 40, 1994: 105–25.

MacMullen, Ramsay. 'Women in Public in the Roman Empire'. *Historia* 29, 1980: 208–18.

Christianizing the Roman Empire (A D 100–400). New Haven and London: Yale University, 1984.

Corruption and the Decline of Rome. New Haven and London: Yale University, 1988.

McNamara, Jo Ann. *A New Song: Celibate Women in the First Three Christian Centuries.* New York: The Haworth Press, Inc., 1983.

Maier, Harry O. 'The Charismatic Authority of Ignatius of Antioch: A Sociological Analysis'. *SR* 18/2, 1989: 185–99.

The Social Setting of the Ministry as Reflected in the Writings of Hermas, Clement and Ignatius, Dissertations SR 1. Waterloo: Wilfrid Laurier, 1991.

Malherbe, Abraham J. 'In Season and Out of Season: 2 Tim 4:2'. *JBL* 103, 1984: 235–43.

Moral Exhortation, A Greco-Roman Sourcebook (Library of Early Christianity). Philadelphia: Westminster, 1986.

(ed.). *Cynic Epistles: A Study Edition.* Missoula, MT: Scholars, 1977.

Malina, Bruce J. 'The Social World Implied in the Letters of the Christian Bishop-Martyr (Named Ignatius of Antioch)'. In P. J. Achtemeier (ed.), SBLSP 1978, 71–119. Missoula, MT: Scholars, 1978.

The New Testament World: Insights from Cultural Anthropology. London: SCM, 1983.

'The Social Sciences and Biblical Interpretation'. In N. Gottwald (ed.), *The Bible and Liberation: Political and Social Hermeneutics,* 11–25. New York: Maryknoll, 1983.

Bibliography

Christian Origins and Cultural Anthropology: Practical Models for Biblical Interpretation. Atlanta: John Knox, 1986.

'Mother and Son'. *BTB* 20, 1990: 54–64.

Malina, Bruce and Jerome H. Neyrey. *Calling Jesus Names: The Social Value of Labels in Matthew.* Sonoma, Calif.: Polebridge, 1988.

'Honour and Shame in Luke-Acts: Pivotal Values of the Mediterranean World'. In J. H. Neyrey (ed.), *The Social World of Luke-Acts: Models for Interpretation*, 25–65. Peabody, Mass.: Hendrickson, 1991.

Martin, Dale B. *Slavery as Salvation: The Metaphor of Slavery in Pauline Christianity.* New Haven and London: Yale University, 1990.

May, Margaret T. (trans.). *Galen on the Usefulness of the Parts of the Body.* Ithaca, NY: Cornell, 1968.

Meeks, W. 'The Man From Heaven in Johannine Sectarianism'. *JBL* 91, 1972: 44–72.

'The Image of Androgyne: Some Uses of a Symbol in Earliest Christianity'. *HR* 13, 1974: 165–208.

The First Urban Christians: The Social World of the Apostle Paul. New Haven and London: Yale University, 1983.

Meier, John P. 'On the Veiling of Hermeneutics (1 Cor. 11. 2–16)'. *CBQ* 40, 1978: 212–26.

Ménard, J. E. *L'Evangile Selon Thomas.* Leiden: E. J. Brill, 1975.

Meyers, Carol. *Discovering Eve: Ancient Israelite Women in Context.* New York and Oxford: Oxford University Press, 1988.

Moxnes, Halvor. 'Honour, Shame, and the Outside World in Paul's Letter to the Romans'. In Jacob Neusner (ed.), *The Social World of Formative Christianity and Judaism*, 207–18. Philadelphia: Fortress, 1988.

Muir, Steven C. 'Rebellion, Debauchery, and Frenzy in the Septuagint'. *Nuntius* 162, 1993: 19–21.

Murphy-O'Connor, Jerome. 'The Divorced Woman in 1 Cor. 7. 10–11'. *JBL* 100, 1981: 601–6.

Murray, Robert. 'The Exhortation to Candidates for Ascetic Vows at Baptism in the Ancient Syriac Church'. *NTS* 21, 1975: 59–80.

Musurillo, Herbert (ed.). *Acts of the Christian Martyrs.* Oxford: Clarendon, 1972.

Newsom, Carol A. and Sharon H. Ringe (eds.). *The Women's Bible Commentary.* Louisville Kentucky: Westminster/John Knox, 1992.

Newton, M. *The Concept of Purity at Qumram and in the Letters of Paul*, SNTSMS 53. Cambridge University Press, 1985.

Neyrey, Jerome H. 'Bewitched in Galatia: Paul and Cultural Anthropology'. *CBQ* 50, 1988: 72–100.

Paul, in Other Words: A Cultural Reading of His Letters. Louisville, Ky.: John Knox, 1990.

Bibliography

'Maid and Mother in Art and Literature'. *BTB* 20, 1990: 65–75.

'What's Wrong With This Picture? John 4, Cultural Stereotypes of Women, and Public and Private Space'. *BTB* 24/2, 1994: 77–91.

Pagels, Elaine. *The Gnostic Gospels*. New York: Vintage Books, 1981.

'Christian Apologists and "The Fall of the Angels": An Attack on Roman Imperial Power?' *HTR* 78, 1985: 301–25.

Adam, Eve, & the Serpent. London: Weidenfeld and Nicolson, 1988.

Pamment, Margaret. 'Witch-hunt'. *Theology* 84, 1981: 98–106.

Pantel, Pauline Schmitt. 'The Difference between the Sexes: History, Anthropology and the Greek City'. In Michelle Perrot (ed.), *Writing Women's History*, 70–89. Cambridge, Mass.: Blackwell, 1992.

Peristiany, Jean G. (ed.). *Honour and Shame: The Values of Mediterranean Society*. London: Weidenfeld and Nicolson, 1965.

Peristiany, Jean G. and Julian Pitt-Rivers (eds.). *Honour and Grace in Anthropology*. Cambridge University Press, 1992.

Pilch, John J. and Bruce J. Malina (eds.). *Biblical Social Values and Their Meaning: A Handbook*. Peabody, Mass.: Hendrickson, 1993.

Pitt-Rivers, Julian A. *The Fate of Shechem; or, the Politics of Sex: Essays in the Social Anthropology of the Mediterranean*. Cambridge University Press, 1977.

Pomeroy, Sarah. *Goddesses, Whores, Wives and Slaves: Women in Classical Antiquity*. New York: Schocken, 1975.

'The Relationship of the Married Woman to Her Blood Relatives in Rome'. *Ancient Society* 7, 1976: 215–27.

Portefaix, Lilian. *Sisters Rejoice: Paul's Letter to the Philippians and Luke-Acts as Received by First-Century Philippian Women*. Stockholm: Almqvist & Wiksell International, 1988.

Radice, Betty (trans.). *The Letters of the Younger Pliny*. Harmondsworth: Penguin Books, 1963.

Remus, Harold. *Pagan-Christian Conflict over Miracle in the Second Century*. Cambridge, Mass.: Philadelphia Patristics Foundation, 1983.

Resseguie, James L. 'Defamiliarization and the Gospels'. *BTB* 20, 1990: 147–53.

Robertson, R. 'The Salvation Army: The Persistence of Sectarianism.' In Bryan Wilson (ed.), *Patterns of Sectarianism*, 49–105. London: Morrison and Gibb, 1967.

Robinson, James M. (ed.). *Nag Hammadi Library in English*, third edn. San Francisco: Harper & Row, 1988.

Rodd, Cyril S. 'On Applying a Sociological Theory to Biblical Studies'. *JSOT* 19, 1981: 95–106.

'Sociology and Social Anthropology'. In R. J. Coggins and J. L. Houlden (eds.), *A Dictionary of Biblical Interpretation*, 635–9. London: SCM Press, 1990.

Bibliography

Rosaldo, Michelle Zimbalist and Louise Lamphere (eds.), *Woman, Culture, and Society*. Stanford, Calif.: University, 1974.

'The Use and Abuse of Anthropology: Reflections on Feminism and Cross-Cultural Understandings'. *Signs* 5, 1980: 389–417.

Rousselle, Aline. 'La Politique des Corps: Entre Procrétation et Continence à Rome'. In Georges Duby and Michelle Perrot (eds.), *Histoire des Femmes en Occident, L'Antiquité*, vol. 1, 319–59. Paris: Plon, 1991.

Porneia: On Desire and the Body in Antiquity, trans. F. Pheasant. Oxford: Basil Blackwell, 1983.

Schaberg, Jane. *The Illegitimacy of Jesus: A Feminist Theological Interpretation of the Infancy Narratives*. San Francisco: Harper and Row, 1987.

Schmithals, W. *Gnosticism in Corinth*. Nashville and New York: Abingdon, 1971.

Schneider, Jane. 'Of Vigilance & Virgins: Honour, Shame and Access to Resources in Mediterranean Society'. *Ethnology* 10, 1971: 1–24.

Schoedel, William R. 'Theological Norms and Social Perspectives in Ignatius of Antioch'. In E. P. Sanders (ed.), *Jewish and Christian Self-Definition, vol. 1: The Shaping of Christianity in the Second and Third Centuries*, 30–56. Philadelphia: Fortress, 1980.

Ignatius of Antioch: A Commentary on the Letters of Ignatius of Antioch. Philadelphia: Fortress, 1985.

Schürer, E. *The History of the Jewish people in the age of Jesus Christ*, vol. 2, revised edition, edited by G. Vermes, F. Millar, M. Black. Edinburgh: T&T Clark, 1979.

Schüssler Fiorenza, Elisabeth. *In Memory of Her: A Feminist Theological Reconstruction of Christian Origins*. London: SCM, 1983.

'The Ethics of Biblical Interpretation: De-centring Biblical Scholarship'. *JBL* 107, 1988: 3–17.

But She Said: Feminist Practices of Biblical Interpretation. Boston: Beacon, 1992.

(ed.) *Searching the Scriptures: vol. 1, A Feminist Introduction*. New York: Crossroad, 1993.

Scroggs, Robin. 'Paul and the Eschatological Woman'. *JAAR* 40, 1972: 283–303.

Selwyn, Edward G. *The First Epistle of St Peter*. London: MacMillan & Co., 1958.

Siegel, Rudolph E. (trans.). *Galen, On the Affected Parts*. Basel/ N.Y.: S. Karger, 1976.

Simon, Marcel. "Apulée et le Christianisme", in Antoine Guillamont and E. M. Laperrousaz (eds.), *Mélanges d'Histoire des Religions*. Paris: Presses Universitaires de France, 1974, 299–305.

Smith, Morton. *Jesus the Magician*. San Francisco: Harper & Row, 1978.

Bibliography

Snyder, Jane M. *The Woman and the Lyre: Women Writers in Classical Greece and Rome*. Carbondale: Southern Illinois University, 1989.

Stendahl, Krister. 'The Bible as a Classic and the Bible as Holy Scripture'. *JBL*, 103 (1984) 3–10.

Stevens, Maryanne. 'Paternity and Maternity in the Mediterranean: Foundations for Patriarchy'. *BTB* 20, 1990: 47–53.

Temkin, Owsei (trans.). *Soranus, Gynecology*. Baltimore: Johns Hopkins, 1956.

Theissen, Gerd. *The Social Setting of Pauline Christianity: Essays on Corinth*. Edinburgh: T & T Clark, 1982.

Thurston, B. Bowman. *The Widows: A Women's Ministry in the Early Church*. Minneapolis: Fortress, 1989.

Tolbert, Mary Ann. 'Social, Sociological, and Anthropological Methods'. In Elisabeth Schüssler-Fiorenza (ed.) *Searching the Scriptures: Vol. 1, A Feminist Introduction*, 255–71. New York: Crossroad, 1993.

Torjesen, Karen Jo. *When Women were Priests: Women's Leadership in the Early Church and the Scandal of their Subordination in the Rise of Christianity*. San Francisco: Harper & Row, 1993.

Turner, C. H. 'Ministries of Women in the Primitive Church'. *Constructive Quarterly* 7, 1919: 434–59.

van Bremen, Riet. 'Women and Wealth'. In Averil Cameron and Amelie Kuhrt (eds.) *Images of Women in Antiquity*, 223–42. Detroit: Wayne State University, 1985.

Verner, David. *The Household of God: The Social World of the Pastoral Epistles*, SBLDS 71. Chico, Calif.: Scholars, 1983.

Veyne, Paul. 'The Roman Empire'. Trans. A. Goldhammer, in Veyne (ed.), *A History of Private Life, vol. 1.: From Pagan Rome to Byzantium*, 5–234. Cambridge MA and London: Belknap, 1987.

Vööbus, A. *Celibacy, A Requirement for Admission to Baptism in the Early Syrian Church*. Stockholm: Papers of the Estonian Theological Society in Exile, 1951.

Walzer, Richard (ed.) *Galen on Jews and Christians*. London: Oxford University, 1949.

Wartelle, André (trans.) *Saint Justin, Apologies*. Paris: Etudes Augustiennes, 1987.

Weems, Renita. 'Gomer: Victim of Violence or Victim of Metaphor?' *Semeia* 47, 1989: 87–104.

Whelan, Caroline F. 'Amica Pauli: The Role of Phoebe in the Early Church'. *JSNT* 49, 1993: 67–85.

Wilken, Robert L. *The Christians as the Romans Saw Them*. New Haven and London: Yale University, 1984.

Willis, Wendell Lee. *Idol Meat in Corinth: The Pauline Argument in 1 Corinthians 8 and 10*. Chico, Calif.: Scholars, 1985.

Bibliography

Wilson, Bryan. *Patterns of Sectarianism*. London: Morrison and Gibb, 1967. *Magic and the Millennium*. New York: Harper and Row, 1973. *Religion in a Sociological Perspective*. Oxford University Press, 1982.

Wilson-Kastner, Patricia (ed.) *A Lost Tradition: Woman Writers in the Early Church*. Lanham, New York and London: University Press of America, 1981.

Wire, Antoinette Clark. *The Corinthian Women Prophets: A Reconstruction through Paul's Rhetoric*. Minneapolis: Augsburg Fortress, 1990.

Witt, R. E. *Isis in the Greco-Roman World*. Ithaca, N.Y.: Cornell, 1971.

Yarbrough, O. Larry. *Not Like the Gentiles: Marriage Rules in the Letters of Paul*, SBLDS 80. Atlanta: Scholars, 1985.

271

Index

Index

Index

Index

patriarchy
  concept critically examined, 26, 185–6,
    188, 257
  early Christian literature, 10, 183–4,
    247, 248
  Greco-Roman society, 122
patronage, 35, 43, 76–80, 102–4, 121
Paul
  communicator of cultural values,
    28–30, 180–1
  ethical teaching, 129–56, 180–1, 184,
    189–95, 210, 237, 244
  missionary circle and activities, 36,
    54–5, 79, 216–17
  missionary priorities, 10–11, 66, 118
Pauline communities, 129–54, 189–95,
  230–40
  women active in, 78, 79, 138, 192
persecution, 62, 71, 176, 205, 209, 214,
  246
1 Peter, 8, 9, 30, 44–6, 50, 127, 159, 187,
  194–207, 212, 215, 231, 244, 245,
  255
Philemon, 30
Philippians, 36
Philo of Alexandria, 32, 86–9, 93, 94, 166,
  169
Pliny, 12, 51–9, 86, 121, 123, 128, 158,
  221, 235, 256
Plutarch, 3, 7, 186, 236
polemic, 1, 61–5, 67, 84, 97, 100, 112,
  122
Polycarp, 219, 225, 227, 231
  see also Ignatius of Antioch
Porphyry, 50
power, 26, 41–7, 105, 126, 150, 202
  relation to authority, 41–2, 73, 101, 117,
    123–4, 199, 245, 255
  relation to influence, 5, 33, 42, 45, 81,
    123, 150, 244
prophecy, 4–5, 66, 103, 114–15, 145–6,
  166
prostitution 55, 57, 103, 224, 228, 239
Pseudo-Lucian, 69, 73
public/private dichotomy
  Acts of Paul and Thecla, 171, 173
  1 Corinthians, 145, 154
  cultural anthropology of Mediterranean
    societies, 26, 29–30, 37–9, 112, 151
  Greco-Roman world, 30–7, 39–41, 56,
    90–1, 181, 218, 243–4
  pagan criticism of early Christianity,

60–2, 67–70, 81, 111–12, 232, 251,
  254
Pastoral Epistles, 62–4, 164–6
1 Peter, 203
public opinion, 5–13, 166, 249–58
  evidence in early Christian texts, 142,
    157, 158, 178, 188
  pagan criticism of early Christianity, 49,
    70, 84, 100, 125, 196
  relation to honour and shame, 29, 147,
    153–4
  see also rumour, stereotypes

Revelation, 4, 83, 210
ritual, 68, 70, 75, 100, 145, 164, 166
  agape meal, 55, 56, 64, 66, 68, 69
  baptism, 52, 66, 92
  Eucharist meal, 56, 66, 68, 118
Romans, 30, 78, 215, 218
Rosaldo, Michelle Z., 41–2
rumour
  as problem for church communities,
    127, 156–7, 171, 198
  concerning church ritual, 66–7, 145,
    236
  in the ancient world, 12, 73, 120,
    127–8
  influencing pagan critique, 52, 67,
    232
  see *also* public opinion

Schaberg, Jane, 96, 97
Schoedel, William R., 215, 224, 225, 233
Schüssler Fiorenza, Elisabeth, 17, 23, 183,
  184, 216, 217
secrecy
  accusation against early Christians,
    60–3, 99, 104–5, 110, 112, 232
  in marriages between Christians and
    non-Christians, 71, 195, 245
  relation to women's religious activities,
    3, 71, 123, 160, 254
  see also evangelism
sects, 128–30, 143, 151, 153–4, 201, 235,
  252
shame, *see* honour and shame
Shepherd of Hermas, 4, 16, 75, 76, 79, 132,
  206, 219, 220, 222, 225, 226, 235,
  241
Sibyl, 4, 114
silence, of women, 162, 236
slander, *see* public opinion

Index

slaves
  Greco-Roman perceptions about, 57, 224
  influence of, 51–4, 121
  social conditions of, 167, 220–5, 229, 231, 240, 256
Smith, Morton, 97, 107, 108
social sciences, 14–16, 22–3, 41, 144, 153
  methodology, 15–21, 24, 37, 38, 43, 185
  models, 14–17, 20–2, 25
  see also honour and shame, power, public/private dichotomy, sects
sociology, *see* social sciences
sorcery, *see* magic
stereotypes, 6, 20, 65, 67, 120
  women's attraction to new religious groups, 2–4, 7, 60, 74, 198, 232
  women's vices, 69–70, 73, 244, 258
  see also public opinion
subversion, accusations of,
  Christian teaching in response to, 233, 246, 254
  pagan criticism of early Christianity, 55, 59, 112–13, 119, 158, 250
  Roman opinion of Eastern religions, 49–50, 98, 122
superstition, accusations of, 3, 51, 57

Tacitus, 7, 39, 40
Tertullian, 58, 70, 76, 113
Thecla, *see Acts of Paul and Thecla*
Therapeutae, 87, 88, 93
1 Thessalonians, 130, 131, 136, 141, 142, 149, 230, 242
Thurston, Bonnie Bowman, 51, 227
1, 2 Timothy, 5, 7, 8, 17, 36, 37, 45, 53, 62–4, 75, 77, 79, 127, 137, 138, 152,

154–79, 203, 212, 214, 219, 221, 225–8, 231, 233, 243, 253, 254
Titus, 62, 63, 79, 155, 163, 227, 231
Tolbert, Mary Ann, 15, 22
Torjesen, Karen Jo, 34, 36
travel, 76–9, 121, 207

Valentinus, 66, 83, 91–4
  see also gnosticism
violence, 166, 176, 212, 246, 253
virgins, 122, 255
  Acts of Paul and Thecla, 170–82
  Celsus, 114
  1 Corinthians, 28, 134–43, 147–50, 162, 178–82
  Ignatius of Antioch, 213–14, 225–6, 247
  Philo of Alexandria on, 87–9

widows
  1 Corinthians, 10–11, 131, 133, 137–8, 152
  Ignatius of Antioch, 177, 183, 213–14, 225–30, 236, 256
  Lucian of Samosata, 74–81, 121–2, 256
  social condition of, 137–8, 152, 167, 248
  1 Timothy, 63–4, 157–66, 171, 177, 181, 253
Wilken, Robert L., 50, 84, 85
Wilson, Bryan, 128, 129, 131, 201
Wire, Antoinette Clark, 37, 134, 135, 191
witchcraft, accusations of, 108, 115–20, 250
  see also magic

Yarbrough, O. Larry, 130, 137, 191